MAKE IT COUNT

How to Generate a Legacy
That Gives Meaning to Your Life

JOHN KOTRE, *Ph.D.*

THE FREE PRESS

THE FREE PRESS
A Division of Simon & Schuster Inc.
1230 Avenue of the Americas
New York, NY 10020

Designed by Carla Bolte

Manufactured in the United States of America

10 9 8 7 6 5 4 3 2 1

Library of Congress Cataloging-in-Publication Data

Kotre, John N.
    Make it count: how to generate a legacy that gives meaning to
your life/John Kotre.
       p. cm.
    Includes bibliographical references and index.
    1. Adulthood—Psychological aspects. 2. Adulthood—Psychological
aspects—Case studies.   3. Children and adults. 4. Children and
adults—Case studies. I. Title
BF724.5.K668 1999   99-25231
155.6—dc21   CIP

Permission has generously been granted to reprint or adapt material by John Kotre that was published previously in a different form: *Generativity and Adult Development*, pages 367–389 (adapted), copyright © 1998 by the American Psychological Association, adapted with permission. *Outliving the Self: Generativity and the Interpretation of Lives*, various pages, copyright © 1984 by the Johns Hopkins University Press. *Seasons of Life: The Dramatic Journey from Birth to Death*, various pages, copyright © 1997 by The University of Michigan Press.

ISBN 978-1-4516-8236-6

*f*P

FOR JACOB

and all the others of his generation

Contents

Acknowledgments

IT WAS AT A DINNER in Toronto, and I had been explaining my difficulty in coming up with a working title for this book. Almost without thinking, a graduate student named Jay Azarow said, "The Generative Way." Although "The Generative Way" did not survive as the book's title, it did become its guiding metaphor; in a very real sense, it enabled the book to be written. Needless to say, I am grateful to Jay Azarow for his timely suggestion.

That brief exchange illustrates the kind of influences that have come to bear on this work. When you are writing about generativity, as opposed to creativity, you realize how extensive these influences are and how impossible it is keep track of them. So when the time comes to give them their due, you are keenly aware of the phenomenon of "source amnesia."

But let me do the best I can. I owe special thanks to the readers who reacted to various parts of the manuscript as it was being developed and who urged me to be more directive. They are: Jason Cline, David Kotre, Stephen Kotre, Gina Magyar, Alane Mason, Tom Meloche, Michelle Puzzuoli, Aideen Weickert, and Adrienne Wisok. These were "lay" readers, three of them my own adult children. When the manuscript was nearly done, I turned to professional consultation, first from historian Gerald Moran, who had just written about generativity (and the lack thereof) in early American colonists; then from psychologists Dan McAdams and Ed de St. Aubin, who had just edited a multidisciplinary volume of research on generativity, the first of its kind; and then, for a chapter entitled "Of Skin and Spirit," from Ronald Manheimer, a gerontologist with a background in the history of consciousness. The responses of all four scholars were both prompt and, in the very best sense of the word, critical. They helped with the finishing touches.

Acknowledgments

There are other kinds of debts: to Dan Patterson for the author's photos he took on a Sunday afternoon; to Philip Rappaport of The Free Press for guiding this book from manuscript to market; and especially to my literary agent, Donald Cutler, for his understanding of what I was trying to accomplish. It was his suggestion that eventually led to the title we adopted: *Make It Count.*

Finally, to my family near and far, and in particular to my wife, Kathy: I cannot pinpoint all the ways they are "in" this book, but their presence is unmistakable—one of those mysteries of generativity I will never understand. To them, and to all the unknown and unseen contributors to these pages, I extend my thanks. And I ask forgiveness for any source amnesia that still lingers.

A WORD AND A WAY

1

The Idea Whose Time Has Come

THERE IS A WORD that puts a finger on a dilemma that individuals and society at large increasingly experience in their lives. A woman, 35, told me about her life as a business consultant, in particular about sitting in a motel at the end of a grueling day and asking herself why her clients were paying $275 an hour for her services—and why she was prostituting herself to provide them. She had been thinking about all the bits and pieces of her life—about the pet she had just lost, about the children she never had, about her husband telling her to quit, about the one time in a previous job when she actually saw her efforts make a difference in people's lives. But now . . . what was the lasting value in all this? Did it matter to anyone? Who cared? She didn't use the word, but there was a void in her "generativity."

A man of 64 spoke of a similar unhappiness that had afflicted him some ten years before. He hadn't heard of the word "generativity" either. He had worked as a journalist in his young adult years but then took a job with a public utility company at the age of 43 because he wanted more security for his family. He began writing and editing for the company's news and information service, developing stories about ordinary workers who sometimes took heroic risks, or about small, out-of-the way communities his company served. He loved being a kind of Charles Kuralt "on the road." But then in his mid-50s he realized how unhappy he was becoming.

The company had shifted emphasis, wanting hard facts now, not soft "people" stories. He found himself working on briefing books that didn't reflect *him*. "Anybody could do what I was doing." In a cost-cutting move, the company offered early retirement. He didn't accept it the first time around, nor the second, but he did the third. He parted from the company at age 59, and the separation had a lot to do with his "generativity."

You can tell that generativity—this feeling of mattering, of creating lasting value, of passing your very self on to others—was at the heart of these dilemmas because of what followed. Within a year the business consultant had quit her job, adopted two puppies, sought medical help to become pregnant, and begun to put together plans for her own consulting firm. "I wanted to create something that would have a life and an identity outside of me," she said—something authentic. Upon his retirement, the former journalist answered an ad for child care help. He became a substitute grandfather for two young boys, then for a 10-year-old with severe cerebral palsy, then an 11-year-old who was the son of a lesbian couple. Ever the writer, he took notes on his workdays to give to the parents of the children and then got the idea of collecting them into a book, a kind of daily log of fatherly fun and wisdom. He published the book himself and followed it with a book of letters to his own adult sons. This writing was worlds apart from what he had ended up doing for the utility company. It was warm, emotional, and full of people. "Boys, I wish you could have seen me when I ran like a gust of wind, and I wish all sons could see their dads when they could steal a base, catch a long pass, or win a race."

The word "generativity" has been in existence for half a century now, coined in 1950 by the eminent psychoanalyst Erik H. Erikson. But the world was not ready to hear it back then, though it eagerly embraced other concepts of Professor Erikson, most notably that of the identity crisis. Erikson defined generativity as "the concern in establishing and guiding the next generation," but the idea is both deeper and richer than that. It revolves around the fact that we are reproductive beings who wish to be fertile, who have been told in sacred scriptures and urged by our very genes to multiply and fill the earth. But as humans we do that in more than a physical sense. We do it with our craft and our care, with our hands and our genius. We do it as parents, teachers, shepherds, guardians, and guides; as artists and scientists and enactors of ritual; as responsible citizens and movers in our businesses and communities. We do it when we bear fruit, sow seeds, create legacies, leave the world a little better off for our presence in it.

A quarter of a century after Erikson, in 1975, I began to write about the reverse of generativity, about the sterility that had crept into notions of self-actualization and self-fulfillment. Of immense influence, these psychologies held up as a goal of development a self that was focused on the here-and-now, skilled at severing old connections and moving on to new ones, "liberated" from tradition, unencumbered by duty, "open," and "fluid"; those were the very virtues preached. But it was a self that lacked any instinct to beget and had hardly a provision for caring for what it might beget. (I wasn't alone in my critique: at the time, the so-called "Me Decade" and "narcissist society" were coming increasingly under attack.) There was a practical side to my thinking as well: self-actualization wouldn't get anyone past the age of 50. Why put so much effort into actualizing something that was going to die anyway? I thought. If I was going to end up dead, I didn't want to be a dead end.

I went on to write a book, *Outliving the Self,* that profiled eight individuals whose lives revealed facets of generativity, and followed it up with occasional articles in scholarly journals. Quantified research on generativity began to appear. But the idea that could lead from Me to beyond Me had not yet captured the public imagination. Now, at the end of the century, the climate appears to be changing. Perhaps it's because seventy-six million members of America's baby-boom generation are entering the second half of their lives. Born between 1946 and 1964, they form a huge population bulge that continues to work its way through the stages of life, changing American culture as it goes. In the late 1960s, the leading edge of the baby boom went to war and protested the war; in the 1970s, it both accepted and criticized Meism. Now the bulk of this massive cohort is reaching middle age, a time in life when people normally become aware of their mortality and sense the possibilities offered by generativity. The baby boom, in other words, may now be ready to hear.

Ready or not, the baby boomers—and indeed all of us—*need* to hear. For the boomers will soon accelerate a trend that is deeper, of longer duration, and global in nature—the aging of populations all around the world. In 1900, only one out of every twenty-five Americans was 65 or older.

Today, one out of eight or nine is that old; and by 2030, when the last of the boomers has crossed 65, one out of five will be. And there are countries—Japan, Sweden, Canada, Italy, for example—where populations are even older than they are in the United States. In 1994, one of them—Italy—became the first in the world to have more people over 65 than under 15.

These figures describe what is known as the "Age Wave," and as it hits nations around the world, it will raise the question: where shall our resources go? To the old, whose political power will only increase, or to the young? The old, not the young, will decide. How seventy-six million baby boomers decide in the United States will have far-reaching effects. There could be a healthy generational flow in the century to come, but there could also be generational war.

And so I return now to the subject of generativity with a greater sense of urgency, a sense of mission almost, wanting to be—at one and the same time—both more idealistic and more practical. My goal in this book is to take what I have learned over the past two decades and cast it in the ancient metaphor of the *Way*. I want to show you a path to an interior state of great value not only to yourself, but also to your family, your neighborhood, your nation, and your very world. A state of great joy, too, for in it one draws on the deepest wellsprings of life.

In describing this inner journey, I augment the metaphor of the Way with a more contemporary one, that of *steps*. I have picked out eight of them, and they form the heart of this book. These are not "self-help" steps; they are not terribly distinct; and their sequence can vary somewhat. But they do bring out certain aspects, certain phases even, of the generative process. They are markers. You can see a particular episode of your life in terms of them, or your life as a whole. You can go through them—travel the Way—more than once. And though I call them steps, they do not always involve an active doing. Often on the road I describe there are moments of standing still as well as walking, of being passive as well as active, of receiving as well as giving. We do not always dictate the terms of our generativity, in other words. Sometimes we have to let those terms come to us.

The eight steps on the Way—talking to your past, stopping the damage, finding a voice of your own, blending that voice with another's, creating, selecting, letting go, and responding to outcome—are mapped out in Chapters 3 to 8 of this book (Part II). The map is preceded by two brief chapters that comprise Part I; their goal is to provide conceptual clarity regarding generativity. The map is followed by four chapters of reflections (Part III). They look at generativity in relation to the adult life span, to the problem of evil, and to the broad progression of life on earth. The last of the reflections is a parable that summarizes the message of the book.

Let me say at the outset that it will take some fresh *seeing* if we are to follow this "Generative Way," or even discover where it begins. We—psychologists and lay persons alike—will have to become aware of the sterility and fertility *in* lives and of their reflexive impact *on* lives. We will have to name dilemmas of generativity for what they are. There are times when these dilemmas stare us in the face, and we cannot miss their true nature. A woman unable to conceive after two miscarriages, a woman who suffered tremendous losses in her early twenties, writes at her lowest point that she feels "less like a woman than like a useless, empty womb. . . . My whole life is a miscarriage, an abortion, dead before birth." Another woman who lost her only son in his teens, a woman for whom family was everything, says, "Now, I'm just a cut-off branch of a very large tree." And a man, living in very different circumstances, fathers five children who live but sees his existence in the same cut-off way: "My life has been so sterile, so useless, so unhappy, that, *por Dios,* sometimes I wish I could die," he tells Oscar Lewis in *The Children of Sanchez.* "I am the kind of guy who leaves nothing behind, no trace of themselves in the world, like a worm dragging itself across the earth. I bring no good to anybody." These individuals articulate suffering that is easy to see and name: something is deeply wrong with their fertility.

But we may not so readily identify the assault on generativity in a young computer scientist who pours himself into the creation of a new piece of software only to see his company destroy 90 percent of it—and, so it seems, of him. Or in a middle-aged man whose great idea, whose "baby," never gets off the ground. Or in a minister who sees each new congregation to which he is assigned slowly but inexorably grow smaller. Or in any worker, blue-collar or white, who cannot wait to retire from a job. It will take a fresh approach on the part of counselors, on the part of any of us concerned with lives, simply to recognize the generative dimension of a person's presenting "symptoms," to relate these symptoms not just to what has gone into a life but to what is (or is not) coming forth from it, and to consider no therapy complete until the entire flow of life is restored, including its flow into a generative outlet.

The path opened up by this kind of seeing is not an easy one. There are twists and turns and hidden dangers along the way to generativity, and difficulties from the very beginning. At the start we must come to terms with what we have been given by previous generations: how do we deal with what has been sown in us? If it has been crippling, how do we prevent it from making us sterile or jading our perspective? Then we must find a voice, *our* voice, and blend it with another's. Not an easy proposition. Add the uncertainty of the future: what acts of faith will be required to produce things that will one day escape our control, whose ultimate fate we will never know? How do we surrender our children and our products to a world that seems more threatening every day? What inner temptations—to fear, to pride, to negligence, to selfishness—must we overcome throughout the time of begetting and selecting and letting go? Suppose our children do not "turn out"—or never stop draining us. Suppose posterity wants nothing of the products of our hands. Suppose our gift is squandered, misappropriated, put to wrong purposes, or put to right purposes that are not our own. And what about the evil we inevitably sow with the good?

Throughout this book I will treat generativity as a virtue, but I will not neglect its "dark side." One of the most poignant sentences I've ever heard consisted of just five words: "It was all from me." The speaker was referring to a baby, her first, who was neither healthy nor attractive, and who eventually died. Her words expressed her profound feeling of producing something that was damaged. "It was as if my husband had not contributed at all to the appearance of this child," she said. "It was all from me." In 1995, a former secretary of defense for the United States looked back on a deadly and divisive war that he had helped to wage some twenty-five years before and realized that it too (though not all of it) emanated from him. His feelings must have been akin to those of a fashioner of the atomic bomb, who witnessed its first explosion and quoted the Hindu *Bhagavad Gita:* "I am become death, the destroyer of worlds." These individuals understood that evil could result from their best efforts and live after them. But others remain blind, unaware of the poison they spread and the lasting damage they do.

So there are dangers and corruptions as well as joys and blessings that line the way of one who would be generative. To illuminate them I will draw upon my own discipline of psychology, where interest in generativity is growing at last, but I will also go far beyond it to consult the witness of history and literature, as well as that of ordinary people who have lived through a variety of generative experiences. I will mix in teaching stories, or what I regard as such, extracting from them the wisdom that has accumulated in their characters and plots. The stories will range from fairy tales for adults to the parables of the world's religions. The latter is an especially intriguing prospect, for psychology and religion tend to pick up opposite ends of the stick when it comes to human lives. Psychology emphasizes what goes into them (childhood experiences); and religion, what comes out of them (their fruits). There are many issues that psychology and religion can address in tandem, but none is more important than the subject of this book—our attitude toward future generations and the future of the world.

It is my conviction that what takes place in the inner life of adults of all ages—the young, the middle-aged, and the elderly—has a significant bearing on the generation now coming into being and on the whole progression of life on this planet. Speaking of sexual intercourse, Mahatma Gandhi once said, "The physical and mental states of the parents at the time of conception are reproduced in the baby." One need not take his statement literally to realize its symbolic value: if we in the older generation wish to develop virtue in the young, we must first develop corresponding virtue in ourselves. This is evident in the lives of our great spiritual teachers, who went to a place apart and faced temptation before going forth to spread their message.

Deep satisfaction can come when a life is lived with generativity in mind—a sure knowledge that one's life has "counted." A man approaching 70 visits a public park and lake he helped to create years before as a state legislator. Once it had been a place of abandoned oil wells and strip mines, but now it was a place where generations to come could "go to dream— one of the best fishing lakes in western Pennsylvania." "I was only a little cog in the wheel that made it possible," he says, "but I appreciate the part I was able to play."

A famous worker of wood, 82, speaks of giving trees that will die a "second life": "If I can bring the nature and the spirit of a tree back, the tree lives again." He, too, is but one cog in a great wheel, one element in the continuity of life that "sparks," he says, from one thing to another. "It's a great, great feeling to be part of that—to be a part of nature and to be a part of life itself."

And a 90-year-old arthritic woman reflects in Robert Coles's *The Old Ones of New Mexico:* "I am rich with years, a millionaire! I have been part of my own generation, then I watched my children's generation grow up, then my grandchildren's, and now my great-grandchildren's. Two of my great-grandchildren are becoming full-grown women now; they come visit me, and will remember me. Now, I ask you, how much more can a woman expect?" She was another who had never heard of the word "generativity," but then she had never needed to.

2

What Is Generativity?

BEFORE SETTING OUT on the Generative Way, we need to explore in greater depth the meaning of this word "generativity." Once we understand what it is and what it is not, once we identify its various kinds of expression, we will be able to see which paths are open to us and which are closed. Each of us has a unique life history and a unique cultural history, so one person's approach will not be another's. The one each of us chooses will relate to where we are in life and what has brought us to our present place.

In the years following Erikson's original definition of generativity as "the concern in establishing and guiding the next generation," psychologists introduced some interesting variations in their understanding of the term. Some who did statistical research shaped it to questionnaires they were creating or to data they already possessed and said it meant "providing for the next generation" or simply "responsibility for others." In 1984, when I wrote about eight generative individuals, I defined it as "a desire to invest one's substance in forms of life and work that will outlive the self." These variants, along with Erikson's original, have circled over the same target, some coming closer than others, but all intent upon a basic drive in humans to be fertile in both body and soul, and to be fertile as part of the larger progression of life on this planet.

Generativity, then, is the force behind all our human forms of reproduction, from the most biological to the most spiritual. And what's behind reproduction, of course, is the fact that we die. Whether we think of the human gene pool or of its pool of cultures, collective life on this earth is maintained through the coming and going of individuals. You can almost picture these pools as living things in themselves, with streams of individuals entering at birth and exiting at death. Perhaps things are different in some far corner of the universe; perhaps there is no need for individual reproduction because there is no death. But anything that we earthlings know of life also involves death. Hence the need for all kinds of generativity.

"All" these kinds may be distilled to four: biological, parental, technical, and cultural. The first, *biological,* refers to the begetting, bearing, and nursing of children—the passing on of living substance (genes and blood and milk) from one generation to the next. In this kind of generativity, the target of concern is not only what is conceived—the growing fetus, the newborn—but also the genetic line from which it springs. We are aware of biological generativity when we see our parents' physical traits in us, or when we see ours in our children. Biological generativity is awake and alert for about three decades in the lives of women and four, five, or even more in those of men, although in practice its expression is concentrated into far shorter segments of lifetime.

The biological domain is the setting of a story I will cite later in this book. A young husband discovers that he is the carrier of a chromosomal abnormality; his wife becomes pregnant on three occasions; and each time the couple decides upon amniocentesis to determine if their baby will be affected by the abnormality. The mother-to-be learns the results of one such test:

> The phone rang and when I talked to the nurse, I tried to read into her voice whether it was good or bad. And she said, "I've got good news. Everything is fine." The baby was not even a carrier. And then I asked the sex. I thought if any human being knows, then I'm going to know. So we found out it was a boy. We started planning and we started coming up with names. When he was born, they took a blood sample and double checked. He was perfectly normal.

The second kind of generativity is *parental,* which involves the rearing of children and the initiation of them into a family's way of life. This kind is distinct from the first because people sometimes raise children who are not their biological offspring. One day in May a mountain woman in North Carolina breast-feeds her infant son—an example of biological generativity —and places him on the ground, fondling him with her toes. It is the first time she has done so. "This is your land," she says to him, "and it's about time you started getting to know it." Then she tells Robert Coles in *Migrants, Sharecroppers, Mountaineers:*

> The first thing I can remember in my whole life was my mother telling me I should be proud of myself. I recollect her telling me we had all the land, clear up to a line that she kept on pointing out. I mean, I don't know what she said to me, not the words, but I can see her pointing up the hill and down toward the road, and there was once when she stepped hard on the earth, near the corn they were growing, I think it was, and told me and my sister that we didn't have everything that we might want and we might need, but what we did have, it was nothing to look down on; no, it was the best place in the whole world to be born—and there wasn't any place prettier or nicer anywhere.

This is a clear example of parental generativity. What a young woman received from her mother she begins to pass on to her child. And there's more than feeding, clothing, and sheltering involved. This young mother is also instilling a sense of pride in a family's place and its traditions. All are targets of concern: the child, the family, and the traditions.

The third kind of generativity is *technical.* This refers to the teaching of skills and procedures—how to play games, how to work with wood, how to write, how to handle money, how to repair a car, how to perform surgery, how to program a computer, and so on. It also refers to the crafting of tools to accompany such skills, and with passing the tools on. An old man of 76 has vivid memories of receiving technical generativity when he was apprenticed as a boy to a barber named Antonino:

> He would ask me to watch him. "You doing anything? Why don't you watch me cut hair?" He showed me how to hold the comb. You cut the hair over the comb and make sure that the scissor doesn't slip under. You figure out how many inches you want the hair off the scalp, you get the hairs, you put them in between your fingers, you cut them all around the head on the top.

I had to learn how to strap the razor. I had to watch how he would hone it. He would put a drop of olive oil in the stone and then he would hone the razor back and forth and try it on his nail to see if it would stick. I had to keep an eye at what he was doing. "Keep on watching me and pretty soon, before you know it, you're gonna shave people." Later he asked me to shave, and I thought I was not yet ready. I was eight and a half years old. I said, "I don't know. I'm afraid." He said, "Oh, you shave now. I told you what to do. Put the razor flat. Don't put it on an angle. Put it flat with the face and glide. It'll shave." By golly, it was too. The way he was teaching me was the truth.

As this example makes clear, there are two targets of concern in the technical domain. One is the person of the apprentice; the other, the skill that is being taught. Sometimes teachers must choose between the two. Favoring the skill, one decides that if a student cannot fully master technique, he will have to be dismissed. Favoring the apprentice, another decides that he will only teach students what is in their capacity to learn, and compromise technique if necessary. The tension between the two targets of generativity disappears only when a follower appears who can fully command technique and carry it to new heights.

Finally, there is *cultural* generativity—conserving, renovating, or creating a meaning system and passing it on to others. A meaning system is the "mind" of a community, just as skills are its "body." One teaches not only how to do things (technical generativity) but also what beliefs inform them, what values sustain them, what theory lies behind them, what they "stand for," what their "soul" or "spirit" is. A culture can be religious, scientific, political, ethnic, artistic—or simply the common sense shared by a particular group of people.

When it came time for Maestro Antonino's apprentice to do his own teaching about barbering, he was explicit about respect and courtesy, both abstract elements of culture. Without such elements, technique is hollow:

I tell young barbers to respect their trade. I tell them to be courteous, to ask the people, "Do you want me to trim the hair from your ears or from your nose?" "You have one eyebrow that sticks out. Should I cut it off?" Don't cut it! *Ask* the customer if he wants it cut, and if he tells you to cut it then you know he's going to be happy.

This 76-year-old man had more advice for young people in general. He was concerned about them but also about the values of a bygone era. Both were the objects of his generative impulse. He wanted both to live on:

> Whenever I get in contact with them, I tell them about obedience. I tell them they've got to be obedient to their father and mother. In the old ideas, obedience was something that had to be carried out. People obeyed the elderly people. I tell them about the Commandments. "Love thy neighbor." . . . If you haven't got that and you think you can do without, I think you're wrong. If you're doing anything wrong, your conscience will bother you, you don't sleep well, but if you're at peace with everybody you meet, everybody you meet is your friend, then you sleep well.

The targets of cultural generativity are both the meaning system and the disciple, and a mentor must hold the two in balance. If the mentor wishes to develop the potential of any and all disciples, she may neglect or dilute her culture's central symbols. But if the preservation of culture is paramount, she may ignore the needs of disciples. The trick is to offer an engaging vision of who the disciple might become, a vision that is true to both the disciple's and the culture's potentials. Under ideal circumstances, one and the same act prepares the ground for identity formation in the follower and serves the mentor's stewardship of her culture.

As one moves from biological to cultural life, the distance between the giver and receiver of generativity becomes greater. In biological life, the two are so close that living matter passes from one to the other. The transmission of living matter disappears in parenting, but touching and close physical contact remain the rule. In the passing on of skills, touching is greatly reduced and may not occur at all. The teacher is present to the learner through a medium—the material that is touched by both. Finally, in the transmission of culture, even the mutual presence of giver and receiver is not essential. Predecessors may speak to successors across oceans and over centuries of time. Seeds that were once physical are now symbolic.

When I was defining generativity on one occasion for a group of middle-aged and elderly adults, they asked if it were ever "accidental" or "unconscious." My answer, of course, was yes. But then it struck me that their question was far more interesting than any answer I might give, for the question told me that Erikson's term was enabling them to *see*. And what they saw was much more important than any definition—that actions of theirs had far-reaching and long-lasting consequences, many of which they would never know about. They had created waves and ripples with their lives and were still doing so. There were even possibilities that lay ahead.

A Case in Point

In actual lives, the four types of generativity move about in intriguing ways. Their domains overlap. In one person you see them emerge separately, each dominating for a while and then moving on. In another, you see them arrive in pairs, or even all at once, to live at one another's benefit or expense. A life in which their interplay (along with their dark side) is clearly seen is that of architect Frank Lloyd Wright. In the words of psychologist Ed de St. Aubin, who has recently made a study of his life, Wright was a man of generative "extremes." "Arguably the most influential American architect ever," he was also a "self-serving prevaricator whose narcissistic tendencies stifled his generative potential."

Wright was born in a small Wisconsin town in 1867, the son of a remarried Baptist minister and his Welsh wife. He spent much of his childhood moving from place to place as his father's work dictated. When he was 18, his parents divorced and his father abandoned the household. Wright spent a year as a student at the University of Wisconsin, where he received some training in civil engineering. Then he moved to Chicago to find work. A year later, he was hired as a draftsman in the architectural firm of a rising star by the name of Louis Sullivan, whom he later called "Lieber Meister." He, Wright, was Sullivan's "pencil."

But the pencil moonlighted, designing projects on his own, and was eventually fired for doing so at 26. From that time until his death at 91, Wright worked independently. Overall he designed more than 600 buildings and saw 430 of them actually constructed. His legacy is visible throughout the world. Generativity of one kind or another was operative for seven decades of his life.

It was operative, first of all, in the *biological* realm, where Wright was prolific. He married in 1889 at the age of 21, and had his first child, Frank Lloyd Wright, Jr., a year later. Over the next thirteen years, his wife gave birth to three more sons and two daughters. After several sexual affairs, some of which were publicized in the tabloids of the time, he divorced his wife in his mid-50s. He married a second time, then divorced again at 60. Two years before that divorce, a 27-year-old lover had given birth to another daughter, the seventh and last child that Wright sired. The period of his biological generativity had covered more than thirty-five years.

Wright married his lover when he was 61 and adopted her older daughter, an expression of *parental* generativity. But in this domain much of Wright's legacy falls on the dark side. He was nongenerative, even antigenerative. He indulged his children but saw them infrequently while they were growing up. "I had affection for them," he said, adding that he thought of them as "play-fellows." Basically, Wright's children were abandoned for his projects; they were humiliated by his affairs and felt sorry for their mother. When his first wife died at 91, just a few weeks before Wright himself did, his son David deliberately waited a full day before telling him the news. When Wright asked why, David replied, "Why should I have bothered, you never gave a god-damn for her when she was alive."

Wright's eldest sons, Lloyd (Frank, Jr.) and John, followed him into architecture. Their paths illustrate that relationships can contain generativity of all four types, that one can be a parent and a teacher and a mentor to the same person. Not that the mix is without danger: Lloyd and John were often belittled and bullied by their father. Wright would blame them for his own failings with clients. "You will say a thing is so when you only think it is so," he once wrote to Lloyd. "You will promise and not keep it. You will buy when you can't pay. You will attempt anything and blame failure on others. . . . You are quick to impute to others the quality that is rankling in your own soul." All of these charges could aptly be directed at Wright himself, describing qualities "rankling" in his own soul. (He had been buying and not paying since his students days at Wisconsin.) In the heat of one dispute with his son John, Wright sent him a bill for all the expenses that he, Wright, had borne as a parent, including the cost of the birth itself.

Some of his children remained unforgiving of Wright's failures as a parent. Some were torn. Only Lloyd, the oldest, maintained an undying loyalty. Wright himself was rarely able to acknowledge the pain he had caused, preferring to remain blind to the trail he had left. In what de St. Aubin considers a self-protective device, Wright said only that he lacked a fathering instinct:

> Is it a quality? Fatherhood? If so, I seemed born without it. And yet a building was a child. I have had the father-feeling, I am sure, when coming back after a long time to one of my buildings. That must be the true feeling of fatherhood. But I never had it for my children.

In the *technical* realm, Wright's genius was unsurpassed. As an architect, he embraced the latest material technologies: the "miracles" of steel and reinforced concrete, which he turned into "textile" blocks, slender "lily pad" columns, "cantilever" roofs with their long overhangs, and staircases that spiraled into ever wider circles. In his designs he played with abstractions from nature (trees, cacti, seashells) and from geometry (the use of "crystallized rotation," for example). And he concerned himself with detail —octagonal copper bathtubs in Japan's Imperial Hotel, art-glass windows and peekaboo wood screens in his "prairie" homes. His innovations are so distinct that today even a lay person can recognize his style. But technical innovation—creativity—is not by itself generativity.

It becomes so when innovations are passed on. Wright did most of his teaching through the Taliesin Fellowship, a community of assistants and apprentices that he established at his Wisconsin home in 1932, when he was 64. It was as close as he got to forming his own school of architecture. Generativity prompted the creation of the Fellowship, but so did a need for funds in the aftermath of the stock market crash of 1929. At a time when Wright was bringing in few commissions, Taliesin fellows paid tuition for the privilege of working for him.

Wright intended the Fellowship to pass on more than technique, and here he entered the domain of *culture,* the domain in which one propagates soul and spirit. For Wright, the soul of architecture was captured in his motto "Truth Against the World." "Truth," of course, was what *he* possessed: a vision of architecture as a way of life. The "World" consisted of the architectural conventions of the times: classicism, commercialism, and academism. In architecture, truth meant that your inspiration came not from previous designs but from nature. It meant that your design fit the landscape, that it was "of" a hill rather than "on" a hill. It meant that your building materials were indigenous to the setting—sand-based concrete, for example, in the Arizona desert. And the materials themselves were to be pared down to their essentials. They were to represent themselves and nothing else. That was the embodiment of truth.

In books and lectures Wright developed his vision of truth, calling it "organic" architecture. It formed the basis of his utopia, a hypothetical society known as "Usonia" whose capital was "Broadacre City." The name Broadacre referred to the fact that every citizen would be given one broad acre on which to live. So there would be no skyscrapers, no "artificial verticals." Politically, the society would be as decentralized as it was architecturally. Educationally, there would be no universities, only "father confessors" to bring out the originality of students. All citizens would benefit from living in the midst of great architecture and from the wisdom of great architect-leaders.

Usonia was the cultural ideal. But it was not realized at Taliesin, for Wright was no father confessor—a tyrant, rather, says de St. Aubin. Wright once joked that a "perfect democracy" existed there: "When I get hungry, we all eat." He did not train his students but adopted instead what one biographer has called the "watch the genius" method. Wright "performed" greatness and others were expected to absorb it. One of the Taliesin rituals came on Christmas morning, when the Master would open presents prepared by each of the fellows. Inside each was a model someone had designed and built. Wright would inspect the model, say something like "It looks upside down," and move on to the next one. So focused was he on *his* techniques and *his* vision that he failed to see originality in students. It is a measure of his teaching that few of them ever achieved significance as independent architects.

If Wright did not produce great students, he did produce great buildings—the Frederick C. Robie House in Chicago; Fallingwater in Bear Run, Pennsylvania; the Johnson Wax Building in Racine, Wisconsin; New York's Guggenheim Museum; and many, many more. Even after they were completed, he regarded them as his, as extensions of *him*. On one occasion, he walked unannounced through the front door of a house he had designed years before. Not even greeting the owners, he led an entourage through each and every room, pointing out details and noting what he would now do differently. Then he left without even bothering to close the door.

When Frank Lloyd Wright was 47, death made a horrendous impact on his life. A handyman at his Wisconsin home bolted its doors and windows, set it ablaze, and attacked its inhabitants with a hatchet. He killed Wright's mistress, her two daughters, four employees, and finally himself. Wright, who was away at the time, was devastated but eventually rebuilt his house and his life, perhaps with more conscious thoughts of legacy making. Near the end of his own life, he was asked if he was afraid of death. "Not at all," he answered. "There is not much you can do about death. What is immortal will survive."

What Generativity Is Not

From the life of Frank Lloyd Wright we can learn much about the complexities of generativity—about the conflict between generative domains, about the mix of constructive and destructive tendencies, about the sheer amount of time in which generativity is possible in a life. And we can use these complexities to sharpen our definitional focus. Having said at the outset of this chapter what generativity is, let me now spend a few moments on what it is not.

Generativity, first of all, is not *creativity*, even though it covers a lot of creativity's conceptual ground. I used to look to the past for a way of distinguishing the two: generativity meant that something old was passed on, whereas creativity meant that something new was made. That was clear enough but there was a problem: creators have a notorious habit of forgetting the "old" sources of their "new" ideas. Frank Lloyd Wright was 65 when he first published his autobiography. "By then," says a biographer, and a sympathetic one at that, "he was unwilling to concede that he had ever been helped, or that anyone whose ideas predated his own could possibly have influenced him. He came from nowhere and out of nothing, a full-fledged genius."

If you poke around in history a bit, you'll begin to see how old some new ideas really are. Nicolaus Copernicus, for example, is given credit for coming out of nowhere with one of the most revolutionary concepts in the history of the world—the notion that the sun, not the earth, is the center of our planetary system. But his idea was actually proposed by Aristarchus (and neglected by Greek science) almost two millennia before his time.

And Copernicus's system was only a modified version of the Ptolemaic system it replaced. The same celestial machinery was involved, orbs of crystal carrying the heavenly bodies on their surface, like knots on planks of wood. Their movements were calculated not from the sun, but from the center of the earth's orbit, which was at a slightly different point. Far from rebelling against Ptolemy, Copernicus spoke of him with reverence and criticized contemporaries who questioned the accuracy of his observations. Indeed, Copernicus himself was later criticized for remaining too close to the system he supposedly had overthrown. There was much that was old in his new idea.

If the past offers a poor basis for distinguishing creativity from generativity, the future offers a better one. To put the matter simply, generativity is creativity *that lasts.* Creativity ends once a product is made, but generativity goes on to take care of the product as it seeks an independent life. It prepares the product to survive the creator's departure, whether through death or simple leave-taking. Thus, if you give birth to a new business, you have been creative. But you are not generative until you pass it on to successors. That's why the Taliesin Fellowship was so important to Frank Lloyd Wright's generativity.

Generativity should also be distinguished from *altruism, responsibility,* and *care,* even though many psychologists and lay persons tend to equate the ideas. In her book *New Passages,* for example, journalist Gail Sheehy defines generativity as "a voluntary obligation to care for others in the broadest sense." That definition is too wide. For the sake of clarity we ought to exclude from the reach of the term any influence that does not extend down the generational chain and ultimately survive one's death. Thus, altruism and responsibility and care are not, by themselves, generative. Nor is the activity of a 10-year-old instructing her 70-year-old grandfather in how to use a computer, admirable though it may be. Or that of a middle-aged housewife caring for an elderly parent, unless it serves as an example for her children. Generativity, as the word's root implies, involves influence that proceeds downward through the generations.

Longings for generativity and *immortality* also have much in common. Many people see themselves as "living on" in their children, in the work of their hands, in their influence. But as concepts generativity and immortality are distinct. One is not the other. The individual life cycle consists of birth, growth, reproduction, and death. Generativity is about the third phase of the cycle, not what may or may not follow the fourth. Think of a plant that sprouts, grows to maturity, goes to seed, and then dies. Generativity follows the seed, not the fate of the plant as it lies withering on the ground. Or think of comedian Woody Allen, who once said, "I don't want to achieve immortality through my works. I want to achieve immortality by not dying." I myself would be pleased to know that, years from now, you remembered some ideas from this book, but I would not derive therefrom a sense of not dying, nor assurance that I would have a conscious afterlife. For me, writing is a matter of generativity, not immortality.

Once the concept of generativity becomes clear, we can appreciate its relationships with other human qualities. We can see that it gives one person a sense of immortality and another something else. We can see when creativity, altruism, responsibility, and care are generative and when they are not. It is fascinating to tease out all the ways in which individual people put together their impulse to generate, their artistic sensibilities, their fear of death, and their wishes to be helpful, dependable, and nurturant. Here's a firefighter talking to Studs Terkel in his book *Working*:

> The firemen, you actually see them produce. You see them put out a fire. You see them come out with babies in their hands. You see them give mouth-to-mouth when a guy's dying. You can't get around that shit. That's real. To me, that's what I want to be.
>
> I worked in a bank. You know, it's just paper. It's not real. Nine to five and it's shit. You're looking at numbers. But I can look back and say, "I helped put out a fire. I helped save somebody." It shows something I did on earth.

This man is describing a heroic form of altruism with a generative component: he rescues babies and knows that his rescuing matters in the big picture. "It shows something I did on earth." He is expressing a parental generativity toward children who are not his own—a wonderful mix of generativity and altruism that assures him his life has made a difference.

In psychological research, generativity has appeared in a number of guises. Erik Erikson saw it as a *stage* in life; it defined the task of the middle years and represented a desirable achievement. More recently, researchers have treated it as a personality *trait*, the idea being that some people, no matter what their age, have more of it than others. Generativity has also come out as a *motive,* as in definitions (my own included) that call it an inner desire or need. There is another possibility, that in a given life generativity may define neither a lengthy stage nor a permanent trait nor a hardy motive, but rather a single *moment.* It may also denote a *relationship,* something like the attachment that develops between infants and their mothers; and it is indeed true that children call it forth from parents, students from teachers, audiences from performers, and societies from their citizens.

These distinctions may seem academic, but they have a practical side as well, for they can help to illuminate the course of a particular life and point out the possibilities that remain. A person in advanced old age, for example, may never have reached the stage of generativity and never have had the trait, but still be capable of a single life-defining moment. And if we are to judge from religious myth, the most mature form of generativity—that which exists only at path's end—finds the individual living from moment to moment, concerned simply about the integrity thereof.

In all its guises generativity is always considered a *virtue.* To the extent that Frank Lloyd Wright acted selfishly, therefore, building monuments only to his ego, his work does not merit the label "generative." What was it then? What shall we call the opposite of generativity, the *vice* in legacy making? Erikson said it was personal "stagnation" or "self-absorption." The implication was that you either impressed the next generation for good or you ignored it; you were either caring or uncaring. Erikson's choice of words, however, overlooked a more pernicious opposite: the possibility of leaving a heritage, not just of neglect, but of active destruction. It overlooked the fact that curses leave marks as lasting as blessings, that, in the words of Shakespeare's Mark Antony, "The evil that men do lives after them."

More than semantics is involved in the matter of defining generativity's opposite. What's at stake is seeing or not seeing the trail you leave. When a man says, as in Chapter 1 of this book, "I am the kind of guy who leaves nothing behind, no trace of themselves in the world, like a worm dragging itself across the earth," we ought to spend some time with his children. We ought to ask them, "Did he really leave nothing, or did he leave a mess?" His "stagnation" or "self-absorption" is likely to be his children's nightmare, as it was in Frank Lloyd Wright's family. What is generativity's opposite? To keep an eye open to all we leave behind, I prefer to speak of the "dark side." It is here that damage is passed from one generation to the next, that curses leave their lasting marks, that evil lives on. It is a side we should be alert to before embarking on the Generative Way.

Are Societies Generative?

How many people "have" generativity? In a long-term study of men that defined generativity as responsibility for others—whether as a parent, a supervisor, a coach, or the like—31 percent of a working-class sample was found to have reached a *stage* of generativity by the age of 47. In a similar study of Harvard-educated men (they were preselected for mental health), 41 percent were found to have reached a stage of generativity by the age of 47, and 83 percent by age 60. In another study that used a different definition, 20 percent of a sample of midlife men and women were found to have a high level of the *motive* in their future plans, and another 46 percent a moderate level. The remaining 34 percent evidenced no generative concern at all. While broad generalizations cannot be drawn from these investigations, it is reasonable to conclude from them that most adults know from experience what it means to be generative. It is also reasonable to assume that nearly everyone is capable of significant generative moments. And much depends upon one's age.

The generativity of individuals, of course, has a cumulative effect on those around them. So societies must "have" generativity, too, in varying degrees, and they must also have their dark side. Consider, for example, two groups of English settlers in America who were recently studied by historian Gerald Moran. The one established Colonial Virginia in 1607 and the other developed New England in the 1630s. Having sought the New World for different reasons, the Virginians and the New Englanders showed starkly contrasting attitudes toward the young under their care.

On the dark side were the free-lancers, adventurers, and traders who landed in Virginia looking to make a profit for investors back home. When they discovered how much money could be made growing tobacco, they turned land into plantations and imported young men from England to work it, taking them on as indentured servants for contracted periods of seven years. In England, the young men would have been covered by labor laws regulating the treatment of "life-cycle servants," but in Virginia they were offered no such protection. In this new society they were at the mercy of masters who were free to exploit them.

The results were lethal. Over half the indentured youth died before their seven years were up, and few of the remainder married or had children, mainly because women were so scarce. Those who did marry were unlikely to see their children reach adulthood. In one county, 20 percent of children lost both parents before they turned 13, 37 percent before they were 18. Colonial Virginia was hardly the place for biological or parental generativity.

Nor was it the place for the transmission of culture, a process that is severely tested by any experience of migration. When they crossed the Atlantic Ocean, those who became Virginians cut off their connection to the past. Nor did they seek to restore it. "Each generation of Virginians seems to have started anew, paying little attention to what had preceded it," observes historian T. H. Breen. "[They] focused their attentions on what they called the colony's 'present state.'" And they made little effort to teach the young. Even when Virginia became more stable in the mid-1700s, it failed to establish a school system. Some planters hired tutors to teach their sons, but many children never learned how to read or write.

In its origins, Colonial Virginia was the "antithesis" of a generative society, says Moran. When the system of indentured servitude was abolished, prospects seemed to brighten for its exploited youth. But indenture was soon replaced with something far worse—slavery. "That by the 1770s over 40 percent of Virginia's population was enslaved boded ill for the future of generativity in that society."

On the other side of the Generative Way stood the Puritans of New England, who began to arrive in the 1630s. They came not to produce a profit for investors but to find a haven for their children. They wanted to get away from England, where "most children . . . are perverted, corrupted and utterlie overthrown by the multitude of evil examples"—the words of the first governor of Massachusetts Bay. Twenty thousand came in the 1630s, an enormous number at the time, and they came in organized family groups, not as isolated, indentured youth. Culture was paramount, and they carried it across the ocean. "As a Biblical people," says Moran, "they viewed the family as God's vehicle for perpetuating faith and religious obligations." The family was a "little monarchy" headed by a father who had absolute authority and exacted unquestioning obedience. Puritan fathers were responsible for all four kinds of generativity, begetting children, feeding and clothing them, teaching them how to read and write, and seeing to their religious and moral education. A mother was her spouse's "helpmeet"—so it appears in one recitation of duties—"educating . . . her children, keeping and improving what is got by the industry of the man."

In New England, the Puritans found abundant land, stayed relatively free of disease, and created a society whose generativity scholars can measure. Writes Moran:

> That New Englanders produced completed families averaging in excess of seven children made their region a unique demographic environment; nowhere else in England, Europe, or in the West for that matter did completed families approach the size of those in Puritan America. . . . In some communities, the under age ten population was as high as 35 percent of the total, and the under age twenty population was as high as 60 percent of the total. . . .
>
> In one New England community, over 80 percent of children and youth under the age of 19 had at least two living grandparents. . . . So different was New England in this regard that it "might have been responsible," according to one historian, "for a simple but tremendously important invention, at least in terms of scale—grandparents."

In 1647, Massachusetts passed a law requiring every town of fifty families to appoint a teacher of children and every town of a hundred to set up a grammar school capable of preparing students for a university. A decade before, while immigrants were still arriving by shiploads, Harvard College had been created—an unparalleled achievement in the history of colonization. From the very beginning of the New England settlement, all the domains of generativity were accounted for.

Even though Puritans raised their children in ways that now seem harsh to us, they actually took steps to protect them, enacting in 1641 a document on the "Liberties of Children" that gave them "free libertie to complaine to Authorities for redresse" from "any unnatural severitie" on the part of their parents. It was the first act of its kind in the Western world. They also made changes in inheritance practices. Instead of conferring land only on the eldest son, the colonists created a system of partible inheritance, in which a double share would go to the eldest son and single shares to his brothers and sisters. It was a radical break with English law and not without self-interest. Fathers could now use the promise of land to control *all* of their children for *all* of the father's life.

All of this concern for posterity had variable outcomes. The early school laws were gradually ignored and Harvard declined both quantitatively and qualitatively. Puritan fathers proved quite willing to disinherit the child who chose the wrong occupation, married the wrong spouse, or in other ways displeased them. As the second generation became adults, many failed to follow the religious path of their parents. One historian explains why: "Only unusual Puritans seem to have been capable of raising children who knew how to love their fathers. In the absence of this love, full conversion became difficult for most and impossible for many." The ultimate legacy of Puritan society was as mixed as that of any individual. But for a good portion of the seventeenth century, its generative intensity was unrivaled—and worlds apart from that of Colonial Virginia.

Three and half centuries later, we can ask the question: does the nation to which both these colonies gave rise "have" generativity? We can, in fact, ask the question of any nation on earth. And each will have to provide its own answer. Each will have to look at all the pockets—ethnic, religious, civic, occupational, recreational—that make it up. Some of them may be experiencing moments of intense generativity. Others may be on the dark side.

For the United States, as for many countries, the real test is yet to come. An Age Wave as real as any wave of immigrants will soon crash upon its shores. It has already hit Florida, where one in five residents is over 65. By 2030, perhaps earlier, it will have washed over the entire United States. Then the whole country will look like Florida, a New World indeed.

What will those who ride the Age Wave in be seeking? Returns on their investments? Havens for their children and grandchildren? Will they—will *we,* for I will be one of them—use the growing power of our numbers to demand more *from* society or to give more *to* it? Will we treat the young as indentured servants, demanding that they pay for our "entitlements," or regard them as vital links in the chain of life? In the midst of the Second World War, the German theologian Dietrich Bonhoeffer once said, "The ultimate test of a moral society is the kind of world that it leaves to its children." Bonhoeffer was describing a test of generativity, and the one we face is unprecedented in human history.

PART

II

STEPS ON THE WAY

CHAPTER

3

Talking to Your Past

SOCIETIES MAY HAVE their Generative Way, but this book is about individual paths and what to expect if you set off on one of your own. However long your trek will take—a moment, a season, or a lifetime—the first thing to expect is a meeting with your past. You may welcome this meeting, but then again you may dread it. In either case I hope you remember the story of "The Fisherman and the Djinni."

This story comes from the Arabian Nights collection, the one in which the maiden Scheherazade keeps herself alive by telling the king stories every night for 1001 nights. It is one of the oldest and simplest stories in the entire work. Scheherazade's tale begins with a poor fisherman standing on the shore and casting his net into the sea. He is "getting on in years," the story says, but he still has a wife and three children to support. So he needs a good catch. When the time comes to pull in his net, it won't budge. So he stakes part of it to the ground, takes off his clothes, and dives in after the rest. He finally manages to haul everything in, only to discover that the net contains nothing but the carcass of a dead ass. Disappointed, he cleans the net and throws it in a second time, this time praying to Allah for good luck. Now his net strains even more than before. The fisherman thinks it is teeming with fish, but once he gets it up on shore he sees that he has dredged up a huge jar full of sand and mud. He makes a third cast, but all he gets this time are the shattered remains of pots and bottles.

In despair, the fisherman prays again to Allah and makes his final cast of the day. This time, when he pulls in his net, he finds in it a small copper bottle sealed with lead. It appears to be very old. The fisherman digs out the seal with his knife, shakes the bottle, and out comes a column of smoke that turns into a huge and terrifying djinni (or genie) who was imprisoned eighteen hundred years before by King Solomon. Enraged at having been confined so long, the djinni looms over the fisherman and threatens to kill him. "Prepare to die," he says, "and choose the way it will happen."

But the fisherman is clever. "I can't believe you fit in that little bottle," he says, and soon he has tricked the djinni back into the bottle and reinserted the lead stopper. "Now you choose the way *you* will die," he declares, and threatens to throw him back in the sea. "I will stay on this very spot and warn everyone who passes of your treachery."

The djinni struggles to escape but cannot. So he tries a different approach, begging humbly for his life. Then a curious thing happens. The fisherman tells him a story.

"You deserve the fate of the king in the tale of 'Yunan and the Doctor,'" says the fisherman.

"How does it go?" asks the djinni.

So the fisherman tells him a long story that turns out to have stories within the story. (Each of the stories, of course, keeps Scheherazade alive for another night.) When the fisherman is finally done, the djinni offers to tell a story of his own. Gradually, the two become acquainted with each other. The fisherman relaxes his guard, the djinni promises him no harm, and the fisherman cautiously reopens the flask. Then the djinni takes him on a magic journey that eventually leads to the freeing of the fisherman's land from the spell of an evil sorceress.

Although this tale was never intended as such, I have found it to be a wonderful metaphor for the first phase of the generative process (or the first step on the Way): talking to your past. In the tale, a man retrieves from the sea—a symbol of his own inner depths—legacies left by previous generations. He is fishing for something to sustain himself and his family, but all he gets is brokenness (the pottery shards), burden (the urn filled with mud), and death (the carcass of the ass). Waste, all of it. Then he comes to the smallest of the legacies and the only one that is sealed up. When he breaks the seal, terror leaps out and overpowers him. But the fisherman takes the time to talk to the terror and to learn what lies behind it. After a while, the contents of the bottle seem less frightening. When the fisherman releases them, they become life, powerful and energetic life, and they steer the fisherman into a kind of generativity he could not have imagined. In the end, he reaches far beyond his family and liberates his land for future generations.

In "The Fisherman and the Djinni," these events occur in the life of an older man, but they can take place at any point in adulthood. At any point we can cast a net into memory and see what it brings up. At any point memory itself can wash an old flask up on our shore. Should we open it up? If we are to be generative, the answer is yes. The sea is an essential source of our creativity.

What might we find if we open a bottle? The djinni in Scheherazade's story had been put in the copper flask eighteen centuries before by King Solomon. The length of time involved and the status of Solomon suggest that the legacy in question was cultural. But legacies come in all sorts of guises, good as well as bad. The symbolic bottle may contain talents or diseases encoded in our genes (in the case of biological generativity), a history of family love or violence (parental generativity), a mentor's approach to solving a problem, whether elegant or awkward (technical generativity), or an artist's view of good and evil (cultural generativity). Some of these legacies—our genetic makeup, for example—go back millions of years, while others—beliefs about good and evil—go back thousands. Still others are the remnants of the many experiences we have had in our own short lifetime. A bottle containing a legacy may be stopped up by deceit, fear, pain, guilt, shame, anger, or simple ignorance. Opening it may mean nothing more than learning what was distinctive about our upbringing or our people's history. And that may take a long while: in the well-known maxim, the fish is the last to discover the water.

A 38-year-old woman I once wrote about drew up from her sea a legacy of deceit. "My mother was a liar," she said. "Her whole life was a lie, even, from what I can piece together, down to the last minute." The biggest lie concerned the identity of this woman's father; it was neither the stepfather who had raised her nor the man whose name she bore. She had not learned who it was until she was a teenager in the middle of the Hungarian Revolution, and she was never able to communicate with the man until she was an ocean away and filled with anger. Ever since, she has kept turning over "blocks" in her mind, trying to understand the reason for the lies, trying to arrange what she learns into a story with which she can be at peace. "The blocks have so many sides! If only I knew which side of each was supposed to face me, if only I could right the pieces, then the puzzle would have meaning. It would be whole." Righting the blocks "means something in my future," she said.

I cite this example not only for its imagery of the blocks but also for the phrase "means something in my future." The *juxtaposition* of the two is critical. Freud acquainted us with the fact that mental life can be full of sealed bottles, but not with the potential for generativity those bottles contained, not with their meaning for the future. The concept of sublimation, of "higher" outlets for "lower" instincts, is as close as he got. The story of the fisherman makes explicit the connection missed by Freud, for in the story the old man's newfound energy flows into a channel that is clearly generative. He uses the inner djinni to leave the legacy of a reformed society. Leaving the legacy is Freud's missing link; it completes the cycle of life. There is no other way but to create a heritage out of the one we have received.

How do we do so? Much depends on the nature of our djinni. Of three possible responses to a legacy, let us now consider two, saving the third for the next chapter. On the one hand, if a legacy is benevolent, we can *repeat* it—"model" it, in the language of psychology. We can be as upright as our father or as nurturing as our mother. We can pass on the values that our mentor has instilled in us. If a legacy falls on the dark side, however, we can *rework* it, taking what we have received and transforming it, so that evil becomes good and lemon lemonade.

In either case we have to find the power of the djinni, who is nothing more, in my interpretation, than a symbol for generative life. The djinni represents a living presence—a unique presentness—of the past. Not all in our history is endowed with such life; much is as dead as the broken pottery, the mud, and the carcass of the story. And that which is so endowed seems often enough to be locked up, sealed in a bottle like the energy compacted into a hard-shelled seed. It is no easy trick to capture the bottle that comes from the sea, and it is harder still to learn to talk to what it contains. But if we do, Scheherazade's story tells us, the power we find will sweep us along the Generative Way.

Repeating a Legacy

I know of no better example of power released than that of 37-year-old Herb Robinson, a short, athletically built African-American who received a legacy of value. His earliest memory of life is being in church on a Sunday morning, a small church with dark, high-backed pews. There he is held securely in his mother's arms while he looks up in awe at his father, who is preaching the word of God. Herb's story is about the way we "take in" progenitors, assimilating them in such a way that they become not only an inner presence but—in the most complete "taking in"—the *I* that is aware of that presence. This is the *I* that repeats a legacy.

Like many first memories, Herb Robinson's stands for much in his life. It speaks not only of a particular father but of a legacy of fatherhood that goes back many generations. It speaks of a cultural legacy, too, of a tradition of preaching in black Baptist churches that descends from an African slave tradition, an older Christian tradition, and an even older Judaism. The same Solomon who figures in the story of the djinni is part of that mix. Herb's father has preached about Solomon, and Herb himself has studied the record of his deeds. Traces of Solomon's wisdom have filtered down through the centuries and become his own. There are many legacies in the conscious and unconscious memory of this 37-year-old man that go back hundreds and even thousands of years.

When Herb was 4, he had an experience that now seems foundational. He can date it because his mother was pregnant with his younger brother. "I was wandering through the house and I heard a voice call my name. I was surprised to hear it because I knew my father wasn't home. It was a masculine voice and it said, 'Bene't,' which is my middle name and what my mother called me. I know I heard the voice because I stopped immediately and looked around to find it, but I couldn't. I looked around again and heard the voice again, and it said, 'You're going to be a preacher.' I was frightened and I ran upstairs to my mother. I told her there was someone downstairs. She said that maybe I was dreaming. I said, 'No, Mom, I heard a voice.' And I told her what the voice said. And she said, 'Well, don't worry about it, just lie down and take a nap.' "

Herb looks upon that experience as his first call to do the work his father does. For twenty-five years he wrestled with the questions it posed.

Was he *truly* called, and, if so, when would he answer? And could he even come close to being as great as the man he looked up to? His struggle was with a legacy of value, one worth passing on. But such legacies have their own problems. To a young man, a great father can be as imposing as the djinni encountered by the fisherman. How do you become your own person when you stand in awe of such a man? How do you put your voice—not his—into your generativity?

I cannot imagine forces of modeling more powerful than those in the Robinson home. Herb was the oldest boy and had been given his father's name. Herb, Sr., was "stern" but not "strict." An excellent bowler and golfer, he taught his son baseball, basketball, and football, and Herb played them all. This is the ordinary stuff of male generativity, but in Herb's case there was more. As few boys do these days, he saw his father outside the family context, saw him at work—witnessed individuals coming forth, trembling, in response to his call, witnessed entire congregations being raised by him to a climax of dancing and shouting and ecstasy. "Years ago, my grandmother told me, 'There's something special about your father. He's a blessed man. So you just pay close attention to him.' " Herb did just that, making even loftier identifications. Seeing his father cry over the assassination of Martin Luther King, he began to draw comparisons. "I used to put my father and Martin Luther King in the same category because someone once told me that they were just alike, but one had fame and the other didn't."

When he was nine, just before Reverend King's assassination, Herb heard the voice again. "It was late at night and I was awakened out of a deep sleep. In my doorway there was a figure in a purple smoking jacket with black slacks, and for a head it had a ball of fire. I was terrified. I rubbed my eyes to be sure I wasn't dreaming. When I realized I wasn't, I put my head under the cover and I prayed and I pulled the covers back again. The figure was still there. It said to me, 'You're going to be a preacher.'

"It was the same voice that I had heard as a 4-year-old. The only reason I didn't think it was my father is because it was very late at night. All I can remember is the darkness and waking up in the middle of the night and the figure telling me, 'You're going to be a preacher.' And I dozed off to sleep."

When Herb told his parents of his childhood callings, they were encouraging but noncommittal. It proved to be a wise position, for in his adolescence Herb became "bullheaded." "When my father would tell me to turn right, I would go left. If he'd tell me to go straight ahead, I'd back up. All because I wanted to be my own man." Still, at age 19, he announced to his father that he wished to be a minister. He told him why: "People were saying I looked like a preacher, I acted like a preacher, I talked like a preacher, I sang like a preacher. So I might as well be a preacher. My father said, 'No, son, that's not it.' He rebuffed me. He sent me away. At first I felt rejected. But then I thought, well, maybe I'm not supposed to be a preacher. Maybe the voices I heard in the past weren't real."

But the memory of those voices stayed with him as he left home and went off to college. From 19 to 28 Herb worked, mostly full time, and took courses at several colleges. He no longer lived under the direct, daily influence of his father. "I put the ministry on the back burner because I would look at the humbleness of my father and say, well, Dad doesn't have all the money that I would like to have. I didn't see how the ministry could get me what I wanted out of life." But there was a greater obstacle. "I never thought that I could be the preacher my father was. He's humble. He's not money-hungry. He's satisfied with his life the way it is. I could never be as great as he is. I thought that if I achieved the status that he had, I would ruin it by my love of money."

Psychology has a number of *i*-words to describe the process of "taking in" other people. *Incorporation, introjection, imitation, internalization, idealization,* and *identification* are six listed by psychoanalyst George Vaillant. Vaillant likens them to ways of digesting food. At the one extreme—incorporation—we take in a presence whole but fail to metabolize it. We are like the boa constrictor who has just swallowed an elephant. With introjection, we take in only parts of the elephant—facets of another person—but even those parts remain foreign to us. In imitation, we *act* like the other person ("I talked like a preacher, I sang like a preacher") but we do not *become* like them. Internalization and idealization are terms for the actual becoming; in the latter instance, we use the internalized presence to represent what we want to be. Identification, says Vaillant, is the most graceful way of "digesting" others. The metabolism is both selective and complete. Elephant turns into snake; the other becomes the very bones of our subjective self. "Incorporation and introjection are ways of believing that one *has* the other person. Idealization and identification are ways of *being* the other person and yet being oneself at the same time. . . . With identification we can say to ourselves, 'He did it and, if I choose, I can do it too.'" The *i*-process leads to an *I*—a miracle that, more and more, I stand in awe of.

By the age of 28, Herb Robinson had been away from home long enough to actually *identify* with his father—to take, eat, and assimilate him. He was ready to say, "He did it and, if I choose, I can too." That year of his life proved to be critical. Herb was told by his girlfriend of five years to make up his mind; it was now or never regarding their marriage. In a culture where spiritual calls were both valid and valued, he was also told by his God that it was now or never. Would he be a minister or not?

This time the voice came when he was reading the Bible. Herb had been reading about one of Jesus' disciples raising a woman from the dead. The voice said, "'Why is it that you don't think you can do these things? You don't have to be Christ to raise the dead.' And I took that to mean that you don't have to be Jesus Christ to preach the Gospel. Because He did say in His Word that the things that we have seen Him do, we would do greater things." The voice also said, "'This is your life.' I took that to mean that if I didn't answer the call into the ministry, my life would soon end. There was no need for me to continue living because I wasn't serving the purpose that I was sent to earth for. I was terrified about what could happen.

"I told my father that I was now ready to accept my calling. I felt that if this is what God wanted me to do, He would give me the tools I needed. We announced it to our church and they gave me a date for a trial sermon. I delivered a trial sermon and they gave me a license to preach. Five years later, I was ordained by the same church, and I'm still a minister." Before Herb turned 29 he had answered his call, married, and moved, geographically, back to his father's church and his direct influence. He was now ready to continue the legacy.

Doing so in his 30s, Herb has learned that he does not have to measure up to the daunting figure of his father. His job, rather, is to "be what God has made me." In that effort, God will give him what he lacks. Herb now sees ways in which he differs from his father—regarding church rules about women's attire, for example—and even sees areas in which his father is lacking. Herb would be more "economically aware" than he, investing church monies in businesses that would employ its members, for instance. He would do more financially for his own family.

Yet even with a sense of being his own man, Herb at 37 still looks up to his father the way he did in his first memory of life. When I asked him if his father, now 67, was a great man, he quietly admitted to feeling that he was "the greatest I've ever known." But this father seems to know what helps in the turnover of generations. "My father has already told me that I'll be greater than he is. He bases that on the fact that he sees me doing at my age things that he didn't do until he was in his late 50s. There was one particular situation where he had me preach on Easter Sunday. He had told me that it was one of the most difficult times to bring a message. You get a lot of people who come to church on Easter Sunday who don't come during the year. The sermon that I preached, I think it was my third sermon, got an overwhelming response from the congregation. He told me that he had never seen anything like that before at an Easter service. It encourages me, but it frightens me at the same time."

In the story of the copper bottle, the fisherman had to get the djinni down to size before he could release his power. Herb had to do something similar with the figure of his father. He had to seal it up for a while, become "bullheaded" until he found out who he himself was. Then he could say, without being overwhelmed, "The father is in me, but I am not the father." And even, "I will be greater than he."

Once he did that, he discovered the power. "I know it's the power of God. It builds up. There's nothing I could say or do to make people react the way they do." Just as Herb has felt the power enter him, so he has seen it leave when his "ego wants to step forward." His greatest fear is not that he will lose the power, but rather that he will corrupt it.

What Herb sees as the power of God is also the power of generative life, and there is more to its release than changes in Herb's relationship with the past. There is the gaining of voice, the establishment of intimacy, the arrival of children, the faith in something transcendent—all to be discussed in subsequent chapters. But here the focus is on Herb's repeating of a legacy.

Today, Herb's father remains more than an internal presence. He is an external reality—a pastor, a sponsor, a director in matters spiritual. He reviews the contents of Herb's sermons. He goes over Herb's invitations to preach at other churches, some of which come because of his own reputation. And when it comes to golf, he's still coaching. "He told me that if he keeps watching me, he's going to be picking his head up every time he swings at the ball too."

For thirty-seven years the two Robinsons have experienced a relationship in all of generativity's domains. Herb may be 50 or 60 before his father's guidance finally ends, before death seals his legacy. At that time he will take his father in one more time and begin to talk to him in yet another way, as did this woman of 19 I visited after her father's death:

> The night of the wake he was out in the living room and I couldn't sleep. I didn't know what to do, so I got up and washed my hair. My sister was sleeping. I came out, and the casket was there. I stayed away from it. I just sat there and said, "Well, you've got a lot of pull now, so do something. Send up signs. Do all these wonderful things." Then I'd say, "I'm really stupid! I'm sitting here talking to this dead body." So I'd run into the other room and I'd lie down, and come back out, and each time I'd get closer until finally I was just sitting there saying, "Well, you know you're going to be watching." And I had this great vision that he was going to be on my right-hand shoulder for the rest of my life. I thought, "Okay, I'm being watched over." And things got much easier then. . . .
>
> Since then unbelievable things have happened. I'm a straight A-B student. Before it was C's and D's. I've finished a major and a half already and I'm going to finish two majors. I used to run away from everything, but now I say, "That's not the way to do it. You face everything head-on 'cause you can beat it. You're bigger than it." Sometimes I feel it's unfortunate he isn't seeing this progress. But he is. He's on my shoulder, every day, every night. I feel I'm so much of him, so much of him is me!

The process of identification leaves the other in you, as part of you; yet it also leaves you distinct from the other. This is the kind of "taking in" that enables one to repeat a legacy. The djinni is not only someone you talk to but also, in a mysterious way, the you that does the talking.

But only part of you. Herb Robinson, Jr., is far from a clone of Herb Robinson, Sr. His genes come from two people, not one, his voice from many more. All of these influences are *in* him. Some of them *are* him. And he in turn will leave influences of his own.

"Is he a preacher?" I asked of his 1-year-old son, Herb's second child.

Herb smiled. "My wife tells me not to say that. When I was younger, people used to tell me I was going to be a preacher. I used to deny it. 'No, I'm not. No, I'm not.' But anything that he can hold in his hand that resembles a microphone, he'll grab it and act like he's talking or singing. Every morning he climbs up on the piano and just bangs away on the keys until we pull him down. I will try to influence him to preach, but I want him to make his decision on his own, just like my father let me."

Reworking a Legacy

Robert Creighton is another African-American man I got to know in his 30s. The heritage he received from the past was also about fatherhood, but it was just the opposite of Herb Robinson's. So Robert had to find a different way to generativity, a more difficult way. He could not identify with the contents of his bottle; he had to defend against them. He could not repeat a legacy; he had to rework it.

Ironically, Robert's earliest memory of life is a lot like Herb's. In it, Robert's father—a tall, lanky man who smelled of cigarettes and mechanic's grease—appears as a hero in the eyes of a small boy. "I was sick. I don't know what was wrong, but my entire body had swollen up. My mother called it a spasm, so I guess I was jerking. I remember being a little butterball lying in bed with all these lights on me and all these adults standing over. And they said, 'Well, let's call Will.' My father's name was William, and he lived on the other side of town. When my mother called him, he came over in fifteen minutes. I remember him picking me up and taking me to the hospital in his car—a black, shiny Plymouth. Beautiful!"

All that followed in Robert's life was a betrayal of that memory. In the apartment where he lived, his mother had two small signs. In glitter glued on blue cardboard they said, "God Bless Our Home" and "What is Home Without a Father?"

"As I grew up I was much aware of not having a daddy. And people used to say, 'You're silly. You have a daddy. Everybody's got a daddy. How could you be born without a daddy?' They knew what we meant by not having a daddy. Other kids' daddies would come home. They would eat and smoke and get clean and shave, and then they'd go in their car and take their brood with them, right? Well, where was my daddy? He had his nice car. Kids would brag about their daddies. My daddy could do this and my daddy could do that. Well, where was my daddy? I better not say anything about my daddy—I didn't have one. And you know kids are often cruel. They'd say, 'Where's your father? You ain't got no father. I bet he didn't even marry your mother.' My cousins, especially the ones close to my age, would ask, 'Why your daddy's like that?' And, well, usually you defended your father. You thought that's what you should do. Everybody else defended his father. But the difference was you didn't live with yours, right? So I felt punished. Why me? You know, why can't I have a daddy?

"I used to do things to provoke him and make him whip me. Anything to get this man's attention. I would stick out my lip and pout. I would grumble under my breath, loud enough to make him say something. And he'd say, 'Who do you think you're talking to? I'm your daddy!' Pat phrases—that's all he ever said. And I'd make smart remarks like, 'You ain't my daddy.' And he'd drop it.

"I didn't want him to drop it. I can remember his cigarette stains on the face bowl on the commode. In the morning I'd get up and I'd trace the stains, and I would smell the oil and the dirt. Anything just to get close to him. But he would not have it. In fact, the more he knew I stood in awe of him, the more he backed up. He didn't want that responsibility. 'Hey, kid, don't be like me.' "

At 12 Robert finally got the message. "The memory I have is of asking him if he would allow me to come to his garage every Saturday, just to learn the trade. And he told me, 'Hell, no. You can't come. You talk too much. You ask too many questions.' And I said, 'Well, just please let me come. I swear I won't say anything.' 'No, you can't come. Just don't come back.' I mean, it was all he could do just to keep from chasing me out of the place. And I was devastated. It was then that I knew he didn't like me. Before I just never knew what was going on."

Robert's mother was the other side of his legacy from the past, the other half of what he called a "double consciousness." She was the one who held him and comforted him and told him stories. Robert had "explicit faith" in her, not only as a safe haven, but also as a teacher. "I mean, she used to preach *all* the time. That's the way she was. Talk, talk, talk. She pointed out when several white kids raped and killed this woman. They were smokin' reefer. That was a bad thing, them reefer. And she'd point that out to me. She'd wake me up in the middle of the night and point out gangs roaming the streets, throwing things. 'That's the kind of thing you shouldn't do.' I can remember stealing at the A&P. She made me take it back. I can remember stealing from a bakery—those little tags you get to wait in line. I showed Mother, and she said, 'Take them back.' I took them back, and the lady was so pleased she gave me some apple turnovers. People used to praise me about how good Mother was. She was special, and everybody told us that."

In his late teens, however, Robert's mother had little influence on him. He found himself full of uncontrollable anger, "bombarded with emotions I couldn't handle." It was 1961, and he began to pour that anger into the civil rights movement. I remember the way his jaw thrust forward when he spoke of that time, just as it had when he spoke of the father of his boyhood. "In my recurring dream I was strapping bombs and bullets and hand grenades to me. I figured if I could end the whole world that would be it. Maybe if I killed myself through killing other people, that would be it.

"I can remember one vigil downtown. You know downtown Chicago. You got these big tall buildings. You stand in the middle of LaSalle and say one word, you can hear it all over the place. I remember tons of cops lined up along City Hall. Tons of marchers walking—we taking shifts, you know. I gave a dialogue. I was a nigger and I was a white and I was playing these roles, assuming different voices. Jumping up on the police cars. I just absolutely flipped out. And when I finished, I was sweating. I was shaking. It was as though I had delivered a sermon. I was just wiped out completely."

Thirty days in jail with books and a journal calmed Robert down and gave him time to think. He reentered the maternal side of his double consciousness. "I was frustrated, and I saw no real reason why things were the way they were. I said, God, it would be great if I could make a change, and the way I saw myself making a change was this bomb bit. But even concurrently I think I was saying, man, I just want to get away from it all. I don't know whether I got it from Martin Luther King or not, but he used to talk about going on the mountain. And for years my metaphor for getting myself together was to take my mother and my portable typewriter and sit on top of a mountain."

Robert never actually went to a mountain, but at the age of 21 he met a white woman who listened to him talk and tell stories. Peggy was timid and shy, and the very first night they met, he talked until morning. Their conversations continued for weeks and then months. "I never hid anything. I never pretended. I mean if something would upset me and I couldn't deal with it, I'd cry. I recognized, too, that my talking was a way of dealing with a lot of my problems. She recognized it. I talked about why I talk so much, why I talk loud, why I talk incessantly. I knew why. It wasn't a way of putting others down or saying look at me, I'm good, I'm better. It was just a way of keeping myself from blowing up."

Two years after they met, Robert and Peggy married, and a year after that Robert finished college and began graduate school in English. He wanted to be a writer, to pour all that talking and all that anger onto the printed page. By the age of 27 he had a master's degree; for several years, he tried to go further but was unsuccessful. In his early 30s, he and his wife were able to make a down payment on a large house in a neighborhood with deflated property values. Both worked, Robert as a part-time college instructor and substitute high school teacher.

He was 27 when the first of two sons was born. With them came the chance to rework the legacy he had received.

"Noah cried from the day he was born to the day he was 2, it seemed. Man, oh man, it was almost unbearable! I could not even think of this kid hurting himself without just feeling my heart . . . breaking, you know. I wanted to protect this kid from everything. I remember looking at him when he was on the bed when he was so little. His head was squished in, and he was grimacing because he had colic, and everything was wrong. You see this kid lying on the bed, and you're feeling so sorry for him. You know, what can you do?

"We had said from the start, when Noah was born, we knew what we were going to do with our babies. Peggy went to school and I kept Noah, or I went to school and Peggy kept Noah. Everywhere we went, Noah went. If we went to a restaurant, he went. If he couldn't go, we didn't go. It was as simple as that. I remember reading William Blake to this kid. I mean, I used to write papers with this kid on my desk. And we treated Matthew the same way we treated Noah. We took Matthew everywhere, we did everything with Matthew. I mean, we didn't separate the two."

The birth of his first child rekindled a hope in Robert: maybe generational links could now be established; maybe his own father would now connect to him. Robert's father met his grandson for the first time at a Christmas gathering. "Noah was a little baby, and he held him a bit, but you could see that he didn't want to. We ate, we were talking and milling around, and in the middle of the festivities he jumps up and he goes. That's what he did when I was a kid. So I start crying, and I say, 'God, he's never grown up. Maybe if I weren't there he would have stayed.' I cried then and I cried when I was a kid. It's just like you're there, you know, your kid, your wife, and your relatives, right, and you're having a good time, and all of a sudden he jumps up and says, 'Hey, I'm going. I'm leaving.'

"I've always shied away from identifying the source of my anger. My brothers used to tell me, and my wife did too, 'Maybe if you stopped saying you like your daddy, you'd be all right.' But I never admitted to myself that I dislike him. I once bought him a present, and I didn't send it to him, and then I did it to be mean. Now I think if I buy him something or send him a Father's Day card, it will really hurt him because he knows this is mockery. It wouldn't be on my part. But to him . . . What have I ever done for this kid for him to say, hey, happy Father's Day? I think he'd just be overwhelmed. He couldn't take it."

Seven years after that Christmas get-together, when Robert was 35, his father called. "After all these years this cat just gets on the phone from Chicago and says, 'Hey, I'm coming over. Something told me to come and see you.' I said, 'Okay, you can come.' I had mixed feelings about it, but my wife was furious, *furious!* She said, 'I'm not going to let him do to the kids what he did to you.' She didn't want me to be hurt, and she saw his coming here so suddenly and his having done nothing for us ever as maybe we're going to start this same thing in a new generation. My kids are going to say, 'Oh, this is my granddaddy,' and they're going to get hooked up with him and he's going to do the same thing. He's going to withdraw. And she didn't want that. She said, 'No, no, no, I don't want the kids to get to know him.' She was going to stay with some friends while he was here, but I convinced her not to because that would embarrass me. But she stayed in the bedroom the whole weekend. He's saying, 'Where is your wife?' and I'm saying, 'Well . . .'

"We went on a drive, he and the kids and I, and I cried and told him what was happening. I told him about the hang-up of not having a father and about some of the quirky things he's done all of his life to us. And he said, 'Aw, man, forget that. You grown now, you got your own kids.' There was no way he could deal with it. He's an older man, and he's built up such a great defense that now he's not going to let anything penetrate. He's lived all his life with the notion of being a rat. That's what we called it. Not taking any responsibility for his kids, not even letting them know that he exists and that he cares about them. He wasn't going to get into that. I brought it up very briefly, and he just didn't want to talk about it.

"Finally I told him why my wife hadn't shown up and he was fit to be tied. He was furious! He wanted to leave right then, that night. I said, 'No, wait until the morning,' and he finally waited.

"The following day he went back to Chicago, and he talked about it. He couldn't understand. He didn't even know my wife. How could she have anything to do with it? Certainly he understood how people could have feelings and want to protect those they love from being hurt, but the irony is that he had done just the opposite. He had said, 'Aw, forget those kids. I'm a man, I made three babies.' I'm sure he was bragging just like everybody else who never did anything for their kids, you know, street corner men. Now he's a little bit older and all of his children are grown, and he looks back on it and says, 'Hey, maybe it could have been different.' "

Robert was 42 when I saw him once again—saw that his anger toward his father had become quiet pity, saw what a difference he was making in the next generation. His two sons were with him on that occasion. At 14 and 10, both were aware of their growing size and strength. When it came to wrestling, said Matthew, the younger, "We can skin him. He doesn't have a chance against us because we're so big." There was no mistaking Robert's involvement in their lives—it was almost too much. Their dad was "maybe a little paranoid," the boys said. He talked too much. He hollered and got "hyper."

"Kind of like me," Noah added. "He gets furious when I do it but I get it from him."

Robert wanted to talk about other facets of their relationship. "We say we love each other a million times a day. I mean, this kid calls me and says, 'I love you, Dad.' I'm sitting in my office with these college kids and they think this is a girl I'm talking to until I say his name."

I wondered aloud if either of the boys would like to be a father someday. Too much of a commitment, said Noah. Right now he'd rather be an uncle with lots of nieces and nephews. He loved kids but he wasn't ready for the responsibility of parenthood.

His younger brother didn't hesitate. "I'd love to be a dad."

How many kids would he want?

"Two."

"What would you do with them?"

"What would I do with them?" Now there was a dumb question. "I'd give them all the love and care I had to give. I'd tell them how the world is, tell them the facts of life, tell them how to survive. I'd teach them how to get through school and help them decide what they want to be. I'd do all that you had to do to be a parent—and be a dad." It was utterly obvious to this young man what a father does, and what he would eventually do. When you think back to his grandfather, you realize what it means to rework a legacy. You appreciate what the man in the middle has done.

Mature Defenses and Coherent Memories

The story of the fisherman and the djinni can enlighten the conditions of Robert Creighton's generativity, just as it did Herb Robinson's. But we must remember that Robert's djinni was different from Herb's. While Herb's inspired awe, Robert's created anger and pain. Robert's illustrates how nongenerativity is felt by offspring to be antigenerativity, how a father's neglect becomes a child's hurt. Robert "took in" his father, but the *i*-process never went beyond incorporation: his father remained foreign to him, like the elephant in the boa constrictor before it is digested. Robert had to defend against a presence within him, not identify with it. He had to say it was *not* I.

Psychoanalysis has identified a number of mechanisms that help in such defense, and research has now confirmed that some are better than others. Some are healthier, less deceptive, more mature. In fact, to an outsider, some of the very best defense mechanisms—*altruism, anticipation, humor*—may not sound defensive or mechanistic at all. They are protective strategies that have evolved into something higher, even in an ethical sense. As George Vaillant says, "Often such mechanisms are analogous to the means by which an oyster, confronted with a grain of sand, creates a pearl."

The story of the copper bottle may be taken as a parable about the maturity of defenses and their relation to generativity. In it, the fisherman recovers something that was either *repressed* or *suppressed* (we do not know how tightly the bottle was corked) and then *sublimates* it. Repression means that a legacy from the past is so tightly bottled up that it is nearly impossible to open; suppression, that it can be opened and closed at will. Sublimation is akin to channeling the energy of the djinni into a noble cause like the liberation of a country. On a scale of maturity, repression occupies an intermediate position; suppression and sublimation are higher up. They enable us to have a conversation with legacies that are buried within us, a conversation that is safe because it is indirect, just as the tales the fisherman tells are indirect.

In the course of the story, the fisherman's defense mechanisms mature. They become healthier. Repression turns into suppression and then into sublimation; energy that was once dammed up is now channeled. In Robert Creighton's 20s, there was an equally creative transformation, though we can only guess at its intricacies. As he entered that decade of his life, he says, he was "bombarded with emotions I couldn't handle." But he gradually learned how to handle them. A "handle" is an everyday word for a defense mechanism. So is a "grip," as in "getting a grip." A psychoanalyst might say that Robert's anger, which on the streets was the subject of *acting out* and *displacement* (immature mechanisms), was rather suddenly *suppressed* and *sublimated*. It was turned on its head (psychoanalysts call this *reaction formation*) and became *altruism*—love for his sons. As these changes were taking place, Robert stopped *denying* its true source and true target. It was his father.

In a study that followed 95 Harvard men from their college years to middle age, Vaillant and other researchers found a pattern strikingly similar to that in the story of the fisherman and in the life of Robert. Men's defenses matured as they got older. Most of the change took place during the years of early adulthood, as it did for Robert, but in a few instances it waited until middle age. Only in his late 40s, for example, did one man describe his mother as "pathetic, hypochondriacal, hateful, and threatening" (in adolescence he had spoken of her with reverence). Only at 50 did another subject reveal that his mother had committed suicide when he was 14. To these men, maturation was like opening the seal on an awful—and awesome—djinni that had been left in them by another. They had learned to talk, in other words, with inner realities that had once terrified them.

It is not surprising that the ability to have such conversations was associated in Vaillant's research with positive life outcomes, or that a lack of the ability was associated with alcoholism and chronic depression. But Vaillant also found that maturity of defenses in the 20s and early 30s made for generativity in the 40s. (Generativity was defined as a *stage* characterized by "sustained responsibility for the growth, well-being, and leadership of others.") Of the men with predominantly mature defenses by their mid-30s, 64 percent were generative at age 47. Of those with predominantly immature defenses, 0 percent—none—were. A similar (although not predictive) relationship between maturity of defenses and generativity was later found in two other samples, one of women and one of men. The timing varied, but the rule held: when defenses mature, generativity flows. And when generativity flows, the defenses mature.

That rule held in another line of research, although the terminology employed was quite different. In London, psychologists asked one hundred pregnant women about their memories of childhood, using a protocol called the Adult Attachment Interview (AAI). The AAI asks about the bond one formed with one's parents. How close were you to your mother and father? Did you ever feel rejected? To whom did you go when you were upset or hurt? The questioning takes anywhere from a half-hour to two hours, the average being about forty-five minutes.

Some of the expectant mothers had pleasant memories of childhood; others had memories that were troubling. Would this difference predict the quality of the attachment the mothers would soon have with their babies? There was a second difference. About two-fifths of the mothers had *incoherent* memories, whether pleasant or not. About three-fifths had *coherent* ones. Would this matter?

Incoherence was not a matter of having a poor memory but rather of having one with poor connections. Some of the incoherent mothers, for example, spoke only in generalities about their parents. When asked for specifics, they remembered little, even though many had a history of rejection. They also dismissed the value of attachment and distanced themselves from the emotions of childhood. Other mothers were flooded with specific memories but could not make general evaluations. They were so enmeshed in their past experiences, so preoccupied with anger or passivity, that they could not get a handle on the past. The former group defended against specifics in their memories of attachment, the latter against generalizations. If you read an interview transcript from either group, you would have serious doubts about the conclusions the narrator was drawing. If you were a psychoanalyst, you might spot a number of immature defense mechanisms.

Coherence meant that generic memories, whether of loving or rejecting parents, were supported by specific examples. There was more objectivity and balance in coherent stories, less distortion and self-deception. Connections drawn between past and present made sense. The narrator seemed free of unresolved concerns and was in control of her memories, not at their mercy. If you were to read a coherent transcript, you would most likely agree with its conclusion. If you were a psychoanalyst, you might spot few defense mechanisms, a sure sign that the defenses were mature.

Fifteen months after the AAI interviews, the mothers returned with their year-old babies. Now the researchers could determine the quality of the attachment the two had developed. They did so by using the "Strange Situation" procedure, a standard measure of attachment. The procedure takes about twenty minutes and is conducted in a laboratory playroom the child has never seen before. A mother brings her child into the playroom and allows him or her to explore. A few minutes later she walks out the door. Then she returns.

Researchers focus on the return. Securely attached children, who may or may not have cried when their mother left, are happy to see her come back. They want a hug and are easily comforted when they get one. Insecure children respond in one of two ways. Some simply ignore their mother's comings and goings. Others become distressed, even inconsolable, when their mother leaves. Once she returns, they seek contact, then angrily push her away or squirm to get out of the her arms. They cannot be comforted.

Common sense suggests that mothers with good memories of attachment would produce securely attached children, and that mothers with troubling memories would create children with insecure attachments. Not so. The content of a mother's memories mattered far less than their coherence. Of mothers with coherent memories, 75 percent had securely attached babies. Of mothers with incoherent memories, 73 percent had babies who were insecurely attached.

This is a finding worth thinking about, long and hard. A mother-to-be tells a researcher some stories of childhood that hold together and make sense, and fifteen months later her baby seeks a reassuring hug—even if the stories were painful. Another mother-to-be tells incoherent stories, and fifteen months later her baby avoids or resists her. The prediction pans out about three-quarters of the time, a figure that has been replicated in subsequent research. It's an almost literal confirmation of those words of Gandhi: "The physical and mental states of the parents at the time of conception are reproduced in the baby."

Why should mature defenses and coherent memories be associated with generativity? For one thing, both are associated with mental health. But there's a more direct link. When memories have mature defenses, they become coherent. There is good internal communication in the system they create: you can talk to the djinni in the bottle. When you put your memories, even bad ones, into good shape, you put *yourself* into good shape. You make yourself coherent. And when you're coherent, the next generation can trust you.

Putting memories into good shape, however, is not altogether a matter of conscious effort. You cannot "work" on it by reading a few books, attending some seminars, or even having psychotherapy, though all of these can help. So can the outside perspective that a good friend brings. There are many "natural" therapists, in fact, who do what professionals do without even knowing the names of defense mechanisms. Robert's wife may have been one of them. She listened with love as he talked; as he talked, he got to know himself; as he got to know himself, his memories became more coherent. His transformation illustrates one side of the coin: when the defenses mature, generativity flows.

But Robert's development also illustrates the coin's other side—a second dynamic that professional therapists would do well to take more advantage of: when generativity flows, the defenses mature. Robert found an outlet for generativity in his children. They became someone he could sublimate *for,* someone he could be altruistic *toward.* What any good therapy does is redirect the flow of life in a person. It removes a dam here, inserts one there, alters a channel, eliminates a massive eddy. But no matter how coherent the redirection, no matter how well it is defended, inner life will not flow unless there is a place to receive it. Hence, the value—the absolute necessity—of having an outlet.

Whatever side of the coin you begin with, it is probably fruitless to work directly on defense mechanisms. Their genius, after all, lies in indirection. And it is just as fruitless to try to force memories into coherence. Time and again on the Generative Way we will be reminded that progress is not simply something we make but something that happens to us. To a very real extent, there is *nothing* you can do to make your defenses mature and your memories coherent. There's a passivity involved, a receptivity: the doing will be done unto you. A woman of 23 who inherited a vulnerability to depression and anxiety has the right idea: "I've been trying to overcome my problems for so long so that I can make something of myself. But maybe, instead, *they* will make something of me." She went on: "Once you find an outlet so many problems solve themselves."

This woman's is not a *helpless* passivity. It's the relaxing of a grip, a yielding to and acceptance of the truth. It's listening to the past, not just talking to it—the standing still that I referred to in Chapter 1. When a person surrenders in this fashion, defenses mature. A dam comes down, a channel appears, and water, with all its power to renew, begins to flow.

What Robert Creighton was able to do so naturally with his sons is not as rare as you might think. In fact, psychological research is showing quite conclusively that there is a natural resilience that comes with each new generation. With regard to fathering, we now know that "positive modeling" is stronger than "negative modeling." Good fathers like Herb Robinson's, in other words, are more likely to produce lasting intergenerational effects than poor fathers like Robert Creighton's. As psychologist John Snarey has concluded from reviewing the research, "The great majority of men with childhood experiences of a severe or inadequate parent do *not* go on to replicate this pattern in their own childrearing behavior." Nor do most abused children become abusive parents, despite public perceptions to the contrary. It's a good bet that those who break the cycle of abuse have mature defenses that enable them to remember their past in a healthy, coherent way.

Enormous satisfaction can come to those who rework a heritage of parenting—or any heritage, for that matter. When you do what your parent never did, you do it vicariously *for* your parent. At the same time, when you produce a child that is free from a scar you have, you remove it vicariously from yourself. Reworking a heritage, you master pain and even execute a kind of vengeance on its inflicter. You stand cured in the reflected light of progeny and have a latent wholeness confirmed by them. Many kinds of emotional gratification are obtained by creating legacies out of just those elements that are missing from your own inheritance.

It is true that being a good parent will never change the way one's own parent was. But I have learned from listening to stories of generativity that when people feel something must be done about damage inflicted and hurt received, they can act as if restitution were owed to life itself and it does not matter which particle of life gives or receives payment. If I cannot alter what my father was, I will take his place and become his opposite. There is no reason to this substitution, but there is a good deal of rhyme. People derive a sense of closure, as when the last word of a couplet falls into place, when they play a painful record over—and get it right—in a new generation.

4

Stopping the Damage

WHEN A LEGACY must not be repeated, when it cannot be reworked, what are we to do? In this not uncommon instance, another response is possible. I once saw it articulated very powerfully for a television audience by a woman near death from AIDS. She had already lost her husband to the disease, and she herself had little time left. But she drew a great deal of strength from knowing that when she died, the HIV virus would die with her. There would be a little less of it in the world. The damage, and the sequence of injustice that brought it to her, would not be passed on.

Many people—probably more than we imagine—receive a crippling or even life-threatening legacy from the past, absorb it, and try to live so that none of it infects others. These people, like the woman dying from AIDS, possess extraordinary generative qualities. But, paradoxically, they express those qualities by *not* passing something on. Though they themselves may bear scars, they say of a sequence of intergenerational damage, "It stops here. It ends with me." I call these people *intergenerational buffers.*

Intergenerational damage is passed down on generativity's dark side, so it's no surprise that the world's myths, so sensitive to this side, abound in stories of its transmission. In the Greek myth of Orestes, for example, the original sin is that of Tantalus, who tries to feed the gods his murdered son. The gods punish him with eternal thirst and hunger, and plague his descendants in the house of Atreus with complex intrigues of betrayal and murder. In the third generation after Tantalus, a wife kills her husband. In the fourth comes Orestes, the one who breaks the curse.

Orestes is an innocent man who inherits an impossible dilemma. It is a son's sacred duty to avenge his father's death, yet nothing is more abhorrent than the killing of one's mother. What is he to do? Paralyzed with doubt, he consults the god Apollo, who tells him to "atone for death by death." He kills his mother, even though at the last minute she shows him the breast that nursed him. Now he absorbs the generational curse. He is attacked by Furies, cackling women with snakelike hair who torment him with guilt. No one else sees them; they are a private hell that follows him everywhere. Orestes wanders for years until, worn out by suffering, he asks the gods to reconsider his fate.

At the ensuing hearing, Apollo speaks up for him. "Orestes killed at my command. It is I who must answer for what he did."

"Not so!" shouts Orestes, stunning the assembly. "*I* killed my mother, not any of the gods!"

There is a dead silence as Orestes' words sink in. No one in the house of Atreus had ever assumed responsibility for a crime. They had always been "victims" who blamed the gods. The gods are so moved by this change in outlook, by this break with tradition, that they absolve Orestes, transforming the Furies into loving spirits, and removing forever the curse from the house of Atreus.

As curses have their breakers, so damage has its buffers. It has those who stand up and take responsibility the way Orestes did. What follows in this chapter are the stories of four of them, one from each of generativity's domains. Two of the leading characters bear the scars of intergenerational damage, but they see that their children do not. The other two bear no scars, but as vicarious buffers they speak for those who do. Different though their situations may be, they all stand up to damage and say, like the breakers of curses, "It stops here. It ends with me." Not all of us have to do what they did, but their actions are distinctive enough to be considered a second step on the Way.

"You Never Think It's Going to Happen to You"

The example involving AIDS at the outset of this chapter brings out, for one person, the meaning of arresting the spread of biologically infectious material. The first story is analogous. It takes place in the realm of biological generativity, though the material involved is not a virus but defective genes.

A young couple I once interviewed—I will call them Karen and Don—wanted to start a family but were troubled by a puzzling coincidence. A few years before, Don's sister had given birth to a daughter with abnormalities that matched a pattern in Don's younger brother: a heart defect, a double thumb, a club foot, and severe mental retardation. One child like this in the family could be attributed to "accident" or "fate," thought the couple, but two could not. Karen and Don went to a human genetics clinic and began a process of discovery. With the help of a counselor, they constructed a family tree, identified potential carriers of the disorder in Don's family, and persuaded them to get a blood test. Don's test confirmed the couple's worst fear: he was a carrier and potential children were at risk.

The disorder in question was a chromosomal translocation. At some distant point in Don's genetic past, a piece of one chromosome had broken off and become attached to another. Copies of the misplaced material had been passed on for generations in his family, manifesting themselves from time to time in abnormalities like those suffered by his younger brother and niece.

The impact of these discoveries on Don's family was profound. When blood testing revealed that his mother was not a carrier, she was relieved of a burden of guilt she had secretly carried for years. She had always thought that she was the cause of her son's and her granddaughter's abnormalities. The same information implicated Don's father; his reaction to it can be gauged by his refusal to have a blood test. Don's sister, who had just given birth to a normal child, had a tubal ligation. Don himself fell into a guilty silence. Not only was he the carrier of a genetic defect; he was disappointing his wife, who desperately wanted to have a baby. He thought of artificial insemination, rejected the idea, and came close to abandoning altogether the idea of having children.

Then, suddenly and surprisingly, after beginning to look into adoption, Karen discovered that she was pregnant. (The couple had also been having problems with infertility.) When she came to this part of her story, Karen's words were ominous: "You never think it's going to happen to you."

Now the process of discovery was extended one generation down, as Karen underwent amniocentesis to determine the status of her unborn fetus. Along with discovery there occurred a process of definition: "damage" would be considered a child with the same pattern of problems that existed in Don's family. Definition is important because in matters of buffering people often make different and even conflicting judgments. Karen's mother is an example. She would not tolerate an abortion, Karen told me. "She kept saying, 'There is no way that you will terminate your pregnancy if you get bad news. There is just no way.' She didn't tell anyone I was pregnant." To an opponent of abortion, "damage" is not a child with an abnormality but the ending of fetal life. And so one who buffers damage in one domain and from one point of view inflicts it in and from another.

A process of intervention began for Karen and Don when the amniocentesis revealed that theirs was to be a child with severe abnormalities. "Maybe I should go ahead and have the child," she remembered thinking, "because it could be the only one I'll ever have." But they had already decided under what conditions they would terminate their pregnancy. "If the fetus had been a carrier, then we were going to go ahead and go full term and have the child. But we did not want to have a child that we knew would have physical deformities and be mentally retarded." They had to inform their families of their intentions, and that included Karen's mother. "When we called and said, 'It's bad news and I'm terminating the pregnancy,' she just couldn't believe it."

Karen's abortion was no easy matter for her. "It's not like I just lost the baby, I had a miscarriage. I willfully went in and terminated a pregnancy, and it was hard for people to deal with it. Some people think it was the kind of thing . . . you go in and you're knocked out and you wake up and you're not pregnant anymore. And that's not the way it was at all. They induced labor, and I was in labor for ten hours and I delivered a child. I was awake. My mother called to find out how I was doing afterwards but then dropped the subject. When I went back to work, everyone acted like things should be normal, like nothing had ever happened, and I was definitely mourning."

The experience left Karen more determined than ever to have a baby. She and Don talked again of artificial insemination, but Don knew he could not accept a child she conceived through that process. Karen had corrective surgery to help her become pregnant and began taking fertility drugs. Three months later she conceived once again. "Although the odds were that it wouldn't happen again, we were very, very reserved. I never thought past the amniocentesis. It was: I'm not going to buy any baby clothes. I'm not going to get a crib. I'm not going to do anything until I know everything is okay." They got the results from amniocentesis on a memorable Friday morning. "The phone rang," said Karen, "and when I talked to the nurse, I tried to read into her voice whether it was good or bad. And she said, 'I've got good news. Everything is fine.' The baby was not even a carrier. And then I asked the sex. I thought if any human being knows, then I'm going to know. So we found out it was a boy. We started planning and we started coming up with names. When he was born, they took a blood sample and double checked. He was perfectly normal."

Karen later gave birth to another child—a girl whom she and Don knew would be a carrier of the family's genetic defect, though she herself would not be affected. One of their reasons for going through with the pregnancy was a belief that advances in genetic medicine would give their daughter far more reproductive options when she herself became an adult.

In this first story, the damage in question was biological and hidden. In the next—an example from the domain of parental generativity—the damage was a family tradition plain for all to see. That made matters of discovery and definition quite different.

"I Was Robbed"

"Growing up in my family was pretty scary," said a middle-aged woman I will identify as Sandra. Her story illustrates how one can stop a tradition of damage in the raising of children. It also illustrates how buffering differs from reworking. The term "reworking" is best applied to legacies that are a combination of good and evil, whereas "buffering" is best reserved for those that are purely malignant—here, two abusive parents rather than one.

Sandra's father was a violent man. As a child she would wait each evening to see when he would come home and in what state, attentive to "messages"—how he pulled into the driveway, how he approached the door—that revealed how drunk he was. "It was my responsibility to read those messages and get everybody out of danger," she recalled. That responsibility was not occasional but a way of life. Sandra remembered the night her father broke an iron skillet with a swing meant for her mother. She recalled the many times she and her younger sisters thought they were going to die—and the one time her father actually said they would. "He was screaming, 'I'm going to kill you all,' and he broke a lamp and cut himself, and he seemed to get real fascinated with his own blood, and he was flipping his arms around, and the blood was splattering all over the walls and all over us." On another occasion, Sandra thought he had actually killed her mother. During the fight, Sandra had been cowering behind a chair in the corner of the room, her little sister behind her, terrified at the grotesque shadows created by a fallen lamp. Her mother was trying to phone for help, but her father ripped the phone off the wall—it was a heavy, old-fashioned phone—and beat her unconscious. Eventually an ambulance came and took her mother away. She was pregnant at the time, and Sandra did not know if she was dead or alive.

Horrendous as this legacy was, what Sandra received from her mother may have been more insidious, because it was so deeply internalized. Her mother constantly disparaged Sandra. She was too short, too dark, too coarse, too stupid, too "plain." Sandra remembered being six years old and shining her shoes with a sponge applicator. When she got the black polish all over herself, her mother became furious and used a stiff brush to scrub her face with bleach and bathroom cleanser. Once adolescence came along, Sandra's mother repeatedly told her that no boy would ever want her. Her younger sister was attractive; the boys were "hot" for her but not for Sandra. "Maybe there's something wrong with you." Even when her first boyfriend date-raped her, Sandra's mother thought she was a fool to "let him get away" because he was from a family who had some status in the community.

Sandra's mother convinced her that she was inadequate, but Sandra, the oldest of four, was actually the family's "little adult." A memory from the age of five has her sitting on the couch with her mother, listening to a tearful litany of complaints, patting her mother on the back, and assuring her that everything would be all right. "I was my mother's mentor," she said, looking back from the perspective of middle age. By the age of 12, Sandra was earning money doing laundry, ironing, and housecleaning for neighbors. Often it was she who put food on the table, not either of her parents. If her father became angry, it was Sandra's fault; she, the oldest, had forgotten to put something away or to keep her younger siblings quiet.

Sandra found occasional refuge from all this in a church. When she was in kindergarten, she started going to a Pentecostal gathering with a girl who lived near her grandmother's house. Sandra was white; her friend and the church were black. Sandra spoke of the "wild, uninhibited love" in that church—a contrast with the wild, uninhibited violence at home. A gospel passage struck her: "I've prepared for you a room." She thought, "I have a place"—a safe place. In the third grade she was baptized at that church. "I ran home the next day after spending the night at my friend's house, and when I went in the door and said, 'Mom, I'm going to get to go to heaven,' she just flipped out. 'How dare you go to that holy roller nigger church and get baptized? How dare you embarrass us like that?' She beat me with a shoe. It was a long time before I went to church with joy again."

When Sandra reached adulthood, there was no need to discover a legacy of damage or to define it as such. It was evident for anyone to see and judge. That was part of the humiliation: the whole neighborhood had witnessed scenes of vulgarity and violence. Intervention began as soon as Sandra had children. She had gotten pregnant right after high school, married the baby's father, and given birth to a little girl. Four years later, she had a second child, a boy. With blind persistence, she worked at being the opposite of her mother, trying to be perfect to keep danger at bay, trying to instill the sense of safety and well-being that she had missed. "We were always together. I would do special things for them. When I'd make pudding, I'd put it in little cups with little wrappers on top so you peeled off the top. Just motherly things. And learning things—take them to the zoo, take them to museums. I might have overdone it."

Once her children were well along in elementary school, Sandra got a job outside the home. Both she and her husband worked hard and spent carefully. Her husband was unaware of what lay in her background; he simply saw an intense woman who kept a perfect house. But as Sandra was approaching 40, he left her for another woman. Many months later, with a divorce imminent, he decided to return. Sandra tried to forgive him, tried not to "fall apart," but the wound was deep. She began to have a variety of physical complaints: stomach pains, severe headaches, sleeplessness, and fits of uncontrolled crying. When she was promoted at work and given extensive new responsibilities, she began to have panic attacks in which she would "check out" or "float away," dissociating the way she had as a child. At this point she sought counseling. "I figured I was going to die if I didn't get help."

Now Sandra began a different kind of discovery—in the form of recovering memories and trying to authenticate them. She opened the copper bottle. With her husband at her side, she revisited the apartment of her childhood. As memories came to the surface, she made connections. She always had to sleep curled up and facing a wall, with a pillow at her back. Now she knew why: it was a position to protect against a nighttime beating. She connected the feeling of dissociation at work with the feeling in her memory, and she understood why the feeling would come back. She questioned her mother, divorced now from her father, and learned that the history of abuse in her family went back at least one more generation. Her mother was not only a victimizer; she herself had been a victim.

As this intergenerational perspective was developing, Sandra's therapist helped her to see that while she carried the scars of abuse, and probably would for life, she had not passed them on to her children. She had not done what her mother had. This was a redefinition of her place in life that had positive effects on Sandra's self-image. She had been an intergenerational buffer.

At first Sandra resisted seeing herself in that role. She thought of all the occasions on which she had not been the "perfect" mother. But over time she began to comprehend what she had accomplished, what strength of character it took to absorb such badness and give such goodness. She had lived with a sense of dread for her children's future. "Or, as my mom said, 'Someday you'll get yours. You'll understand what I'm going through.' " Even when her children were born, she could not bear to take a first look at them, so sure was she of finding them deformed. But now they were grown, and they had turned out well. How, then, could she be the stupid, inadequate person her mother always said she was?

The realization that she was a buffer allowed Sandra to make peace with herself. Her therapy progressed rapidly after that. The religious dimension of her problem was addressed, as was her relationship with her husband. He had seen so much improvement in her that he was willing to participate in the counseling. Sandra was able to make peace with him, and a short time later her therapy came to an end.

Two questions can be asked of Sandra's story, and indeed of any that involve buffering. The first is: what resources enabled her to buffer? And the second is: what was the cost of the buffering? In the case of Karen and

Don, the most important resource was their unyielding desire to have a normal baby. The cost was estrangement from Karen's mother and the emotional pain of an abortion. Sandra's first resource was religious faith, or, as she said, "Jesus. Finding Jesus very early in my life." She was referring to her childhood experiences in the Pentecostal church. Other ingredients were a dogged persistence and a keen intelligence, though she never knew she had the latter. Her relationship with her husband, strong enough to survive a serious break, was also a factor; it gave her strength and her children a second parent. From a developmental perspective, however, Sandra's most significant resource may have been that she had been a buffer all her life. "I was the one responsible for getting the children out of danger." Her mother had cast her in that role but so had her younger siblings. "On scary nights when we weren't sure what was happening, my sister would come in the top bunk and sleep behind me. Because I would be in front of her, she wouldn't have to worry." When Sandra became a parent, her buffering—already ingrained in her personality—took on an intergenerational character. Now it was her children, not her brothers and sisters, that she was called upon to protect.

The cost of being a buffer all her life was great. Not only did she carry in her person the results of the original damage, she suffered a developmental loss. "I never really felt like a child. I do not know how to relax and play. I spent all of my 20s and half of my 30s not enjoying life like I should have. I was robbed, really robbed. I can make it up, but I was robbed."

A "Close Heart" to Women

It happens that in our third and fourth stories, the lead characters do not themselves bear the scars of intergenerational damage. They witness it in others. And the damage is not passed on within families, either biologically or parentally, but in the wider sphere outside the family.

The third story centers on technical generativity. It involves skills and techniques—here, medical procedures—that one learns from the previous generation and teaches to the next. The procedures in question are two whose use on women has been significantly curtailed: dilatation and curettage (D&C) and hysterectomy. These procedures are related: a D&C

removes the lining of the uterus, while a hysterectomy removes the uterus itself. For a number of years, the routine treatment for abnormal vaginal bleeding was a D&C. If several D&Cs did not solve the problem, the uterus (and often the ovaries as well) was removed. A physician who saw unnecessary risk in these procedures, defined them as damaging when others did not, and found an alternate way to treat his patients was Thaddeus Zwirkoski. Born of Polish immigrants in Winnipeg, Manitoba, Zwirkoski was educated at Ottawa Medical School and completed his residency in Detroit. Now 70, he has practiced in the Detroit area all his life.

The roots of this story go back to Dr. Zwirkoski's reasons for becoming a gynecologist in the first place. He had what he called a "close heart" to women. "My mother was sick since I was three or four years old. My sister suffered from a lot of menstrual cramps. I was a few years younger than she was, and I didn't understand why she was having troubles." Because he didn't understand these things, he talked to women about them—a theme that runs through his entire narration. One of the many part-time jobs he took to help pay his school expenses was singing at parties. When there was a break, "Instead of talking with the men I sat and talked with the women. I wanted to know how married people react, why women were complaining. Is it fact? Is it fiction? Are they making it up?" He had "platonic relationships" with his girlfriends, having vowed not to marry until he became a specialist. So he talked with them about their experience of being female. From very early on, he educated himself by communicating with his future patient population. And he believed what they were telling him. In particular, he believed what they were telling him about their monthly cycles.

This self-education may be seen as a process of discovery. It continued in medical school. The European professors there were strict and uncommunicative, so Dr. Zwirkoski became the "question box," asking what other students were reluctant to bring up. When he wanted to learn more about endocrinology, he took extra courses, connecting what he was learning there with what he was learning from conversations with women. Even before his clinical years, he was making trips to the operating room—to watch technique.

Early in his clinical training Dr. Zwirkoski began to question some standard practices, in particular the automatic use of the D&C. In a D&C, the lining of the uterus is scraped off—this is the "curettage"—and examined for signs of polyps, fibroids, and other abnormalities. Its purpose is diagnostic. But in the 1950s it was also being used as a form of treatment, to stop excessive bleeding. The procedure was expedient; it was financially rewarding; but, in Dr. Zwirkoski's emerging view, it did not address the root cause of most abnormal bleeding, which was hormone imbalance. No one, he recalled, was trying to regulate the endocrine system. No one was taking the time to talk to patients. After three to six months, many of the women who had had a D&C were again bleeding excessively.

As a resident, Zwirkoski came to define what he was being taught as poor technique. Few agreed with him. "I used to argue with doctors. I couldn't figure out why nothing else was done for the woman." The technique was more than poor; it had the potential for damage. There was the risk of a perforated uterus, as well as the risk associated with any procedure that required anesthesia. In Zwirkoski's view, a D&C was "totally unnecessary because the problem could have been corrected by communication with the patient and by medication."

At the time Zwirkoski was turning 30 and developing an alternative approach of using natural hormones to correct imbalances. He had found several local doctors who took that approach and he learned from them. What they were doing proved to be compatible with his own study of endocrinology and with the knowledge he had gathered from talking to women. But as a resident his ability to intervene was limited. He was not the final authority in matters of patient care, nor did the hospital's pharmacy carry the medications he would require. "When I got into private practice, I did it my way." He began his own practice in 1958, when he was 32 years old. What enabled him to buffer from the very beginning—what was a primary resource—was the alternate approach (and hence the identity) that he had already established. At the age of 32 there was no doubt in his mind. He knew himself to be a doctor who listened very closely to his female patients, gave them knowledge about their bodies, and used hormone replacement as a first line of defense. He was "Doctor Z."

D&Cs were in their heyday when he began to practice. "I would do one a week and the other guy would have ten, fifteen, twenty." Zwirkoski's were limited to cases with other than hormonal causes. When he was in a position to supervise residents, he preached the benefits of hormone replacement therapy and, more important, of communication. "I don't think there's 1 or 2 percent of doctors who believe their primary function is to give their patients knowledge and remove fear." When there was no choice but to do a hysterectomy, he would remove the uterus but not the ovaries. "I had a lot of problems with residents and even surgeons who did not respect tissue. The residents would start putting their clamps on and grabbing stuff, and I'd say, 'Who told you we were taking out the ovaries?' " The answer was always that the patient might get ovarian cancer when she was older. "So I said, 'Fine, if you think that way, why don't you get your testicles removed because you might get cancer of the testes? It may not be as common, but you're still at risk.' "

Zwirkoski wanted to keep the ovaries intact because of their role in the endocrine system. He was confirmed in his approach because his patients told him it worked and because he was often called upon to treat the casualties of other approaches. Added confidence in his definition of damage and his ability to repair it kept him on an independent course. When birth control pills came out in the 1960s, he would not prescribe them until the size of the doses came down. Even then he would not use them for hormone regulation. Though the pill form made them convenient for that purpose (at the time, natural hormones required injections), he was cautious about using synthetics. Later, when fetal monitoring became routinely available, he objected to the "skyrocketing" rates of Caesarean sections to which it led. He objected all along to dismissing postpartum depression and what is now known as PMS as problems that were merely "in the head." And he treated postmenopausal women long before the replacement of estrogen in them was considered routine.

Zwirkoski's buffering entered the realm of generativity when he became a teacher of residents. But he was not out to change medical practice on a wider basis. "I figured I was doing better for my patients than other people would, but I couldn't change society." Talking about hormone replacement at conferences was like "talking to air." To have the credibility he needed, he said, he would have had to teach and conduct research at a medical school. "But I have to be with people. People to me are better than any book. And I read many books every day through people." Besides, he was suspicious of academicians. "You think the guy that's got all the degrees knows everything. He knows baloney because he doesn't know how to talk to a woman."

At 73, Dr. Zwirkoski has had the satisfaction of seeing academic research support a number of the stands he had taken earlier in his career. He has seen a decline in the use of the techniques he once warned against: both D&C and hysterectomy now require extensive written justification. He has not, however, seen a corresponding rise in the number of physicians practicing hormone regulation. Medical students are not being taught enough endocrinology, he said. Besides, his approach takes time—time, in some cases, to learn what is happening to a woman almost every day and then to explain it to her. This is one reason his approach is not more widespread. "Ninety percent of the time it's too much work." The time-consuming nature of his approach is one of the costs Dr. Zwirkoski has borne, though cost was rarely mentioned in his narrative. When pressed, he spoke of patients he had lost because he would not do "convenience" hysterectomies and of "hassles" with his peers. But that was all. Had he lost income by doing far fewer surgeries than others? "I didn't go into medicine for money."

It is clear from this story that one does not buffer in the realm of technical generativity without getting into the realm of cultural generativity—into issues of meaning, value, and (in this case) scientific theory. As Dr. Zwirkoski tried to teach his residents, "There's more to medicine than just surgery or lab tests." Convictions about the place of women, the place of patients, and the place of income provided a background for his generativity. So did hypotheses about the functioning of the human body. In the next case, culture comes out of the background and into the fore, where it becomes the direct target of buffering. The buffering does not extend throughout a career, as it did in the case of Dr. Zwirkoski; it occurs, rather, at a particular historical moment.

"Awful Stories"

Cultural generativity refers to the conserving, renovating, or creating of a meaning system. The meaning system may be viewed as the "mind" of a community, just as related skills, techniques, and rituals may be thought of as the culture's "body." Mind and body are virtually inseparable, as I noted in the case of Dr. Zwirkoski and as our final story illustrates. In the 1960s the Catholic Church decided to reconsider its stance on birth control, primarily with regard to the newly developed pill but also with reference to any "artificial" technique. The concrete "how-to's" of contraception were inextricably tied to abstract conceptions of religion, law, ethics, history, and institutional self-definition. Technique was tied to a collective "mind" that had perdured for centuries.

A participant in the process of reconsideration, one of the very few women involved, was Chicagoan Patty Crowley. Though she would not have phrased it as such, she served in the role of intergenerational buffer. Patty and her husband Pat, now deceased, were asked to serve on the Special Study Group on Population and Birth Control convened by Pope Paul VI in 1964. Popularly known as the birth control commission, the group was assigned the task of looking into the matter of contraception, so that the pope, "supported by the light of human science," might decide upon its morality. The church was already on record as being opposed to contraception; in the view of Catholic conservatives, it had spoken infallibly and its stand could not be reversed. Yet the opening of the Second Vatican Council in 1963 had led many Catholics to wonder if this "infallible" teaching could be—indeed, would be—changed.

The Crowleys were in their early 50s when they were asked to serve on the birth control commission. The most likely reason was their leadership of the Christian Family Movement (CFM), an international organization of Catholic lay persons that they had founded almost two decades before. All the other members of the commission were experts of one kind or another, demographers, economists, sociologists, psychiatrists, gynecologists, philosophers, and theologians. The Crowleys were one of three married couples present; Patty was one of five women (out of a total of fifty-seven delegates). Though no one realized it at the time, all three of the married women were incapable of bearing children. When they received the invitation to sit on the commission, the Crowleys were unquestioning believers in the church's traditional teaching. They had never practiced birth control in their marriage and had had no need to: after the birth of their fourth child, Patty had been left sterile by a near-fatal episode of hemorrhaging. Unlike other intergenerational buffers, she herself had borne few, if any, of the effects of the legacy in question.

Because they were the only nonexperts on the commission, the Crowleys decided that their role was to speak for "plain married couples." They began the process of discovery by undertaking, with the help of a sociologist, several surveys of CFM membership and by placing a request in the Catholic press for readers to mail in their comments about the church-approved rhythm method. What the Crowleys discovered about cultural damage overwhelmed them. The general attitude of some three thousand responding couples from eighteen countries was one of controlled frustration. What truly moved Patty, and changed her definition of damage, were the "awful stories" that came in the mail:

> I am on the verge of a nervous breakdown with worry, and my doctor also tells me that it would be unwise to have more children. My husband suffers from colitis, which is a nervous disorder aggravated by continual worry of this immense problem. Total abstinence, is this our only answer? Does the Church approve of this state? If so, we will accept its ruling.

> My husband has a terrible weakness when it comes to self-control in sex and unless his demands are met in every way when he feels this way, he is a very dangerous man to me and my daughters. Apart from these times he is completely normal and tries in every way he knows, such as morning Mass, sacraments, prayers, etc., to accumulate grace.

> Following my 3rd pregnancy in 2 years I almost smothered the baby with a pillow because I couldn't stand its crying. Now in a few years we will have to abstain entirely, perhaps for years, when I become more irregular due to menopause. I am very depressed and becoming more so. What will another baby do to me at this age?

> The maintenance of temperature charts is much too awkward in the social environment of the average Indian home. Where a number of people live and sleep together in one room, a couple have often to choose a late hour at night or a very early hour at morning—say 1 or 2 A.M.—for the conjugal relationship, at a time when everyone else is fast asleep.

It was patent that the writers of these "awful stories" were not ordinary Catholics but among the most devout. Like 78 percent of those in the surveys at large, they believed that the church should change its position. It was also clear that most of the story writers were women. How could the Crowleys bring their voice—the voice of sexual females—into the celibate male bastion of Rome?

The Crowleys sent copies of the letters they had received to other commission delegates in the United States and Canada and to the commission secretary in Rome in the hope that they would eventually reach the pope. At a meeting of the commission in April of 1966, the second they had attended, Patty realized that the time for her intervention had come. But she was still in awe of her surroundings. "Here were all these learned men from all over the world," she remembered. "My inclination would have been to say little and sit down. But I had come a long way at that point." When the women present were asked to address the assembly, Patty presented "A Woman's Viewpoint." "Is rhythm unnatural?" she asked. "Yes," she answered. She read excerpts from the letters she and Pat had received. "No amount of theory by men will convince women that this way of making and expressing love is natural," she said in conclusion. "We think it is time for a change."

Later in the session, a theologian objected. If the church backtracked on contraception, what of the millions of people it had already condemned to hell? Patty shot back, "Father Zalba, do you really believe God has carried out all your orders?"

The work of the panel concluded in early June of 1966 with a report calling for change. It was endorsed, according to some sources, by a vote of fifty-two to four. The Crowleys left Rome with a peaceful feeling that an immense amount of work had born fruit, indeed that they had helped to make history. All that remained was an official proclamation from the pope.

What the Crowleys did not know, however, was that conservative forces connected with the commission were working behind the scenes to undo its work. They had already written a minority report to stand against the majority's. For two years Paul VI agonized over a decision. Then, on July 29, 1968, he announced his conclusion in the encyclical *Humanae Vitae:* the church would not change its position. The Crowleys did not learn of the pope's declaration until a reporter called them at four o'clock in the morning to ask for their comments. They were stunned, incredulous. Within a few weeks they had joined two hundred Catholic scholars in signing a statement that took exception to the encyclical and encouraged Catholics to decide for themselves.

Now the Crowleys began to bear the cost of being buffers. Even before the encyclical, they had tried to share their enthusiasm about the commission's conclusions with a priest who had been their longtime mentor; he reprimanded them and said only, "We'll wait and see what the pope says." After their public stand in opposition to the encyclical, they were cut off from him and from many in the church hierarchy who had been friends, supporters, and guides of the Christian Family Movement. That movement, their "baby," began to lose momentum as married couples became disillusioned with the Catholic Church in general. Today CFM is a fraction of its original size and in the hands of leaders who blame the Crowleys' refusal to accept *Humanae Vitae* for its decline. "I get frustrated when I see what's happened to CFM," said Patty twenty-five years later, adding, "I guess I'm a little bitter. No priest ever talked to me about *Humanae Vitae*. No one ever discussed what we had done or why it turned out the way it did. No one asked how we felt. We never even got a letter of thanks from the Vatican." The stony silence in the wake of the encyclical extended even to their fellow commissioners, with whom the Crowleys lost contact. Three years after the encyclical Pat was diagnosed with cancer; he died in 1974. Says Patty in retrospect: "If Pat and I hadn't had each other, we could never have made it through this period." Her relationship with her husband was one of her primary resources.

When I spoke with Patty in 1995, she was a healthy 82-year-old deeply involved in women's issues. She works part time for her daughter's travel agency, volunteers at a shelter for homeless women that she helped establish in the mid-1980s, coordinates a group of some fifty women who meet in her apartment for "consciousness raising," and visits women in prison every Sunday afternoon. She is still a loyal Catholic and active in her parish. "No one is going to kick me out," she says, though the emotional scars of the commission's aftermath are still with her.

The major source of conflict throughout the Crowleys' experience on the birth control commission was over the definition of damage: church conservatives did not see it the way the Crowleys and the commission did. The former were concerned about damage to a tradition of papal infallibility, the other about damage to married couples. And yet the commission was effective in stopping the damage it saw. It effected change not in the "official" culture of Catholicism but in its "unofficial," popular culture. The fact that a commission was created in the first place had set American Catholics of a particular generation thinking: why would the pope convene such a group if the rule wasn't revocable? The fact that the commission subsequently recommended a change furthered their thinking. By the time Paul VI made his official proclamation in 1968, it was too late. The majority of American Catholics had made up their minds, not only to practice unapproved forms of contraception but to reconsider their view of the pope, their definition of the church, and, in some cases, their affiliation with it. It was a profound cultural shift.

When one serves as a buffer in the transmission of cultural elements, one rarely acts in isolation, simply because the extent of a culture is so vast and its adherents so many. Rarely does cultural change center in one person, as it did in the famous cases—Martin Luther and Mahatma Gandhi—that were the subject of Erik Erikson's biographies. The Crowleys were not the figureheads that Luther and Gandhi were, nor even principal players on the commission. But, perhaps more than any other commission member, they were deeply in touch with the suffering caused by the church's rule on contraception. They played a role in stopping it, though not through the mechanism they would have wished.

Using the Concept of Buffering

It should be clear that I see the removal of a particular moral prohibition from intergenerational transmission in the same light as the removal of a piece of genetic material. There are differences, of course. In one case we are dealing with an abstract element of culture and in the other with a concrete element of biology, in one case with the human spirit and in the other with human tissue. Yet in both instances a buffer says, "The damage stops here." And in both, other people contest the buffer's definition of damage so that moral conflict ensues.

Though I have seen the concept of buffering help a fair number of people, I have also learned that there are complexities to anticipate and care to exercise when introducing it to another person's life. When I explained the concept to a middle-aged woman whose story revolved around parental generativity, for example, her predominant reaction was that she had *failed* to buffer. Sexually abused by her father, she was unable to prevent him from inflicting the same damage on her daughters—his grandchildren. What he had done to her she thought of as an "accident," an exception to his true character; although she was able to end it gradually, she never told anyone about it. "I did not face reality in time to prevent abuse to my daughters." It had never occurred to her that they would be at risk.

When one of this woman's daughters was 11, she told her mother that her grandfather had been acting strangely. An older daughter left a one-page paper entitled "Grandpa" on the kitchen table. "I read, in effect, 'I trusted you and you hurt me.' I knew I had let my daughters down, should have known better, protected them better, asked questions and informed their father of what I knew. I told my daughter I had read her paper, asked her to forgive me for not protecting her, told her I had had enough experience with my father to serve as a warning. And I admitted that I had never told her father, so he had been deprived of the opportunity of protecting her."

For this woman, the impact of her failure to buffer was worse than the damage which she herself had suffered. And yet the pattern of abuse in her immediate family stopped—largely because an 11-year-old did what she herself was unable to do. "She did not deny what happened. She did not make excuses, and she did not choose silence." As an adult, this same child has successfully urged her mother to tell her husband what had taken place within his family. (The secret had been kept from him.) And while this child has let her mother know that the abuse was more severe than she had indicated initially, she has done much to assuage her mother's guilt. "She assured me that I did serve to some degree as a buffer, because she knew I would listen and understand. And she pointed out that the power of a grandfather isn't quite as strong and ever present as that of a father." This woman sees her daughter as "the intergenerational buffer I failed to be."

In this case a sequence of intergenerational damage was stopped because the knowledge of it was passed on. Is this a universal feature of buffering: stop the damage by transmitting the knowledge? Or are there times when the damage is so extreme that even the knowledge of it is crippling? One victim of the Nazi Holocaust began telling her son of her death-camp experiences when he was 4. By the time he was a teenager he was seeing a psychiatrist because of recurring nightmares that were directly related to the stories he had heard. His mother's transmission of knowledge was clearly premature. Sandra waited until her children were in their 20s before beginning to talk about her past. "They're in the safety zone now," she said. This is close to what Sidney Bolkosky, an oral historian of the Holocaust, believes: the late teens are early enough for the children or grandchildren of surviving victims to hear of their forebears' experience. At that point it is safe to *cease* buffering with regard to the knowledge of damage.

Bolkosky has been recording the stories of Holocaust survivors since 1981. Before that time, hardly any spoke of their experiences, except to each other. There were a number of reasons for their silence. As immigrants to the United States, many were told to forget about the past and start afresh. One of them recalled going on a trip to see his cousin in California. He had just gotten off the plane when his cousin said, "I don't want to hear about it. I don't want to know what happened. I've seen the newsreels." Language was another problem, not because of the difficulty of translating into English, but because common, easily translatable words ("bunk," "cold") had such different reference points in and outside a concentration camp. There was the pain and the abject humiliation to which survivors had been subjected, the awful choices some were forced to make. There was the desire to protect their children—and, later, the fear that their children, like everyone else, would not understand.

Around 1980, the silence began to break. A popular television series on the Holocaust in 1978 and a massive gathering of surviving victims in Jerusalem in 1981 provided a cultural impetus. But survivors themselves were also getting ready to talk. They were aging; it was now or never. Their children, now adults, were old enough to hear; the buffering could cease. Many survivors made audio or video recordings of their experiences, and they continue to do so. "So it will never happen again," they say, or "to defeat the Holocaust deniers"—so the damage will stop, in other words. But Bolkosky believes that "never again" is not the real reason why survivors speak. It is because the events themselves were so compelling, because the Holocaust was the most significant thing that happened to them, because their history was a part of History. As they neared the end of their lives they could not *not* speak. And they found various ways of doing so. One woman made an audio tape of her experiences and went for a walk while her children listened to it. They were stunned. They had not even known that she was a survivor.

Each new case makes one sensitive not only to differences of kind in buffering but also to differences of degree. Some individuals have suffered more than others at the hands of previous generations. Some have blocked the transmission of damage more completely. Some have paid a higher price to do so. And some have had experiences so humiliating and so devastating that they cannot, from the inside, sustain a definition of buffering.

Though he did not employ the concept of buffering in his study of Holocaust testimonies, Lawrence Langer brought out the difference between inside and outside perspectives on trauma. From the inside, he noted, in the depths of "unheroic" memory, the victim often feels the concentration camp experience is unredeemable, devoid of meaning, and impossible to restore to generational continuity. Much as an outsider, even a loved one, might wish it otherwise, no generativity is possible. (Nor, I might add, is the consolation of seeing oneself as a buffer.) But interviewers—outsiders—often try to redeem the experience, give it meaning, and restore it to the flow of generations.

Langer provided many illustrations of the contrast between internal and external points of view. In one taped segment he observed two interviewers attempting to make a heroine of a former victim, telling her that she survived through pluck and guts. But she says no, it was through sheer stupidity. The interviewers cannot comprehend, cannot reconcile their perspective with hers, and the interview seems to end, says Langer, "with the defeat of the witness, or at least of her language." Another interviewer tells a survivor, "You are one of the greatest optimists I've ever met"—just after the victim has spoken of harsh truths she knows in her deepest being, of her complete lack of faith in humans, of her extreme pessimism. This interview ends, too, with unreconciled perspectives. Even children who grew up in the homes of surviving victims find it difficult to bridge the gap. The adult daughter of one couple says that her parents' ordeal has left her with strength and a sense of connection with a rich Jewish heritage. But her parents, who from her perspective are the very channels of strength and connection, have no sense of being so. What have they been left with? Loneliness, says the mother. "As long as we live, we are lonely." And the father: "Nothing to say. Sad."

An awareness of differences in perspective should accompany any attempt to interpret another's experience as buffering. The risk in employing the concept is that a person's experience may not be able to bear it, that he or she will not be understood. Its use may reflect our inability as outsiders to hear what lies beyond normal human boundaries. Some of life's happenings are so abject that, in the eyes of the insider, they can never recross the boundary and reenter the flow of generational continuity, not even under the rubric of buffering.

A "Faithful Force"

I would never rule out the possibility of reentry, however. In an in-depth study of ten Holocaust survivors, psychologist Avi Kay discovered something remarkable: generative inclinations far above normal, and far above those of ten Jewish refugees who had fled Germany and waited out World War II in China or the former Soviet Union. The ten survivors had felt their first generative desires as adolescents in the concentration camps:

> In *lagger* (the Yiddish term for "concentration camp") I would go to sleep at night think(ing) how weird it would be not to wake up. But in the morning I'd open my eyes and say: "Hah, they're not going to destroy the whole Jewish people. Some of us will survive. Maybe I will be the lucky one. By me we (the Jewish people) will survive." It made for a future to look for.

Thoughts of a benevolent future helped these young people to disengage from the bleakness of the present, says Kay. They thought of a distant, almost mythical time in which they would once again be surrounded by family. The ones who actually did survive the camps were driven after their release to the most basic kind of biological generativity. They wanted to conceive children, to *establish* a next generation, to restore the genetic links that had been broken. Some would name children after deceased relatives, trying—impossibly—to undo the past. To these, adoption was of little interest. "To put it bluntly," writes Kay, "survivors were less interested in raising 'Jewish children' than in having individuals with 'genuine' Jewish genes repopulating the world."

Raising their children, these ten survivors exhibited a kind of parental generativity that centered on material provisioning—good food, a good roof over their children's heads, lots of possessions. A reaction to their own material deprivation, this emphasis was not without its problems later on. It also overrode cultural generativity, although with time survivors came to place more importance than did refugees on the religious education of their children.

In response to genocide, then, there occurred in these survivors a remarkable surge in generativity, and generativity of the most instinctual kind. What Kay encountered with the tools of psychology has also been described in a literary way. A Jungian psychoanalyst and writer, Clarissa Pinkola Estes grew up in a family that housed refugees from World War II. Even as a child, she got to know of a war that raged inside of them—a war that caused them now to speak of horrific losses, now to remain silent, now to look for redemption and meaning, now to be certain there was none. As she wrote in *The Faithful Gardener,* "In each of our people who had suffered so greatly, there were two struggling persons. One living the life of the new world, the other running, constantly running, from memories of hell that rose up and gave chase."

An Uncle Zovar, who somehow survived a slave labor camp near the Russian border, arrived one day at the train station in Chicago. He was a huge, muscled man with red forearms, eyebrows like wire brushes, and strange smells. Clarissa was only 5 at the time, and she had to tilt her head way back to take him in:

> Uncle set down his little sack of goods and his cardboard suitcase. He slowly took off his hat and knelt before me right there on the concrete walkway. Many shoes and boots hurried around us. I saw the sweat-soaked silver hairs of his sideburns, and the fluorescent silver bristles on his chin and cheeks. Uncle reached out and held my head with one big hand and put his other arm around my body. I will never forget his words as he hugged me close to him: "A . . . living . . . child," he whispered.

What could it have meant to a man burdened by his memories, a man who knew he would always carry them, to see a child in whom they did not exist? Could he rest in her innocence from time to time, be cleansed in some vicarious way? Over the years Uncle Zovar told Clarissa about the war, but only through the lips of an alter ego he called This Man. " 'This Man I used to know, he was haunted by the last images of the old women of the village as the wagon-trucks hauled the men and boys away' "—and so on. Though his life had been destroyed, he was still gentle with children and animals. And he still believed that the land was a living being, that we all stood in the care of its "faithful force." This was his greatest legacy to Clarissa:

I learned the harshest gift-lesson to accept, and the most powerful I know—that is, *knowledge,* an absolute certainty that life repeats itself, renews itself, no matter how many times it is stabbed, stripped to the bone, hurled to the ground, hurt, ridiculed, ignored, scorned, looked down upon, tortured, or made helpless.

Uncle Zovar's "faithful force" is what Avi Kay discovered in ten Holocaust survivors. It is the resilience of life itself—a "process of spirit and seed that touches empty ground and makes it rich again," says Estes. We shall encounter certainty like hers again, for it seems to characterize not only the way generative people think about the past, but also the way they think about the present, and about the identities they construct therein. Those identities are the subject to which we now turn.

5

Finding a Voice of Your Own

I HAVE HAD in my life a very concrete experience of finding a voice—literally. If you've ever listened to the sound of your own voice and not liked what you've heard, you will understand what I am about to tell you.

It happened during the production of a radio series on the human life cycle. I had interviewed hundreds of people, from infants to the elderly, and their voices were being edited, assembled, and shaped into twenty-six programs. The time came to record the host, me, gluing it all together. What would I say, and how would I say it? In the beginning, I didn't say it at all. Someone else did, a writer, and I simply read her script, which a director told me how to read. The result was awful. I cringed when I heard the stiff, unnatural voice. Once, to loosen me up, the director drew a picture of another person, sat it in a chair, and told me to imagine talking to it as I read. It didn't help.

In desperation, I took a microphone home and began to practice reading script into it. It started to sound a little better. Soon I was fiddling with the script, saying things the way *I* would say them, not someone else. I got in touch with my pace, my pitch, my inflection, my emotion. Eventually I wrote the scripts from scratch. A new director began to learn about my voice—the inner, conceptual voice, not just the outer one. He brought it out and refined it. He sat in on the final mixes and supervised its electronic rendition. Now, when someone who has heard the programs meets me for the first time (or, even better, talks on the phone for the first time), they say, "I recognize that voice. It's *you.*"

A voice, such as the one I found in a new medium, is a crystallization of one's inner self. But a voice is also, by its very nature, propagative. It carries through the air; it reaches and enters others. In the sound waves it creates, identity and generativity are one.

In this chapter I look at the role of identity in generativity, at the necessity of finding a strong, clear voice. This is another aspect of the generative process, a third step on the Way. A strong, clear voice is needed to repeat legacies—recall the story of Herb Robinson, who had to create his own out of the sound waves of his father's. It is needed to rework legacies, to stand up to the damage within them and buffer its impact on the future. Thaddeus Zwirkoski found a voice, a particular approach to medical practice, early in his career; it stayed with him throughout. Patty Crowley found a new voice in her 50s; it was suited to a particular historical moment. In one case, identity was established prior to a generative stage. In the other, it was established in the midst of a particular generative episode.

If a voice is weak or muffled, or if there is no one to hear it, generativity will lack identity—a common problem. The journalist I spoke about at the very beginning of this book was happiest in his work when he was writing people-oriented stories that reflected *him.* His crisis of generativity occurred when the company he worked for insisted on hard statistical reports that anybody could do. *Anybody,* not *I.* When God creates Adam in the Book of Genesis, He makes him in His image and likeness: there is a message here about the ideal generative process. Somehow, our image and likeness must appear in the things we create.

The appearance of identity in generativity was the focus of Erik Erikson's book *Young Man Luther.* There, Erikson described Martin Luther's development as the "liberation of his voice." Luther's gift for language was immense. Nietzsche called his translation of the Bible "the masterpiece of German prose," for it had the ability to "grow into German hearts." Erikson regarded Luther's talent as paralleled in English only by Shakespeare's. Like any generative voice, Luther's was ineffectual until it found an audience; once it did, he was able to touch even the least comprehending among them. "You must preach," he said, "as a mother suckles her child." But like few voices in history, Luther's was carried in a medium, print, that was also just finding itself, much like today's electronic internet. A decade after Luther nailed his ninety-five theses to a church door in Wittenberg (the year was 1517), thirty printers in twelve cities were publishing his sermons as fast as they could get their hands on the manuscripts. "He gradually learned to speak a new language, *his* language," Erikson wrote. And then "he not only talked himself out of the monastery, and much of his country out of the Roman Church, but also formulated for himself and for all of mankind a new kind of ethical and psychological awareness."

Not only did Luther find a voice with which to speak, he also found a voice that spoke to him. Luther believed in the Word of Scripture; to hear it, he said, he had to keep "good and open ears." "My conscience is bound by God's words. Retract anything whatsoever I neither can nor will," he told the papal representative at the Diet of Worms. He also had to learn to discern the voices he heard. That of a punitive conscience, no matter how disguised, was not that of God. When "Christ comes and talks to you as if to a sinner and tortures you like Moses: 'What have you done?'—slay him to death. But when he talks to you as God does, and as a savior, prick up both ears." What Luther interpreted religiously, Erikson did psychologically: "Many a young man (and son of a stubborn one) becomes a great man in his own sphere only by learning that deep passivity which permits him to let the data of his competency speak to him."

Mahatma Gandhi, the other historical figure studied in depth by Erikson, was also guided by an inner voice. In Erikson's words, it "would speak unexpectedly in the preparedness of silence—but then with irreversible firmness and an irresistible demand for commitment." It was the same kind of voice that could bind Martin Luther and make him incapable of retraction. But Gandhi had worked out an arrangement with his. While it was a voice he had to act upon, he could make it "hold its breath" (Gandhi's words) until he studied the facts of a situation.

Although these examples come from a religious context, they suggest something more general. They point to a process of identity formation that is passive as well as active. "Receptive" might be a better word: those who become generative seem to experience a kind of inspiration or imperative that claims their inner nature and tells them not only who they are but what they are to do, and what they are to do next. There are things that "need doing," they will say, even "want doing." Or, as Martha Graham said of her identity as a dancer, "It fastens itself to you. You become a channel and are used." When identity formation is both passive and active, the voice that speaks to you becomes the voice with which you speak. Identity becomes a *calling*. It's an old idea; but, as we shall see, it's one that's turning up in the latest research.

The Identities of Generative Adults

"I'm mixed up very bad," Biff tells his brother in Arthur Miller's play, *Death of a Salesman*. At the age of 34, he has tried his hand at twenty or thirty jobs. "Maybe I oughta get married. Maybe I oughta get stuck into something. Maybe that's my trouble. I'm like a boy. I'm not married. I'm not in business, I just—I'm like a boy. " Later, he has a talk with his mother, Linda:

> *Linda:* Are you home to stay now?
> *Biff:* I don't know. I want to look around, see what's doin'.
> *Linda:* Biff, you can't look around all your life, can you?
> *Biff:* I just can't take hold, Mom. I can't take hold of some kind of life.

In the simplest terms, identity means that you know who you are and what you want to do. Biff, of course, knows neither, and so he is an example of everything that identity *is not*. A man of sales, he stands in contrast with a man of "all seasons" who exemplifies everything that identity *is*. That man, Thomas More, is also the subject of a play, Robert Bolt's *A Man for All Seasons*. Bolt describes More in the preface to his work:

> He knew where he began and left off, what area of himself he could yield to the encroachments of his enemies, and what to the encroachments of those he loved. It was a substantial area in both cases, for he had a proper sense of fear and was a busy lover. Since he was a clever man and a great lawyer he was able to retire from those areas in wonderfully good order, but at length he was asked to retreat from that final area where he located his self. And there this supple, humorous, unassuming and sophisticated person set like metal, was overtaken by an absolutely primitive rigor, and could no more be budged than a cliff.

In Bolt's play, as in history, More comes under increasing pressure to sign an oath approving the marriage of Henry VIII to Anne Boleyn. He tells a friend who has already signed, "I will not give in because I oppose it—I do—not my pride, not my spleen, nor any other of my appetites, but I do—*I!*" His daughter pleads with him to save himself from execution, and More explains why he cannot. "When a man takes an oath, Meg, he's holding his own self in his hands. Like water. And if he opens his fingers *then*— he needn't hope to find himself again."

More's self was defined. As the root *fin-* implies, it had the end lines, the boundaries, that made his choices clear. With boundaries you know where you begin and where you leave off. You know you are this and not that, and hence you know you are to do this and not that. You also know that you will last. As Erikson said, identity provides "the ability to experience one's self as something that has continuity and sameness, and to act accordingly." Duration goes hand in hand with durability, with "absolutely primitive rigor," with Luther's inability to retract and Gandhi's irreversible firmness. Your voice does not waver.

The first time in life that we attempt to form an identity is adolescence. Because identity covers so much—who we are as personal, social, sexual, ethnic, religious, civic, and working beings—the task of developing one will be complex and may go on for many years, even in some cases for a lifetime. Identity results from the identifications we have made earlier in life, from the figures we have "taken in" from the past. At some point we unite the voices of these figures, turn them outside in, and then speak with them. They become our own. And so do we—we become our own. We "take hold of some kind of life," see our defenses mature, "acquire" an identity.

Do generative adults have characteristic identities? Judging from three recent studies, the answer appears to be yes. Clarity, definition, and durability—a voice that does not waver—mark their self-concepts, as they did those of More, Luther, and Gandhi. So, in many cases, does the sense of being called.

The first of these studies, conducted by Anne Colby and William Damon, was a psychological investigation of "moral exemplars," people who act in accordance with the highest ethical principles and inspire others to do the same. The twenty-three subjects of the study were identified for

Colby and Damon by independent nominators, and they came from all walks of life. They were individuals like Cabell Brand, the head of a multi-million-dollar corporation who directs programs to give a "hand up" to the poor in Virginia's Roanoke Valley, and Mother Charleszetta Waddles, whose Perpetual Mission in Detroit offers food, clothing, and emergency assistance to 100,000 people a year. Many of the exemplars had taken stands in life that had cost them safety, security, comfort, and friendship. They were altruistic, responsible, and caring; but as concrete embodiments of abstract values, as exemplars, they were also generative.

Nothing in the research literature on moral development prepared Colby and Damon for the first of their findings. As the exemplars told their stories, they revealed an "impervious sense of certainty." They did not agonize over what was right and wrong, struggle with doubt, or question endlessly. *They knew,* and consequently *they did.* "I knew for me the right answers without sleepless nights and indecision," said one man. "I was never tempted to take a contrary course." This certainty was neither rigid nor dogmatic. "Even as the exemplars' grip on their core ideals remained unwavering," wrote Colby and Damon, "they continued to reexamine their most fundamental attitudes and choices at frequent intervals." And, if necessary, they made dramatic changes in their lives based on what they discovered.

A similar finding emerged from the second study, which was conducted by personality psychologist Dan McAdams and his colleagues at Northwestern University. The Northwestern researchers recruited samples of forty generative adults and thirty who were far less generative. The generative sample consisted of schoolteachers and community volunteers who agreed with questionnaire statements such as "People come to me for advice" and "I feel as though my contributions will exist after I die." They also reported that they had recently performed a number of generative acts: teaching someone a skill, producing a piece of art, donating blood, reading a story to a child, and so on. The comparison group were neither teachers nor community volunteers; they agreed with fewer generative statements and reported fewer generative acts. All seventy subjects told their life story in a semistructured interview that lasted two to three hours.

One of the major differences between the two groups turned out to be the "depth, clarity, and continuity" of their core values:

[The] highly generative adults . . . are guided by a clearly articulated and strongly-held ideology that remains steadfast over time. This *moral stead-fastness* survives questioning and doubt and suggests that for all the changes that the protagonist goes through in life, his or her basic values and beliefs do *not* change much. Thus, the hero or heroine in these life stories is not the Sartrean quester filled with existential angst. . . .

A 50-year-old church minister was once a girl scout den mother, then a prostitute, and later a con artist, and she spent two terms in a federal prison. Her life story account is filled with tumult and transformation from beginning to end, but throughout it all "I was always doing ministry."

Whether this woman was indeed doing ministry all her life is beside the point. What matters is that she now sees ministry as something that was in her from the beginning and, by extrapolation, as something that will be in her until the end. What matters is the continuity she feels in her very self.

Like the experience of continuity, the experience of call was common to subjects in both studies I have cited. Among Colby and Damon's moral exemplars, it was sometimes felt to come from God, sometimes from the circumstances of those in need. A woman who took it upon herself to locate sanctuaries for immigrants fleeing persecution said of facing danger, "It's not anything to do with courage or fear. It's . . . I guess it has more to do with obedience. Obeying the call that I hear, and doing what I hear I am asked to do." In the Northwestern sample, as we shall see in a moment, the call often emanated from an awareness that one had been given advantages in life that others had been denied.

In a third study of generative lives, this one conducted by Laurent Parks Daloz and others, similar experiences were uncovered. The researchers interviewed one hundred men and women who had sustained for at least seven years a commitment to causes that involved humanity's global interconnectedness—the earth's common good. The interviewees revealed a "strong moral compass" and a sense of certainty about their mission that some expressed with a double negative: "You can't *not* do it." Once again, investigators heard people speak of a calling: "We didn't ask to be born at this time. And yet we are chosen to be born at this time—chosen by history, chosen by the cosmological process." Or, "I've just been bitten by a bug that says you must contribute." In the researchers' summation:

Whether manifest in action on behalf of better education, responsible business practices, participatory democracy, or environmental sustainability, at its core we heard a thrumming concern for the future in which life, "the most basic, bottom stuff" could flourish—as though they were responding to some call from Life to realize Itself more fully through them.

Other than Erikson's case histories, the studies I have described here are the first to probe in any depth the nature of generative identities. (The first and third did not even consider their studies to be research into "generativity.") The findings are important in their own right, but they are also significant in a larger historical sense.

Scholars argue that the modern concept of identity has existed in the West for perhaps two hundred years. It was born in the midst of a growing skepticism toward religion and other external sources of authority. In the modern view, you actively create your own identity; it is not bestowed upon you. So psychology speaks of "forming" or "shaping" a self the way a sculptor would a statue. It speaks, as Daniel Levinson has done in his books on adult development, of articulating a dream which you then attempt to realize. The process is conscious and deliberate, a task in its own right, like my efforts to fashion a voice on audio tape. In the absence of external authority, the identity you create becomes the ultimate moral source: "To thine own self be true."

But when it comes to *generative* identities, recent research is suggesting that self-creation is only half the story. The other half is receptivity—the passive side of the Way. As you seek to discover who you are, you stay alert to what life is asking of you. You are less self-conscious about it all. You simply take your dream and listen for a corresponding summons. The latter becomes the ultimate moral source: "To thine own call be true."

Not every generative identity hears a call, of course. One of Colby and Damon's exemplars, in fact, was consciously pursuing personal growth, guided by the belief that he had to be true to himself. But he was unusual. In general, recent work is telling us that many people who leave their marks on the world experience identity—or what we moderns call identity—as something that life confers on them. They receive it as a piece of clothing meant for them and no one else, the way Cinderella received her slipper, or the way I once received in imagination a pair of my grandfather's white gloves. In remaining true to the slipper or the gloves, you also remain true to yourself.

These findings on generative identities have additional historical import, offering a challenge to a more recent view of selfhood. Back in 1970 Alvin Toffler argued in his influential book *Future Shock* that durable identities with clear boundaries were a thing of the past. In the future, he said, people would experience a "through-put" of self-concepts in their lives, a "sequence of serial selves." At the same time—this was the Me Decade—advocates of self-fulfillment were coaching their clients to be "fluid" and "open to experience," to focus on the "here-and-now," to continually "expand" the limits of consciousness. Twenty years later, in books with titles such as *The Saturated Self* and *The Protean Self,* scholars called into question the ability of people in a "postmodern" world to be *anything but* a series of selves. "The very concept of an 'authentic self' with knowable characteristics recedes from view," said one of them, Kenneth Gergen.

The challenge offered by the studies I've described is clear: their subjects have a sense of permanent definition; they have a sense of authenticity; and they have it during the time of their generativity. "I was always doing ministry," said one of them, recognizing it in herself. Her definition may change once a particular period of her life is over. It may prove from a historical point of view to be less than permanent. But this woman knows what it takes from a psychological point of view to give an identity roots, to focus one's energies, to deepen one's voice. She knows that something lasting in the world can only come from something lasting in oneself.

The Stories They Tell

One way of telling someone who you are is with a list of roles: I'm a daughter, a student, a fiancée. Or a list of traits: I'm gregarious but I can be moody and aloof. A third way, one championed by Dan McAdams, is with the story of your life. The last approach is intriguing, for if the self is a story, it has certain characteristics. It has a beginning, a middle, and an end. It has duration and durability, but it's also open to revision. It's not surprising that the idea of self-as-story is particularly well suited to the study of generative identities, or that generative individuals tell certain kinds of stories.

McAdams and his colleagues at Northwestern University have identified two kinds of life stories that generative people tell. One, told by those who are essentially repeating a legacy, is the *commitment story*. The other, told by those who are reworking or buffering a legacy, is the *story of reform*. Both require voice, and both reveal a belief in the resilience of life.

The commitment story begins with scenes of blessing—a sense that you were singled out in childhood for some special advantage. A number of subjects in McAdams's generative sample noted that they had been endowed with musical talent, or been given a cherished family name, or been the teacher's pet, or been blessed—so they saw it—by the necessity of having to stand up for themselves. At the same time, they remembered being sensitive to the suffering of others. "We had a retarded kid on our street; I always felt sorry for him." Thus a narrative contrast was set up early in their stories: "I was lucky. Others were not. As a result, I came to believe that I was *called* to service in some manner—that it is my destiny or obligation to be of some good use to other people in life."

This sensitivity to the contrast between one's blessing and another's suffering is something that Erikson found in stories of Gandhi's childhood; it resulted in a feeling of obligation to alleviate the suffering Gandhi saw, an outcome like that in McAdams's subjects. I once found a similar sensitivity in the early memory of a 30-year-old man. As a young child he had received a brand-new bike which was noticeably different from the rusty old bike his friend had. So he feigned an interest in his friend's bike, giving his friend a chance to ride his. When such a theme appears in an adult's early memory, it reveals much more about the identity he currently possesses than about any self-image he may have had as a child. It reveals how he sees life *now*.

From this initial sensitivity, the leading characters of commitment stories go on to make a decision to live in accord with a set of clear and abiding values. As they try to be of service to others (theirs is generativity mixed with altruism) they encounter their share of disappointment and even tragedy, but these bad events are transformed into good outcomes, whether by the protagonists' own efforts, or by chance, or by external design. As they look to the future, protagonists set goals aimed at the welfare of the next generation and the betterment of society.

The most striking feature of commitment stories is their way of juxtaposing events so that good seems to flow out of bad. McAdams called this bad-to-good contrast a *redemption sequence*. The loneliness of my childhood "made me resilient" as an adult, said one narrator. And others: In the aftermath of a divorce, I developed a better relationship with my son. Following a near-fatal accident, I made an amazing recovery. A period of chaos led to the happiest time in my life. Overall, stories from the generative and less generative groups had equal amounts of positive and negative. But as scene followed scene in the generative stories, negative emotions were used to set up positive ones. The last word in a sequence was usually good.

Life stories in the study also contained the reverse: *contamination sequences* in which the last word was bad. I got a stable job, then I was fired. I was enjoying life in the city, then I was mugged. I fell in love with a woman, then she rejected me. There were fewer contamination than redemption sequences in the study's life stories, but almost all of them appeared in the less generative group. If you read transcripts from the generative adults, you would come across five or six redemption sequences for every contamination sequence. If you read transcripts from the comparison group, you would come across fewer than one.

Was this the way that lives had gone or simply the way they had been remembered? We'll never know. Perhaps the generative group had actually been redeemed more and contaminated less. But "redemption" and "contamination" are also perspectives on life, and ways of interpreting one's own. Maybe the generative adults had a penchant for *seeing* redemption, even if there was little of it around. However it came about—through actual events, through interpretation—they worked more of life's resilience into their stories. And so into their selves.

The generative adults, in other words, had what Erikson once called a "belief in the species." They had a certainty about the "faithful force." This conviction surprised Colby and Damon when they found it in their moral exemplars. Sometimes it was a faith in human nature, or in a system of laws, or in a larger "struggle," but for nearly 80 percent of their subjects it was religious faith: "I didn't know how I was doing it or why, but I know the Holy Spirit was leading me." That percentage was nearly identical to one found in the Parks Daloz study, and in both cases it was surprising because religion was not a criterion for those who nominated subjects for interviewing. The faith involved bound subjects to something beyond themselves, something that would survive their death. It explained their disclaimers of courage, their sometimes striking joy, their feeling of gratitude for being where they were. It gave them the ability to go on against daunting odds:

> There is a story that the sky is falling and all the animals were running through the village, the lions and the tigers. In the middle of this dirt road, there was a sparrow with his little legs up in the air. And the zebra runs by and says, "Hey dummy, the sky is falling. Do you think with your spindly little legs, you're going to hold it up?" And the little bird says, "One does what one can." That's me.
>
> I have no illusions. I have absolutely no illusions about who I am or what I can do. I mean, I love the work we do and the thing that keeps you going is that the dragon doesn't win all the time.

Not every generative adult in McAdams's study told a life story with commitment elements. Fewer than half, in fact, had themes of being singled out for a blessing or being sensitive to the suffering of others. So while prototypical commitment stories are likely to be found among generative adults, other kinds of identity stories are likely to be present as well, underwriting generative self-concepts, sustaining generative efforts.

A second prototype has been identified by criminologist Shadd Maruna, who analyzed the published autobiographies of twenty men and women who had gone straight after a life of crime. The autobiographies had remarkably similar elements, creating a quintessential *story of reform.* This story opens with scenes of special *dis*advantage. The eventual heroes or heroines begin life as victims of abuse; they were "born to lose." In adolescence they take up criminal activity as a way of "winning" and even finding a family, then sink deeper and deeper into deviant behavior. Eventually there is a crash, or many crashes, which force them into "moments of clarity" in which they question the direction of their lives and wonder how they can "get the hell out." Words of wisdom come from a trusted source who reminds them of the ideals they already possess. Now protagonists try to reform, but they run into roadblocks. Something keeps pushing them back to their old ways. Finally, in a single dramatic moment, they are redeemed in a way that locks in the reformed identity. The redemption comes from the outside—it happens *to* the protagonist, usually at the hands of a higher power. Now life gives the narrators a second chance. This time they take it and succeed.

Generativity comes at the end of the story. Grateful for what life has given them, narrators now want to "give something back." They help troubled youth or tell their story so that others will not repeat their mistakes. In the words of one author, "I know that one bald-headed old ex-con is not going to convert the world, but I humbly thank God that it is the kind of world where one man *can* make a big contribution—that I can be part of molding plastic, young life."

The reform story contains an identity well suited for those who would rework or buffer a legacy, just as the commitment story does for those who would repeat one. These stories, of course, are pure types—summations of elements found in many individual life stories, none of which fits the summation in every respect. The story that follows, for example, illustrates commitment in response to a call and sensitivity to the suffering of others. But the sense of redemption is absent, and that of contamination present, until the very end.

Florence Nightingale's Calling

The story takes place in the nineteenth century, but the influence of its heroine has reached the twentieth and will surely extend into the twenty-first. Though she never had any children, Florence Nightingale led a generative life—not so much because she cared (that's altruism), but because, as a nurse, she left behind a craft of caring and became a symbol of caring. If you've ever rung for a nurse from a hospital bed, you've been touched by her technical genius—she rigged up some of the very first call bells. And if you've ever made a bar graph or a pie chart on your personal computer, you've been touched once again. A brilliant statistician, Miss Nightingale was the first to present data in pictures, this to make findings on mortality rates in the British Army more compelling.

Florence Nightingale's life has something to say about identity in generativity because she both heard a voice and gained one, and because she nearly went mad before finding an outlet for hers. She experienced demands "from the outside," one from above and one from the graves of dead British soldiers. These calls, and her own iron constitution, were enough to drive her on when she felt utterly useless and sterile. In her most productive years she was steadfast and committed; but she was, paradoxically, alone and bedridden. It is a marvel of generativity that in the middle of the nineteenth century, a voice could travel so far from a room its occupant never left.

We can know a great deal about Miss Nightingale's inner life because from girlhood to old age she poured her feelings out unremittingly in what she called "private notes." "She wrote them on anything that came into her hand," says biographer Cecil Woodham-Smith, "on odd pieces of blotting-paper, on the backs of calendars, the margins of letters. . . . Frequently she repeated a note several times at different dates with only a slight variation in wording." These were not diary entries, although from time to time she kept a diary. They were just scraps of feelings written on scraps of paper—the secret experiences and uncensored opinions of a lifetime. And vast numbers of the scraps have survived for her biographers to ponder.

Florence Nightingale was born in 1820 to a prosperous English family and named after the city in Italy where they happened to be living at the time. In one of her notes she wrote that as a small child she was haunted by the feeling that she was different—a monster, in fact, who might be found out at any moment. Afraid of betraying herself, she avoided strangers and refused to dine downstairs. She also wrote that by the age of 6 her rich surroundings had become distasteful to her. By her teen years, she said, "I craved for some regular occupation, for something worth doing instead of frittering time away on useless trifles." She believed she was singled out, but not for a blessing. Her commitment story would have a darker cast than those of McAdams's research subjects.

"On February 7th, 1837, God spoke to me and called me into His service." Florence told no one of this voice but recorded its message in a private note. It came when she was three months shy of her 17th birthday, and it established as her own the cultural context for her work: she would operate within the framework of Christianity. Florence was to remain constant in her beliefs—morally steadfast—never really doubting them and certainly not departing from them. The voice told her what she was to do, but only in the general sense of serving God. The idea of nursing had not yet entered her mind.

For the next seven years Miss Nightingale led the life her family asked of her, touring the continent, partying, dancing, writing letters, attracting the attention of young men, "shining in society." Her mother and her sister lived for these activities but to Florence they were a prison. In the summer of her 22nd year, when England was gripped in starvation, she became intensely aware of the suffering and despair that lay outside her ambit. "All the people I see are eaten up with care or poverty or disease." Feeling the contrast with what she had, she began to pester her mother for food, clothing, and medicine to take to them. Gradually she determined what she was to do—serve the sick in hospitals. She was certain of her calling at 24, and once she was, she asked her parents for permission to study at a local hospital.

The request set off an explosion. Her mother was terrified, then furious, accusing her of having a love affair with a "vulgar surgeon." Her older sister went into hysterics. Her father, who had been her tutor and intellectual companion, talked of spoiled and ungrateful daughters and left on a trip. Florence was cut off and devastated. She wrote to a cousin: "No one but the mother of it knows how precious an infant idea becomes; nor how the soul dies, between the destruction of one and the taking up of another. I shall never do anything and am worse than dust and nothing."

Still, she tried to educate herself. At 19 she had discovered mathematics and fallen in love with its exacting nature. But her mother could only say, "What use were mathematics to a married woman?" and her father, who had been her personal teacher, "Why Mathematics? I cannot see that Mathematics would do great service. History or Philosophy, natural or moral, I should like best." At 26 she began to study public health statistics. Getting up before dawn and writing by candlelight, she worked in secret, filling notebooks with facts on sanitary conditions in hospitals as far away as Paris and Berlin. But there was as yet no use for what she was learning.

There was little joy in Florence Nightingale at this point in her life. The child who thought herself a monster had grown into a young woman who escaped into sickness and fantasy. She recorded how much "dreaming" had taken over her life. Sometimes it was out of control: she fell into "trances" in the middle of ordinary conversation. Alone, unable to sleep, often confined to bed, on the verge of a complete breakdown, she would have killed herself but for her belief that suicide was a mortal sin. "O weary days," she wrote when 31, "oh evenings that seem never to end—for how many years have I watched that drawing-room clock and thought it never would reach the ten! and for twenty, thirty years more to do this!" In yet another note, she saw herself bitterly as "butchered to make a Roman Holiday."

Sigmund Freud was five years from being born when Florence Nightingale wrote that terse comment, yet the psychoanalysis he created offers metaphors for reflecting on her life. Analyst George Vaillant sees these years of Florence's distress as marked by immature defense mechanisms, especially intellectualization (seen in her obsessive note writing), hypochondriasis (seen in her conversion of emotional problems into physical illness), and schizoid fantasy (seen in her uncontrollable, trancelike daydreaming). But a creative burst would soon erupt in Florence's life and those defenses would mature, would turn into sublimation and channel the "lower" impulses they once dammed into a "higher" call of service. She would find a way of treating the sick instead of being sick. She would acquire a voice to match the one she had heard. More important, she would find what every voice needs: someone to hear it.

The change took place in the summer of her 31st year, and it was forecast in a private note about her family: "I must expect no sympathy or help from them. I must *take* some things, as few as I can, to enable me to live." The first thing she took was a trip to a German hospital to learn about nursing. Years later she would write, "The nursing there was nil, the hygiene horrible. . . . But never have I met with a higher tone, a purer devotion than there." She was happy. She had to return home, but at 32 she could say, "I have come into possession of myself."

Two years later, she had found an outlet for that self. It was November of 1854, and she was on board a ship headed for Scutari, a large village across the straits of Bosporus from Constantinople. There, British casualties from its war with Russia, the Crimean War, were being deposited. The British public had been inflamed by a war correspondent's account of how sick and wounded soldiers were being treated—like "savages," he said in *The Times.* With the backing of the British secretary of war, who was a personal friend, Florence Nightingale was leading a party of thirty-eight nurses to the scene of the outrage.

When the nurses disembarked at Scutari, they were overcome by a stench that reached outside the hospital walls. Inside, thousands of men lay on damp and rotting floors crawling with rats, using their boots for pillows and their bloodied coats for blankets. In the wards, amputations were being performed in full sight of the men who were next in line. In those same wards, tubs holding excrement were spilling over. The cellars of the hospital held hundreds of women, the wives and widows and prostitutes of the soldiers, some of them giving birth, others dying of cholera. Diarrhea in Scutari was killing men faster than war in Crimea.

It was no place for the faint of heart. Miss Nightingale had money at her disposal, some of it collected by herself, and important political connections back home. They gave her the power to cut through red tape, to outflank administrators whose heads, she wrote, had been "flattened between the boards of Army discipline." She bought scrub brushes, clothes, plates, cups, spoons, cooking utensils, towels and soap, operating tables and medical equipment. She established a laundry. She altered the distributions of rations. She started a lying-in hospital for the women in the cellar. Week by week, she set up a machinery of administration and made sure that she was at the center of it, fighting army authorities and her own nurses every step of the way. She had no secretary; all the paperwork was done in her own hand. Letters to officials, letters to the families of soldiers, requisitions, reports, plans for hospital reorganization, compilations of statistics: she would write on and on in the cold of winter, her ink freezing in its well.

In those dark winter months, when Florence made her nightly rounds, a legend was born: the Lady of the Lamp. "It seemed an endless walk," wrote one of her nurses. "As we slowly passed along the silence was profound, very seldom did a moan or cry from those deeply suffering fall on our ears. A dim light burned here and there, Miss Nightingale carried her lantern which she would set down before she bent over any of the patients. I much admired her manner to the men—it was so tender and kind."

Florence vowed that no one under her care would die alone, and she estimated that she witnessed two thousand deaths during her first winter at Scutari. Her influence over the soldiers was enormous. "Nightingale Power," they called it. She gave them the courage to submit to the pain of surgery without anesthesia. She herself dressed wounds with no fear of becoming infected. "She would speak to one, and nod and smile to as many more; but she could not do it all you know. We lay there by hundreds; but we could kiss her shadow as it fell and lay our heads on the pillow again content"—that from the letter of a soldier.

At the end of February a Sanitary Commission arrived from England and described hospital conditions as "murderous." That proved decisive. By spring rubbish had been removed, the hiding places of rats ripped away, sewers cleaned, walls washed with lime, the water supply decontaminated (it had been flowing, the commission discovered, through the carcass of a dead horse). The mortality rate dropped dramatically and instantly—from 43 percent to 2 percent in six months. Florence Nightingale had been a rock—*the* rock—throughout the worst of the crisis.

She would spend another year and a half at Scutari, nearly dying of fever and exhaustion, and ultimately despairing of her mission. The war ended in March of 1856, and the troops that returned that summer turned her into a national heroine. But she would have none of it. "She said she had seen Hell," says biographer Woodham-Smith, "and because she had seen Hell she was set apart." Over and over in private notes she wrote, "I can never forget." Over and over she expressed the belief that she would soon die. Soldiers in their graves called to her: she must effect the health reform of the British Army. "I stand at the altar of murdered men, and while I live I fight their cause." She would adopt the role of buffer.

A strong maternal feeling began to appear in her private notes. She had been "a bad mother" to leave her children in Crimea, lying "from causes which might have been prevented, in their forgotten graves." These were *her* dead. "The real fathers and mothers of the human race are NOT the fathers and mothers according to the flesh," she wrote with bitterness, remembering her own childhood. "For every one of my 18,000 children . . . I have expended more motherly feeling and action in a week than my mother has expended for me in 37 years."

After her return from the Bosporus, Miss Nightingale worked with blind, monotonous persistence. She would never leave England again, would in fact live until she was 90, spending most of her years confined as an invalid to her room. But from that sickly spot, where she insisted on being alone, where she made arrangements for her funeral and wrote letters to be sent after her death, her voice would eventually carry around the world. When a reform commission was established to look into the Crimean disaster, she prepared a report which showed that the hospital in Scutari was more fatal than the battlefield ever was, showed that *even now* army barracks in England were far more lethal than comparable civilian quarters. Now her knowledge of mathematics and her familiarity with public health reports proved to be invaluable. Now, to be even more convincing, she created ways of presenting statistics in pictures.

It was joyless work that produced few tangible results, and none that she herself could see. She suffered from spells of fainting, nausea at the sight of food, and nervous twitches; and she exploited her poor health to keep her mother and sister at bay. But day by day, for years and then for decades, she forced herself to grind on. Call it moral steadfastness, call it an iron will, call it a grim obsession; however you put it, there was something lasting in her—that "primitive rigor" and "metal" that Robert Bolt saw in Thomas More. And it grated others. Florence Nightingale was not merely impatient and demanding but resentful of the sacrifices that she made and others did not. She irritated even her closest supporters.

Her private notes and letters record a trail of despair. "Contamination sequences," narrative psychologists would call them today. She achieves a minor victory, but it's turned into a defeat. She compiles a new set of statistics or drafts a new set of regulations, and they are buried by inertia at the War Office. At various times she writes, "My doctrines have taken no hold," "Not one of my Crimean following learnt anything from me," "I do not wish to be remembered when I am gone." This, despite evidence repeatedly presented to her of what she was steadily accomplishing.

People were listening. When the American Civil War broke out, she was asked for help in organizing the care of the wounded, and she began an extensive correspondence. A few years later she turned to the health of the British Army in India and then to India itself, organizing data collection from great distances, receiving visitors one by one (a rule on which she insisted), and writing endless drafts for the improvement of sanitary conditions. In her solitary London room, she was the hub of a network that covered all of India. And as she exercised her power, she gradually transformed the image of the British soldier from drunken brute to courageous hero.

She also changed the image of the nurse. Before Scutari, nurses were either ignorant, promiscuous drunks or religious sisters more concerned with souls than with bodies. Four years after Crimea, at the age of 40, Miss Nightingale founded the Nightingale School and Home for Nurses at St. Thomas Hospital in London. Here she insisted on education in character as well as skills; students accumulated a "Moral Record" as well as a "Technical Record." In a small book entitled *Notes on Nursing,* she prescribed in minute detail a craft of nursing that was revolutionary in its day and remarkable because it stressed fresh air and sanitation while repudiating the germ theory of disease. Every aspect of the patient's condition was covered. "He should be able to see out the window. . . . Never let a patient be waked out of his first sleep. . . . Keep your patient's cup dry underneath"—or else it will stick to the saucer. This stuff of technique was complemented with elements of culture. What was a nurse to be? Neither the harlot nor the nun; instead a trained, well-paid professional of impeccable character, "a sound, and close, and quick observer, . . . a woman of delicate and decent feeling."

In the last decades of her life, Florence Nightingale began to see and enjoy the fruits of her continual battles with government bureaucracies. She saw the redemption of her work. At 61 she wrote to a friend, "For years and years I used to watch for death as no sick man ever watched for the morning. It is strange that now I am bereft of all, I crave for it less. I want to do a little work, a little better, before I die." An extraordinary peace and benevolence began to flow through her. Never having married, she began to enjoy being a grandmother to the children of friends and relatives. In her 70s and 80s, says her biographer, "She was treated with an almost religious deference—ministers, kings, princesses, statesmen waited at her door, and her utterances were paid the respect due to an oracle." At 75 she herself wrote, "There is so much to live for." At 87, blind and uncomprehending, she became the first woman to receive the British Order of Merit. She died in 1910 at the age of 90. In keeping with her wishes for a simple burial, the family declined offers of a national funeral. The "mother" of modern nursing was buried in the family grave with only a single line on the tombstone: "F. N. Born 1820. Died 1910."

Someone to Hear

If Scutari was the experience that gave Florence Nightingale definition, it also divided her life into distinct periods. Before her trip there, she was restless almost to the point of insanity. She was going mad. Afterwards, she was mad in an altogether different sense—filled with righteous anger. What changed the nature of her madness and steered it to a higher end was finding a way of expressing her identity, a way of answering her call. To be generative (and, I might add, to have her defenses mature), Florence Nightingale needed an outlet. She needed someone to hear.

And heard she was, more widely than she could have imagined. Channels of communication the world was using for the first time—the telegraph, the war correspondent—ensured, as the printing press had for Luther, that her voice was not only carried but amplified. England was well aware of what Miss Nightingale was doing in Scutari when she was doing it, and the country learned more when its journalists and soldiers returned at war's end.

The importance of someone to hear is well known to Alcoholics Anonymous, whose Twelfth Step includes the instructions to "carry the message to other alcoholics." "If you hang on to your sobriety, you'll end up getting drunk" and "Get somebody to work on" are two of AA's well-known maxims. An alcoholic mother I got to know had been sober for only two months when she was asked by a physician to do informal counseling at a halfway house for alcoholics:

> It made it more difficult for me to go out and drink on the weekends, when I was going to go down and talk to those men about sobriety on Wednesday nights. Now when I'm telling somebody about staying sober and how it gets better, I can be having a rotten day. But saying to someone new that it will get better helps me to remember, yeah, this is going to get better, it's going to pass.

Telling those men a story of reform forced this woman to live up to it. It kept her sober self in place.

An audience not only confirms a voice; it elicits and shapes more of it. This was one of the "more counterintuitive observations" in Colby and Damon's study of moral exemplars: "In their transactions with entrusted groups, people who become known as leaders often take direction from their 'followers,' and people accustomed to autonomous, sometimes defiant determinations of right and wrong nevertheless are open to, and deeply affected by, the opinions of certain others." The Soviet human rights dissident Andrei Sakharov is a case in point. The inventor of the Russian H-bomb, he eventually turned against his country's establishment and became a crusader for peace, winning the Nobel Prize for doing so. In his memoirs, Sakharov recalls being told by a friend in a trusted group, "One of the problems in getting involved with us is you do something and we're right on top of you to do something else." Sakharov had his own voice, he attracted and inspired followers, yet at the same time he was transformed by them. He led them; they developed his leadership.

In the exchange between leaders and followers, a collective identity story is often born. Who *I*, the leader, am begins to say who *we* are. Leaders feed the identity story to their followers; the followers release and shape it.

In his book *Leading Minds* psychologist Howard Gardner analyzed some midcentury examples. George Marshall, appointed Unites States Army chief of staff in 1939, had the task of alerting the American people to the Nazi threat in Europe and preparing its army for war. (In 1939, the U.S. Army, numbering 200,000, was only the seventeenth largest in the world.) Many Americans were indifferent to a war on the other side of the Atlantic. So Marshall told an identity story: *we* Americans are a people who defend the values we believe in; we fight for them; and we fight for them wherever they are under attack. The story was not new, but it countered what the isolationists of the day were saying. To the army itself, Marshall told a related story: *we* are nonpartisan professionals ready for any contingency; we represent all of America, not just parts of it (this to sell the draft). Marshall himself embodied these stories, and therein lay their greatest power. He did not vote in political elections lest he be accused of partisanship. His integrity, lack of self-interest, and preparedness were beyond question. In many minds he was America's exemplary soldier.

By war's end Marshall's army numbered eight and a third million, and Winston Churchill had called him the "true organizer" of the Allied victory. But in the aftermath of the war he faced a new problem: many Americans wanted their country to flex its newfound muscle and punish the vanquished. Marshall said *we* are something else. We are citizens of the world who transcend our national interests. We aid the victims of war, even in nations that fought against us. In 1947, as secretary of state, he laid out a plan for the reconstruction of Europe. Senator Joseph McCarthy would call it "America's retreat from victory" and Marshall himself a traitor. But in 1953, when awarding its Peace Prize, the Nobel committee would describe the Marshall Plan as the "most constructive peaceful work . . . in this century."

Another leader studied by Gardner made his impact in the world of business. When Albert Sloan, Jr., took over the presidency of General Motors in 1923, it had almost collapsed. When he retired as chairman of the board in 1956, it was the largest and richest corporation in the world. Sloan initiated the turnaround by giving GM a new organizational structure, making each division responsible for its own profit. He broadened the range of its products, creating "a car for every purse and purpose" at a time when its rival Ford was limiting itself to economy cars. But he also developed an identity story that explained GM's place in the emerging world of transportation.

We, said Sloan, are shaping the new world as members of the most progressive organization on earth. We are a family, a corporate family, that knows how to conduct its business efficiently. Embodying that family identity, Sloan acted the patriarch. During the 1920s and early '30s he traveled the United States in a private railroad car, visiting five to ten dealers a day, hearing from the family's members.

During the war years, GM became the country's leading manufacturer of defense materials. As the corporation grew in peacetime, so did Sloan's audiences, and so did the scope of his story. First it was *we Americans* who believed in business as the key to the good life. Then it was *we humans:* "It is clear that every man, woman, and child, including generations yet to be born, has a stake in the power of General Motors." The capitalistic way of life, Sloan added, "was to advance the economic and social status of humanity more than any other." There were counterstories in abundance —from labor unions, from crushed competitors, from critics of capitalism—and Sloan's identity story eventually lost its power. Today, it might fall on deaf ears, but in the first half of the twentieth century it found receptive ones. It found the right audience, one that could make it their own.

The influence of Marshall and Sloan can be attributed in large measure to their organizational expertise. But we must not overlook the power of a story that people could believe in and become a part of. A generative identity is not merely a matter of finding *your* voice and *your* story; you must also find the place where your story will thrive. As Gardner points out, "Even the most eloquent story is stillborn in the absence of an audience ready to hear it."

The Three Languages

Much of what I have said about voice can be summed up in a tale that comes to us through the brothers Grimm. Not quite two hundred years ago, these law students turned librarians turned scholars collected and edited a number of folktales, calling them *Kinder- und Hausmärchen,* "children's and household tales." The stories were not just for the young, but for everyone who lived under the same roof.

One of the stories in *Kinder- und Hausmärchen* is about a young man coming of age and finding a generative identity. That, of course, is the meaning *I* see in it, which is another way of saying it's the meaning I put into it. The story is called "The Three Languages," and versions of it have been found in many European and some Asian countries. It is a wonderful account of the sources of voice, in particular of a voice's depth and carrying power. It also happens to describe the portion of the Generative Way that we have traveled so far.

The hero of the story is the son of an aging count. Like the ugly duckling of another tale, he appears dull and directionless to his father. Wanting to "knock" something into his head, the count sends him away to spend a year with a famous tutor. When the boy returns, he tells his father that he has learned "what the dogs say when they bark."

Florence Nightingale might just as well have said "mathematics" to her mother. What good were mathematics—or the language of the dogs? The count decides that his son needs a different teacher.

So the boy goes off to live with a new master. After a year he comes back and tells his father that he now knows "what the frogs say when they croak." The count can't believe it: all that time and money down the drain! He gives his son a final chance. If the boy learns nothing useful this time, he warns, "I will no longer be your father."

A year passes, and with it another town and another teacher. The son faces his father a third time. "What have you learned?" the father demands.

"What the birds say when they sing."

It's the last straw. Enraged, the count commands his servants, "Take him to the woods and kill him."

The servants, however, cannot bring themselves to murder someone they love, so once they're in the forest, they let the boy go. They kill a deer instead, cutting out its eyes and tongue and offering them as proof to the father that his son is indeed dead.

Now the story of identity begins. A young person finds himself lost in a dense forest, cut off from all that he has known, confused about what he is to do and where he is to go. In his wanderings he comes eventually to a castle and begs for a night's lodging. "Yes," answers the lord of the castle, "but you will have to spend it in the old tower." There, wild dogs bark without ceasing, demanding every few hours to be fed a live human being. No one knows why, but for a long time both the dogs and the land have been cursed.

"Give me some food to take to them," the young man says, unshaken.

When he enters the tower, the dogs eat what he sets before him. They bark, and he understands their language. The next morning, to everyone's surprise, he comes out of the tower unscathed and tells the lord of the castle, "The dogs are bewitched. They are obliged to watch over a great treasure in the bottom of the tower and cannot rest until it is taken away. They have told me how to do it."

With the lord's blessing, the youth returns to the tower's depths and brings up a chest full of gold. Immediately, the howling of the dogs ceases, and the curse is lifted from the land.

The young man stays in his new surroundings for a while and then decides to go to Rome. Rome is a "high" place, but on the way he must pass through something "low," a swamp where thousands of frogs are croaking. The brothers Grimm are strangely silent about what takes place in the swamp. They say only that the young man listens to the frogs and understands their language. He becomes "thoughtful and sad" and then moves on.

Coming to Rome, the young man at last enters a church where the college of cardinals is convening to select a new pope. Suddenly, two snow-white doves land on his shoulders, and the cardinals take it as a sign that God has chosen him. The young man is startled and mystified, for the frogs in the swamp had prophesied this very moment. But how could he possibly be a pope? He doesn't know what to do. He doesn't know the words.

At this critical moment, the doves begin to sing in his ears. They whisper the words he needs to know, and he understands them. Now he can step into—and up to—his rightful place in life. He can answer the call, don the appropriate vestments, receive an identity. As the story ends, the young man is saying his first Mass, trusting the doves to give him the words.

For the count's son, the path to a generative identity involves three aspects of himself, three inner places he has to visit. The first is the past—an old tower beset by an ancient curse. When he spends a night there, the young man reenacts the fisherman's encounter with the djinni, and with the same result. He calms the dogs, as the fisherman did the djinni, and releases a treasure. At the same time, he breaks a curse that had afflicted a country, becoming a buffer for others. "The Three Languages" tells us that the past is the first source of depth for our voice, but the treasure it contains is often constricted by fear. To lift what is buried into the light of day and open it to generative ends, we must find a way of talking to the fear. We must calm the dogs. Then the fear will cease (the defenses will mature), and the past will be ours to use.

The second source of depth is the swamp. The swamp represents our lower nature: the body, the flesh, the particularities of passion and temperament that make us unique. It is here, not in Rome, that the young count first learns the specifics of his calling. There is an important lesson in that: we need to know our lower nature before we can step up to something higher. Unless we are intimate with our flesh, we cannot express our spirit. An instructor of voice once told me of a student with extraordinary talent who could not sing from her physical depths. Her problem lay in feelings about her body that originated in childhood—in the tower of the story. Her music could not ascend because she could not yet descend.

The experience in the swamp is given short shrift by the Grimms, and this is a tendency of religion—to overlook what happens there, to condemn it as "carnal," to distort what comes from the unconscious. Religion wants to get out of the swamp as quickly as possible. But, "The Three Languages" tells us, you do so at risk to your creativity and your calling. A tendency of psychology, on the other hand, is to neglect Rome or to see it only as elevated swamp, to explain our highest endeavors as the work of selfish genes or selfish ids. Here, religion and psychology have something to learn from each other. Religion needs to learn the language of what is down below in human nature; psychology, of what is up above.

Rome is the end point as well as the high point of the young man's trek to identity. His place in life awaited there, to be filled by a moral exemplar, a spiritual father. In that place the young man does not, in the modern idiom, "create" an identity. He receives it from the outside and puts it on like a cloak. Then, for the first time in his life, the voice that speaks to him becomes the voice with which he speaks. In such a circumstance, his voice—any voice—will carry a great distance, even beyond the grave.

6

Blending Your Voice and Creating

SUPPOSE WE START this chapter (I hope it's not too slowly) with a snail. The one I have in mind, *Potamopyrgus antipodarum,* is found in New Zealand, and in one ecological niche, in deep water where ducks do not feed, it reproduces by cloning. An exact copy of a parent's genetic blueprint is passed on to its offspring. But in a different ecological niche, in shallow water where ducks do feed, *Potamopyrgus antipodarum* reproduces the way we do. Its genetic material is split in two, and one of the sections is joined to a section from another snail. This is an example of sexual reproduction, the word *sex* referring to the fact that something is split or sectioned.

The difference between the snail's two ecological niches is that the shallow water is full of dangerous parasites deposited by the feeding ducks. Evolutionary biologists believe that the snails have responded to the infestations of their bodies by mixing genes. This creates offspring that are different from each other and different from their parents. So there is a greater likelihood that a few of the young snails will be better able to resist the parasites. Sexual reproduction makes for genetic variability, and genetic variability establishes a good defense against threat.

We'll never know for sure if a similar scenario explains the presence of sexual reproduction in humans; but whatever the case, I like to think of this tiny New Zealand snail when entering the next stretch of the Generative Way, where we explore the role of intimacy in generativity. In his stage theory, Erik Erikson stated that one had to establish a close, committed relationship with another before one could become generative. But *Potamopyrgus antipodarum,* in its own little way, is more flexible than that. It can "do it" alone or it can "do it" together. So can other creatures, among them plants, insects, fish, and reptiles. There is a malarial parasite, in fact, that can do it alone *and* do it together. During its journey from mosquito to victim and back again to mosquito, this parasite multiplies asexually; then, splitting into male and female, it does so sexually; and then, in yet another form, it reverts to asexual reproduction.

How do human beings "do it"—in all of generativity's domains, not just the biological? Must we be intimate in order to reproduce? Must we mix our genes, blend our voices? To address these questions, let us explore at one and the same time the next two steps of the Generative Way: blending your voice (the fourth) and creating (the fifth).

The story of "The Three Languages" implies that we can "do it" alone, that intimacy has nothing to do with generativity, for there is no mention of a mate for the young count. He gets to Rome, the place of his generativity, by himself. But just as *Potamopyrgus antipodarum* exists in two versions, so does the tale of the count's journey. In the version I have not told, the lord of the bewitched castle offers the young man his daughter in marriage if he can silence the dogs and recover the treasure. The daughter is a beautiful young woman, so the count readily agrees. After the two marry, they go as a couple on the journey through the swamp. Once they arrive in Rome, the young woman drops out of the story—just before the doves land on her husband's shoulder and summon him to be pope. In this rendition, which Erikson would have surely preferred, intimacy sets the stage for generativity.

In myths about the origins of the world, we find both kinds of creators, those who do it alone and those who do it together. From India, for example, comes the story of a solitary creator named Prajapati. Prajapati hatches from a golden egg that has been floating for a year on a sea of water, all that existed before creation. While still an infant, Prajapati tries to speak: "Bhuh." The word becomes the earth. He tries again: "Bhuvah." This word becomes the air. He utters a third sound, "Svah." It becomes the sky. And then, just as a child struggles to stand up, Prajapati rises to stand on the world he has created.

Eventually he wants to have offspring, and, as the story puts it, "he lays the power of reproduction into his own self." Breathing upward, he creates gods in the sky. With them comes the daylight. Breathing downward, he creates the evil Asuras, and with them the darkness of night. Then he and the gods complete the work of creation.

There are also origin myths that feature creators who act together. In a Mayan account, the forefathers Tepeu and Gucumatz, "great thinkers," come together in the darkness of the night to plan the creation of the world. They talk, they deliberate, they consult with the deity (the "Heart of Heaven"), and they agree that it must happen at dawn. "Thus let it be done!" they say when the time comes. "Let the emptiness be filled! Let the water recede and make a void, let the earth appear and become solid. . . . Let there be light!" Instantly, mountains come out of the water, cypress and pine shoots start to grow, rivers begin to make their way through valleys. The Heart of Heaven comes to make it all fruitful, and the storyteller concludes, "So it was that they made perfect the work, when they did it after thinking and meditating upon it."

In a Zuni account of creation (the Zuni are a Native American people from New Mexico), life on earth begins with the sexual coming together of Earth Mother and Sky Father. The two separate after children are conceived, but before they are born Earth Mother begins to worry. How will her children—human beings—find a place to live? Where will they get their food? She delays giving birth until she can make plans with Sky Father. "Upon me the homes of my tiny children shall be," she says, "and from my bosom they shall draw nourishment." The warmth of her breath mingles with the coldness of his and produces rain, which she collects in the hollow places of her lap. "You will not be the only one to help our children," says Sky Father, filling her wrinkles and crevices with grain. "Even as these grains gleam up from the water, so shall seed-grains like to them, yet numberless, spring up from thy bosom when touched by my waters, to nourish our children."

Creating alone and creating together: both themes appear in nature, in fairy tales, and in religious myth. Do both appear on the Generative Way? Let's turn to the research, which has taken a number of approaches to the question, not always with the word "generativity" in mind. We shall see that, when it comes to generativity, blending is not so much necessary as it is inevitable; sooner or later it will happen. But we shall also see that there are many ways of "doing it" together.

Commitment in the Family

In Erikson's portrait of the life cycle, intimacy was the sixth of eight stages that depicted the tasks of life. It followed adolescence, designated as the time to form an identity, and preceded middle age, the time for generativity. Though he recognized the potential of celibacy, the core of Erikson's idea of intimacy was "mutuality of orgasm with a loved partner of the other sex." But intimacy was not simply sexual. It described a mutual interdependence, physical, emotional, and intellectual, "a counterpointing as well as a fusing of identities . . . in friendship, in erotic encounters, or in joint inspiration." It included the capacity to commit oneself "to concrete affiliations and partnerships and to develop the ethical strength to abide by such commitments, even though they may call for significant sacrifices and compromises." It included, in other words, the same steadfastness and durability that Erikson saw in generative identities.

Almost from the beginning, researchers have tried to test Erikson's theory in a scientific way, but the enterprise has proven to be difficult, for the theory is more an artistic vision than a strict hypothesis. (How do you "test" a Monet or a van Gogh?) Still, there have been some confirmations of the proposed relationship between intimacy and generativity. Returning to three longitudinal samples—one of working-class men, one of Harvard-educated men, and one of intellectually gifted women—George Vaillant first determined who had "achieved" intimacy. His criterion was arbitrary but clear: had the person lived with another in an interdependent relationship *for at least ten years,* and had the relationship brought "unmistakeable, if imperfect, mutual satisfaction?" If the answer was yes, that person had by definition established a long-term commitment, had reached Erikson's sixth stage. For the men in the studies, the other person involved was almost always a spouse. (Men who identified themselves as homosexual were extremely rare; some dropped out of the research.) For the women it was usually a spouse, though for a few it was a close female friend.

Vaillant found that the majority of those who had achieved generativity —it meant being in a position of responsibility for others—had first achieved intimacy. How sizeable a majority is difficult to say, but the findings do square with an incidental result in Dan McAdams's research on the identities of generative adults. Though marital status was not a criterion of selection in that research, 63 percent of his generative sample, both men and women, turned out to be married, whereas only 37 percent of the less generative group were. To judge from both studies, the young count didn't *need* a mate to get to Rome, but it certainly helped to have one.

Rome, of course, stands for the place of one's generativity, and these studies took a broad view, an aerial view almost, of how to get there. Other research has been more specific and down to earth, focusing on the parental generativity that occurs within families. And this research yields a clear conclusion: although there are many ways to raise a child in today's world, there is still a *best* way: in a family where a strong bond exists between mother and father. As a general rule, children in such families experience more warmth, discipline, and consistency than children in other kinds of families; they exhibit fewer behavior problems and have greater psychological well-being. There are many exceptions to this rule, of course, but they do not negate it. Children benefit when there is a bond between parents that is more than just legal.

Children appear to benefit mainly because of the bond's impact on fathers, normally the wild cards in the parenting enterprise. When a divorce occurs, it is usually fathers who move, reducing their involvement with the children or severing it altogether. In one large-scale study that followed the fate of divorced families, 49 percent of the adolescent children had not seen their father during the past year. Few of the fathers had made up for their absence with phone calls or letters, and many had failed to support their children financially. The findings of this study are typical. "Divorce usually leads to the loss or diminished availability of a father and the economic, social, and emotional resources he can provide," concluded a team of psychologists after an exhaustive review of the literature.

In probably the best empirical test of Erikson's theory, psychologist John Snarey concentrated exclusively on fathers, using the same working-class sample that Vaillant did. Going over the fathers' longitudinal reports, Snarey determined whether, and how seriously, they had ever considered divorce. That became his measure of intimacy (he called it marital "affinity" or "commitment"). Snarey also determined how involved fathers had been in all aspects of their children's development—in their social, emotional, intellectual, and athletic upbringing. That became his measure of generativity. In essence, Snarey was asking what turned biological fathers into good fathers.

Because the study covered four decades of the men's lives, Snarey could begin by looking at how they themselves had been parented. He found it mattered hardly at all. The strongest correlate of involved fathering lay not in the past but in the present, and it was marital affinity. As one father's adult daughter said, "My parents made it very clear, without saying it, that each other came first and the rest of us as a group came second." For the typical father, intimacy set the stage for generativity (and generativity no doubt reinforced intimacy). Thus, if you wanted to use Snarey's research to predict the quality of a man's fathering—and you were allowed but one question—you would not ask about his childhood. Rather, you would ask if he had ever come close to divorcing his wife. If the answer was no, odds are that he was a good father.

Contemporary data on fathers should come as no surprise. For all of human history, the challenge has not been to involve mothers in the care of their children (their interest is forged by biology), but to involve fathers. Things go better for children when fathers are invested in their families— when parents, in other words, "do it" together.

While research says what is best in general, it also notes some exceptions. Children in *well-functioning* single-parent and stepfamilies, for example, usually do better than children in two-parent families that are *riddled with conflict*. And some children actually benefit from the transition that a divorce brings. All the single parents who find ways of involving others in the rearing of their children, and all the children who bounce back from marital disruption, demonstrate that remarkable capacity for resilience that characterizes the human life cycle. In our parenting, as in other aspects of our existence, we seem to have the knack of coming up with Plan B when Plan A isn't working.

While there are many ways of rearing a child, there is still only one way, biologically, of having one; and that is through the union of male and female genes. If the day comes when humans are able to drop that requirement (I should probably say *when* that day comes), we may want to pause and remember *Potamopyrgus antipodarum*. This little creature has discovered that it may be a lot of trouble to reproduce by finding mates and mixing genes, but it's certainly worth the effort. Indeed, as a planet-wide strategy, sexual reproduction has not only established defenses against threat; it has led to higher and higher forms of life. If you look at the evolutionary ladder, you will find that nearly all of the planet's most advanced species "do it" together. Within the family, in generativity's biological and parental realms, that seems to be the way to go.

Contact at the Creation

When we move beyond the family into the technical and cultural domains of generativity, however, we are struck immediately by a paradox: many creators who work in these areas lead lives of intimacy that are anything but "successful," at least from the stage point of view. Neither Frank Lloyd Wright nor Florence Nightingale, for instance, "succeeded" at intimacy. Wright compartmentalized intimacy and generativity so well, in fact, that he could wreak havoc in the lives of those closest to him and go on creating in the midst of it. Perhaps he even fed off the chaos: during a tumultuous three-year marriage to his second wife, a marriage filled with hate and occasional violence, he created the magnificent Imperial Hotel in Tokyo. Florence Nightingale separated intimacy and generativity in quite a different way. She was 26, and in the midst of her most troubled period, when she decided that marriage was not for her. In one and the same breath, she was writing in private notes, "I feel as if all my being were gradually drawing together to a point"—a description of identity consolidation—*and* "Oh God, no more love. No more marriage O God." She seemed to sense that to have her voice she could not have intimacy. In the course of her life she would receive three offers of marriage and turn them all down.

The experience of Wright and Nightingale was not unique. Studying the lives of seven creators of the modern world (Sigmund Freud, Albert Einstein, Pablo Picasso, Igor Stravinsky, T. S. Eliot, Martha Graham, and Mahatma Gandhi), Howard Gardner found that most had enormous difficulties with the normal forms of intimacy. Neither of Albert Einstein's marriages was a success; he denied fathering his firstborn daughter, who was born out of wedlock; and his relationship with his two sons, one a schizophrenic, was poor. He did not miss the loss of human contact, often preferring to be left alone: "Isolation is sometimes bitter but I do not regret being cut off from the understanding and sympathy of other men." Mahatma Gandhi, who had entered an arranged marriage at the age of 13, had a conflicted relationship with his wife. He renounced sexual relations in midlife (just as Freud did) and was almost cruel to her when she became sick. His relations with his children were even worse. When they failed to live up to his expectations, he turned on them, disinheriting his oldest son on several occasions. T. S. Eliot was virtually celibate and living in an unhappy marriage during his most creative years. More than once he devastated those close to him by abruptly cutting off all connections. Later in life, when he divorced his wife and remarried, he became much happier—but, significantly, far less productive.

The lack of normal intimacy did not hamper the creativity of these individuals; it may in fact have helped it. In some cases, isolation was an escape from complexity and chaos; it cleared the desk for more important work. In at least in one case, the chaos itself seems to have been stimulating. Pablo Picasso's personal life was a tangle of involvements with women, some of them the wives or lovers of friends. "When I die," he prophesied, "it will be a shipwreck and as when a huge ship sinks, many people all around will be sucked down with it." The prophesy was not far off. As Gardner observed:

> His first wife, Olga, went crazy and died in 1955; his most carefree mistress, Marie Therese Walter, hung herself in 1977; his most intellectual mistress, Dora Marr, suffered a nervous breakdown; his grandson committed suicide by drinking concentrated bleach when he was not allowed to attend Picasso's funeral service; his second wife (and widow) Jacqueline, whom he had married in 1961, shot herself to death the night after she completed the plans for an exhibition of her personal collection of Picasso's works.

One scholar has called Picasso a "tragedy addict" who preyed on fragile women and used them as catalysts for artistic experimentation. Whatever the meaning of his involvements with them, he seems to have thrived on relationships that were anything but committed and steadfast.

In varying degrees, the creators Gardner studied had decided to sacrifice normal personal relationships in order to develop their talent. They had, so to speak, "struck a deal with a personal god," making a pact that resembled "that kind of semimagical, semimystical arrangement in the West we have come to associate with Dr. Faust and Mephistopheles." Gardner called such pacts "Faustian bargains." Faustian bargains are testimonies to the fact that extraordinary gifts come with extraordinary prices.

But one cannot conclude from the price creators pay—and the price they extract from others—that intimacy plays no part in their creativity. In fact, if you look at the moment of creation, and at the period of tension immediately preceding it, you will find striking manifestations of close human contact, whether with a single individual or a small group. There may not have been commitment to the family, but there was contact at the creation. Consider three of Gardner's cases—Freud, Picasso, and Graham—in which the contact involved a single other person.

Freud's legacy to the world is a way of thinking and a set of techniques called psychoanalysis. It has influenced modern life to such an extent that many of its elements—free association, dream interpretation, repression, the unconscious—have become household terms. Psychoanalysis is a specialized movement too, consisting of individuals, training institutes, and associations around the world that still orient themselves with respect to their founding father, whether to accept, reject, or revise.

The 1890s were critical to the birthing of psychoanalysis. Freud was in his mid-30s when that decade began; he had not been particularly successful as a neurologist; and he realized that if he did not make his mark soon, he never would. He was struggling financially yet responsible for a growing family. (He ceased to have sexual relations after his sixth child was born in 1895.) Freud suffered from depression, addiction to nicotine, and chronic stomach pains. Years later he reflected, "At that time, I had reached the peak of loneliness, had lost all my old friends, and hadn't acquired any new ones; no one paid any attention to me, and the only thing that kept me going was a bit of defiance and the beginning of *The Interpretation of Dreams*." *The Interpretation of Dreams*, his breakthrough work, was published in 1899, though dated 1900.

Into that dark yet fertile decade stepped a Berlin physician named Wilhelm Fliess. Freud and Fliess had been introduced by Josef Breuer, who had once been a father figure to Freud. Fliess was developing biological theories that today seem odd, even bizarre. He believed that human life was regulated by biorhythmic cycles of twenty-three days for men and twenty-eight days for women, and that health was governed not only by these cycles but also by the dominant human organ—the nose. Like Freud, he was developing his ideas in isolation. Though their interests were different, each needed a sounding board, a *confidant*—someone to hear his emerging voice.

Freud and Fliess tried to meet at a resort at least once a year to converse in a relaxed atmosphere. They talked not only of scientific theories but also of more personal matters. Their principal medium of contact, however, was the mail: for more than ten years they were in constant communication. Freud supported his colleague during this time and rarely criticized his views; indeed, his own may have seemed equally bizarre. How much Fliess contributed to Freud is hard to say, for Freud destroyed the letters that would have told us. We do know, however, that during their years together Freud dropped some ideas (such as his "Project for a Scientific Psychology") and changed others. Writing to Fliess in 1897, he stated that he no longer thought that early sexual abuse explained adult disorders; in an about-face that ignited fierce debate nearly a century later, he said he now believed that scenes of abuse were products of a child's imagination.

The depth of Freud's intimacy with Fliess was critical to the creation of psychoanalysis, says Gardner. What happened in Freud's life happened in others:

> At times when creators are on the verge of a radical breakthrough, they feel the need to try out their new language on a trusted other individual—perhaps to confirm that they themselves are not totally mad and may even be on to something new and important. This desire to communicate has both cognitive and affective aspects, as the creators seek both disciplinary understanding and unquestioned emotional support.

Confidants like Fliess believe both in the creator and in the work that the creator is trying to bring into existence. In a confidant's presence, the creator can think out loud without fear of disinterest or condemnation. He can experiment with different voices, using the confidant as a sounding board, until he finds the one that rings true.

But the role of confidant is not the only one that energizes creation. In the Mayan story of the world's origins, the forefathers Tepeu and Gucumatz not only think together but act together. They become *collaborators.* Eight years after *The Interpretation of Dreams,* a relationship similar to theirs altered the history of Western art. The collaborators were Pablo Picasso and Georges Braque, and the movement they initiated is known as cubism.

A year apart in age, Picasso and Braque met in 1907, when both were in their late 20s. As different in temperament as they were in appearance— Picasso, the short, expansive Spaniard; Braque, the tall, shy Frenchman— they nevertheless became friends. A year later they began to work together, painting separately during the day, then coming together at night to compare what they had done. As Braque recalled years later, "We lived in Montmartre, we saw each other every day, we talked. . . . Picasso and I said things to each other during those years that no one says anymore . . . things that would be incomprehensible and that gave us so much joy. . . . It was like being roped together on a mountain. . . . We were above all very absorbed." For his part, Picasso was to call this the happiest period of his life. It was the time of his creative breakthrough.

Cubism is a set of techniques for breaking objects down into their geometric forms—into "little cubes," an early critic said disparagingly, giving the movement its name. Initially, Braque and Picasso were inspired by Paul Cézanne, as well as by more distant sources—African tribal masks, Egyptian bas-reliefs—but then, more and more, they fed off each other. "When we invented cubism," Picasso said, "we had no intention of inventing cubism, but simply of expressing what was in us." In some fields (contemporary science is one) such collaboration is the norm, but in painting it is rare. And it was out of character for the egotistical and destructive Picasso, marking the only time in his life when he failed to make regular entries in his written notebook.

Between 1910 and 1912 Picasso and Braque produced paintings so similar that today only an expert can tell them apart. (There were a number that neither painter signed.) Some of the little cubes looked like box kites, so the collaborators jokingly referred to themselves as Orville and Wilbur Wright. Braque was more than a Fliess to Picasso's Freud; he was a co-creator. When Picasso began gluing oilcloth to his canvases to create "collage," Braque began using paper cutouts in the same way, creating *"papier collé."* Then Picasso started experimenting with wallpaper and newspaper, employing decorator techniques that Braque had learned from his father. For several years, says Gardner, their talents meshed perfectly:

As a more proficient depicter of the natural and human worlds, Picasso may have been responsible for the stronger representational aspects, the focus on objects with their idiosyncratic peculiarities, whereas Braque pushed more toward abstraction. Picasso's virtuosity also contrasted with Braque's interest in, and contribution to, more technical aspects, particularly those having to do with the creation of purely spatial effects and experiments with composition.

In this fertile coming together we can see what Erikson meant when he said that intimacy entails "a counterpointing as well as a fusing of identities . . . in joint inspiration." Some of the counterpointing involved competition, and there were times when Picasso and Braque separated, held back on sharing new ideas, and hid their work from each other. As the competition grew, so did the tension between them. But it never reached the breaking point. Their relationship was ended instead by World War I, which erupted in 1914 and called Braque into service. A collaboration that had lasted six years, that had an enormous impact on twentieth-century art, ended quite suddenly. "Thereafter I never saw Braque again," said Picasso simply.

Neither Picasso nor Braque ever found another colleague like the one they had had. Nor, ever again, did either make such radical innovations in art. "It must be left to clinicians to say whether the relationship to Braque replayed Picasso's relationship to members of his immediate family or had homosexual overtones or made it impossible for him ever after to pursue a path that was equally revolutionary," Gardner concluded. But it seemed perfectly evident that in Picasso's most creative moment, he "needed to hold someone else's hand."

In the stories of creators there are endless variations on the theme of holding hands, endless ways of making contact at the time of creation. Martha Graham illustrates a third kind of blending. Born in 1894, she was 5 when Freud published *The Interpretation of Dreams* and 14 when Picasso and Braque began their collaboration. At 17 she witnessed the riveting performance of an exotic dancer named Ruth St. Denis. Alone on stage and lavishly costumed, St. Denis impersonated the Hindu goddess Radha, conveying an aura of spirituality and mysticism. "From that moment on my fate was sealed," Graham recalled later. "I couldn't wait to learn to dance as the goddess did."

At 22, an age considered too old to begin training, Graham enrolled in St. Denis's school. She traveled for several years with the school's troupe, performed in vaudeville for a while, then taught dance in Rochester, New York. In 1926, when she was 32, her own tiny company gave its first performance in New York City. But they still danced in the style of St. Denis.

By this time Graham had begun to work with composer and accompanist Louis Horst, collaborating in a different way than did Picasso with Braque. Horst's medium, music, was different from Graham's, though complementary to it. He was willing to submerge his identity as a composer in order to proclaim Graham's as a dancer. When called upon, he was even willing to write the music for a production *after* Graham had composed the dance. The usual practice was music first, dance second.

With Horst as accompanist, Graham quickly found her voice—in the world of movement. Instead of concealing effort onstage, as had been the convention, she began to display it. She danced in bare feet, slithered on the floor, became more explicitly erotic. She used her torso, more than her hands and arms, as a medium of expression. It was not ballet, but neither was it St. Denis. St. Denis, in fact, would refer to the Graham style as "the open crotch school of music." That remark certainly did not characterize *Lamentations,* which Graham first performed in 1930. Gardner describes the effect:

> A solitary, grieving woman was encased in a tube of stretch jersey, with only hands, feet, and face visible. Seated on a low platform throughout, the mummylike figure rocked with anguish from side to side, plunging her hand deep into the dark fabric. Barely perceptible, the body writhed as it attempting to break out of its habit. As the body moved, the tube formed diagonals across the center of the body. The movements, created through the changing forms of the costume, were prayerful and beseeching, not so much a re-creation of grief as its embodiment.

Horst was more than a complement to Graham. Ten years her senior, he was also a *lover* and a *mentor.* (He had been a lover since her student days at St. Denis's school.) Horst exposed Graham to influences as diverse as European dance and music, the philosophy of Nietzsche, baseball games, and prize fights. As her work became sensitive to contemporary events and took on a distinctively American character, Horst had the job, in

Gardner's words, "of keeping these diverse constituents of the emerging language in mind and helping make them accessible to an audience."

Although long-lived, this relationship of mentor and protégé was tempestuous. Graham had a volatile temper, and their fights sometimes became physical. She would say: "You're breaking me. You're destroying me." He would respond: "Every young artist needs a wall to grow against like a vine. I am that wall."

Graham's relationship with Horst ended when in her 50s she became the lover of a talented young dancer named Erick Hawkins. There was a confrontation at a rehearsal, and then it was over. A month later, in 1948, Graham married Hawkins, forming a union that lasted only six years. Hawkins said afterwards, "I was her equal, and that created a lot of tension, which is why I finally left." Graham never had children and appears to have been celibate after her divorce from Hawkins. She struck the Faustian bargain in earnest at that time, cutting others off, alienating many of her students, giving everything to her talent. She gave her last performance at 74 and died at 96, shortly after returning with her company from a fifty-five-day tour of the Far East. More than any other individual, say historians of the art, she created the body and soul of modern dance.

What of the others Gardner studied? At critical junctures in their creative process, they too had individuals or small groups providing a matrix of support. Einstein had a fraternity of intellectuals nicknamed the Olympiad; Stravinsky, an ensemble of artists gathered by the impresario Serge Diaghilev; T. S. Eliot, the friendship, counsel, and sponsorship of Ezra Pound. Only in Gandhi's case was Gardner unable to identify a clear and significant source of support.

Though none of the relationships studied by Gardner can be considered typical, they reveal many of the ways that life and love are exchanged during times of creation. Not that one individual can offer all of the ways to another, being the confidant, the collaborator, the lover, the mentor, not to say the fellow parent. Most of the time different roles are played by different people, and some may go unplayed.

Still, for a creation to emerge, there must be an exchange of life in its history, and a powerful one at that. Listen again to what these creators have said: "It was like being roped together on a mountain. . . . We were above all completely absorbed." "You're breaking me. You're destroying

117

me." And the response: "I am [your] wall." When life is exchanged, even in a conflicted way, *ideas* are exchanged too. And in the exchange, society's storehouse of ideas (we call it culture) acquires a variability akin to biology's (we call it a gene pool). Creators may find it necessary to go it alone in the aftermath of an exchange, to shape its results in their own unique way, to recover their distinctive outlook. But without a period of blending, their creations would not merely be poorer; they might very well be nonexistent.

Leeuwenhoek's Error

Given all the ways energies are blended in creation, a conclusion is inescapable: no human legacy results from "doing it" alone. "You think you are alone. Then you raise your eyes, and you are surrounded," said Biblical scholar and literary critic Jack Miles, when he had finished the book that won a Pulitzer Prize. Somehow what surrounds a creator finds its way into what he creates.

In 1677, when Antoni van Leeuwenhoek first put human semen under a microscope (he had just ground an astonishing lens), he saw, or thought he saw, complete fetuses. They had round bodies and a long, thin tail that propelled them about. Leeuwenhoek believed that a man delivered these minuscule creatures into a woman's womb, as if he were planting seedlings in the soil. One of them would survive, to be nourished by the woman's egg, which acted a bit like fertilizer. Other scientists of the time saw, or thought they saw, tiny *adult* humans in a man's semen. "Homuncules," they called them. Leeuwenhoek disputed their observations (he saw nothing with his microscope that looked adult), but he nonetheless shared their belief about the role of the male in reproduction.

Leeuwenhoek made many discoveries with his amazing technical innovation. (His single-lens instrument outperformed the compound-lens microscopes of his contemporaries.) He described numerous protozoa and was almost certainly the first to observe bacteria. Many of his observations about sperm cells proved uncannily accurate. But he did make a key error of interpretation. He believed that men left *all of me* in their biological legacy, when in fact they left only *half.* It took another two centuries for the actual union of sperm and egg, the actual combination of two genetic pieces, to be directly observed.

Leeuwenhoek's error occurred in generativity's biological domain, but it appears in others as well. Experiments in psychology have shown that people often misremember the contributions of others as being their own, a phenomenon known as "source amnesia" or "cryptomnesia." They also take more credit for a collective endeavor, if it is successful, than others in their group assign to them. In his autobiography, Frank Lloyd Wright consistently tried to establish that he was a genius who came out of nowhere and drew on nobody else. Scholars are uncertain about Freud's tendencies in this regard, though they have wondered why he destroyed the record of his interchange with Fliess. Martha Graham appears to have been quite direct about her sources: "I am a thief—and I am not ashamed. I steal from the best where it happens to be—Plato, Picasso, Bertram Ross. I am a thief—and I glory in it." But we still do not hear from her about ideas she might have stolen from those closer to home, from students, say, or rival dancers. Among the historical figures I have touched on in this book, only Erik Erikson seems to have erred in the opposite direction, consistently downplaying his own originality. Apparently he feared being cut off from the psychoanalytic community if he departed too extensively from Freud.

Leeuwenhoek's error can be perfectly functional, an illusion with positive effects. Without the belief that it is *up to me*—and no one else—many enterprises would fall far short of completion. Without the anticipation of money, kudos, or a place in history *for me*—and no one else—many would never have gotten off the ground in the first place. But Leeuwenhoek's error is still that: an error. The product you create or the child you raise will only be a fraction of you—and a fraction, perhaps many fractions, of somebody else.

Our status as creators may be diminished by the truth of fractional contributions. We may be "cut down to size." But our responsibility for negative outcomes may also be lessened. Remember the words of a young woman I cited in Chapter 1 of this book. Upon seeing the fragile and "withered" appearance of her premature baby, she said, "It was as if my husband had not contributed at all to the appearance of this child. It was all from me." Hers was another form of Leeuwenhoek's error. For her, the truth of fractional contributions would have been a comfort.

Communion: The Intimacy Within

There have been times in my life when I have suddenly felt incredibly alone. It comes again and again: I realize I am the center of nobody's life. I am a nice convenience, and I'm helpful here, and I brighten this thing up, but if I were to die tomorrow, it wouldn't mean an awful lot. People would grieve, but I'm not sure there would be any profound sense of loss for a very long time. Sometimes I feel, God, I want someone to care more than this.

The speaker is Sister Jo Biondi, a nun whom I interviewed in her early 50s. By reasons of vows freely made, she has never entered a stage of intimacy. But intimacy is *in her,* and it has led to many generative moments. More than anyone else I have interviewed, she embodies the idea of intimacy as a trait. This is the intimacy within; like the intimacy of stages and moments, it has a strong bearing on generativity.

As a trait, intimacy has several meanings. You possess it, first of all, when your defenses are mature enough and your memories coherent enough that you can "talk" to all your inner parts, as the young count did on his way to Rome. I have known people almost desperate to be generative who do not know themselves in this way, and so are unable to connect with others, to be intimate in the more traditional sense. Not knowing their own depths, they cannot reach them in others.

Intimacy is "within," secondly, if you have entered into and know the human condition at large. "Just being in touch with the feelings that come from being a woman and from being human help me to understand a lot about love that is exchanged in excitement and betrayed, about rejection, and about loneliness," said Sister Jo. Her words point to a third meaning of the intimacy within: it exists when love, friendship, caring, togetherness— "being in touch"—are simply on your mind, when you are aware of both their presence and their absence.

In the study of personality, all these aspects of intimacy are today called "communion," and they are set apart from another cluster of traits collectively called "agency." "Agency" and "communion" were originally introduced into psychological discourse in 1966 by David Bakan, who used the terms to characterize "two fundamental modalities in the existence of living forms." Agency, Bakan said, represents the self-asserting, self-protecting, self-expanding existence of the individual. It manifests itself in the urge to master and the quest for power—in the "cold command" of Ozymandias—as well as in the formation of separations and the repression of feeling. Communion represents the participation of the individual in collective life. It manifests itself in contact, cooperation, and openness, in the sense of being at one with other organisms—in the yielding of Kujum-Chantu. Agency says, "Do it alone." Communion says, "Do it together."

Earlier in this book we witnessed expressions of agency in buffers who stood up to legacies of damage and destruction, in moral exemplars who were willing to disregard what other people thought, in creators who ventured into territory where no one else had gone. But we also saw expressions of communion—in data showing the value of commitment to a spouse, in the actions of those very same exemplars and creators who found human support when they most needed it. Agency is manifest whenever we exercise control on the Generative Way, whenever we speak with our own voice, whenever our orientation is active. Communion comes out when we yield control, when we are receptive and surrendering, when our orientation is passive.

Though both agency and communion are needed for generativity, personality psychologists are now asking if there is more of one or the other "in" people who are generative. The preliminary answer coming from research is intriguing: such people have as much agency as others but far more communion.

Going back to the Northwestern samples of forty generative and thirty less generative adults, Elizabeth Mansfield and Dan McAdams looked for themes of agency and communion in key autobiographical memories. They found the same number of agency themes in the two groups, but twice the number of communion themes among the generative—the same amount of power, if you will, but a great deal more intimacy. Even more revealing, the generative adults were twice as likely to *integrate* agency and communion, that is, to have both present *in the same memory*. They were more likely to recall a victory, say, in which there was a powerful feeling of togetherness. For these individuals communion did not rule out agency; it was added to it.

Two previous studies had produced comparable results. In one, power failed to correlate with generativity and intimacy did at a low level. But the *sum* of power and intimacy scores produced a relatively strong association. In the other, a longitudinal study, adolescent women who *combined* power and achievement (signs of agency) with affiliation (a sign of communion) proved in midlife to score higher than others on a measure of generativity. In all three studies the key words have been "integrate," "sum," and "combine." Add communion to a base of agency, add intimacy to a foundation of power, and you add to your generative potential.

A sophisticated account of the addition of communion to agency can be found in the Bible, where it happens to a most unlikely character: God. God begins by "doing it" alone, and doing it with power. He brings light, water, dry land, and plants into being, then sun and moon and stars, simply by calling them forth. "Let there be creatures in the sea, birds in the air, wild beasts upon the earth," He then says; and, in an instant, as though He had snapped His fingers, they appear. At the climactic moment He calls forth humans: "Let us make man in our image, after our likeness. They shall rule the fish of the sea, the birds of the sky, the cattle, the whole earth, and all the creeping things that creep on earth." An agentic creator, God makes humans to be like *Him* and endows them with *His* capacity to dominate. Blending, either with a consort or with His creation, is out of the question.

As the Biblical narrative continues, God the creator becomes a destroyer, a lawgiver, and a conqueror; but not until much later—the second book of Samuel—does He refer to Himself as a father. And only in the Book of Isaiah (it comes earlier in the Hebrew Bible than it does in the Christian Old Testament) does God begin to feel tenderness toward His people. As Jack Miles writes, following the Hebrew ordering, "It is no exaggeration to say that, to judge from the entire text of the Bible from Genesis 1 to Isaiah 39, the Lord does not know what love is." The "love" emotion He felt before was *hesed,* the loyalty or "steadfast love" that binds liege and vassal. But beginning especially in Isaiah 40 God becomes sensitive to another's pain. He develops empathy for the human condition. He acquires the ability, says Miles, "to eavesdrop on the human heart; to note fears, sorrows, confusions, and so on; to be the soul's omniscient companion." He becomes the God of whom the Psalmist sings:

O Lord, you have examined me and know me.
When I sit down or stand up You know it;

You discern my thoughts from afar.
You observe my walking and reclining,
and are familiar with all my ways.
There is not a word on my tongue
But that You, O Lord, know it well.

Before, in the Biblical narrative, humans had to tell God what they were thinking. Now He simply knows. Agency is still in Him, but it has been tempered with communion.

Cross-cultural research suggests that in a man's life agency and communion follow a similar pattern, agency coming first and communion second. An ex-marine who had agentically climbed the corporate ladder and admired "tough-minded" mentors since he was 30, discovered communion in his 40s:

> I think I'm probably as effective as ever, but I don't have the energy or driving ambition to succeed that I used to have. . . . Instinctively, I'm soft and compassionate toward people, to a fault. The hardest thing in the world for me is to sit down face to face with somebody and tell them what they are doing wrong. . . . I had a boss who said the only real problem you have is you wear your heart on your sleeve. I get emotionally upset about people, that is what he told me.

Research also suggests the opposite pattern in women: communion first, agency second. A woman who returned to school at the age of 43 came to realize "that I had some value as a person, that some of my thoughts were pretty worthwhile, that maybe it was worth asserting myself a little." A year later, as agency welled up, she made a family pronouncement:

> The pronouncement was that everyone else, meaning of course, mostly my husband, had to adjust to the fact that I was going to school and that I was going to do something that I wanted to with my life, too, or we would part ways. And I was prepared to back that up, because what I wanted to do was very important to me.

One voice softened; another hardened; each achieved a better balance. Although hormonal shifts have something to do with these changes, although societies have long expected them, they are far from universal. They follow a different sequence, for example, in women who focus on work and career early in their adulthood and parenting later—who start off with agency, in other words. But however the timing comes out in a particular life, it is the eventual balance of agency and communion that seems to make for generativity.

As a nun trained in a particular era, and perhaps simply as a woman, Sister Jo Biondi may have expressed communion in her life before she did agency. When I got to know her, however, the two were thoroughly integrated. She was a woman of personal power who taught, wrote, and broadcast over the radio. "I don't fall apart," she said, explaining why so many people sought her counsel. But she was also a woman who knew the human heart. "I've traveled all over, I've had incredible opportunities to assess the human condition, to see the story of the rich man dining at the banquet and the poor man begging at the gate." Though she had not "achieved" a stage of intimacy, intimacy was *in her;* and, plain to see, it was in her generativity:

> The articles that I write and whose effects I never see, the words I speak on the air that millions of people hear on a Sunday, I don't know where they go, but somewhere in there, there is another touching. . . . I feel very much in touch with a lot of people living and dead who have meant something to me. Our love may not be exchanged in any physical way, but I sense connections. I sense a lot of unexpressed affection, and I know with a certainty that I have mattered.

The Golden Tree

What research has said about the kinds of intimacy that lead to generativity is said as well in a Jewish fairy tale that comes to us from India. It's a story about the love of a man and a woman, about the child that is born to them, about finding the source of life deep within the forest.

The man in the story is the King of the land; the woman, the youngest and most beautiful of his wives. Knowing how much the King loves her, the other wives whisper in his ear, "She doesn't love you." (It was a lie.) "She cannot have children." (It was the truth.) "Get rid of her!" (It was the point.)

Eventually the King listens to the whispers and banishes his youngest Queen, sending her off without money or food. Not knowing where to go, she simply follows the first path she comes across. It leads into a dark forest. When evening comes, she climbs into a tree for safety and listens all night to the howling of wild beasts. Tired and hungry at dawn, she is startled to find an old man standing at the base of the tree.

"Do not be afraid, my daughter," he says, and the look in his eyes reassures her. "My house is not far from here. You can rest there, and eat as much as you like."

The old man takes her to a little hut where he lives as a hermit. There he prepares a meal of nuts and berries and lays out a mat of rushes. The banished Queen eats and then falls into a peaceful sleep. She dreams she has wandered into a beautiful garden and found at its very center, surrounded by a pool of water, a magnificent tree with leaves of gold and blossoms of diamonds. As she stands in awe of it, the old man approaches her in a long white robe. He gives her a golden necklace with an amulet in the very shape of the wondrous tree.

As soon as she places the amulet around her neck, the Queen wakes up from her dream. Then she discovers the necklace is real! So he is to be my guide, she thinks of the old man, and she tells him the whole sad story of her life—about her love for the King, about her childlessness, about the whispers of the jealous wives, about the banishment. This morning, she adds, she has discovered something that makes the banishment even more unfair. "I am pregnant with the King's child."

"Then stay with me," the old man says, "and wait until he comes to his senses."

The Queen agrees, and as she awaits the birth of her child, she watches the old man. She discovers that he is a craftsman who turns precious metals into works of art. Many of his creations are in the shape of the golden tree. But he is an unusual craftsman. Once he finishes something, he melts it down and starts all over again. "Why?" she asks.

"It is the creating that matters to me," he says. "Nothing else."

Finally the wait is over and the Queen bears a son. That very night, far away in his palace, the King has a dream about a magnificent tree with leaves of gold and blossoms of diamonds. On the trunk of the tree he sees the face of his banished wife, but when he reaches out to touch it, it disappears. Now he realizes how much he misses her and what a mistake he has made.

Every night thereafter the King is tormented by the same dream, so he calls for interpreters from far and wide. Some say that his wife must be found, so he sends messengers throughout the land to learn of her whereabouts. But they return with no news. Other interpreters tell him to make a tree like the one in his dreams. But the finest goldsmiths can produce only a pale imitation. The last interpreter says, "You must find this tree for yourself." So the King dresses as a beggar and sets out as his wife had, without money or food. He travels the length and breadth of his land, asking about a golden tree and a young woman, sleeping on the ground, living as his people do. But no one has seen the tree or the woman. Eventually, in the midst of despair, the humbled King enters the forest.

There he meets the hermit. "I can help you," the old man says, "but first you must come to my house."

The King follows him to his hut, where he dines on nuts and berries and notices a woman who stays in the shadows and keeps a veil over her face. He notices a small child as well. The woman recognizes him at once, but she keeps herself hidden. The old man tells the King where he can find the tree he is looking for, but says nothing of the woman.

"It grows in the center the forest. If you follow that stream to its source, you will find it. But be careful. The water there comes from deep within the earth. The closer you get to the tree, the hotter it will be. Many have tried to reach the tree, but all have perished in the boiling waters. But if you wear these shoes"—the old man removes his—"you will be safe."

The King bows in gratitude, takes the shoes, and begins to follow the stream. The water grows warmer, just as the old man had said it would, and clouds of steam start to billow from it. Then, through the hot fog, the King sees a distant flash of gold. He remembers the shoes, puts them on, and walks through the boiling water until he is standing at the center of a spring. He looks up and realizes that he is under the tree of his dreams! But it's not a tree exactly. It's a fountain, rather, of liquid gold constantly flowing upward and outward, each spray forming a branch, each droplet a leaf, its diamonds catching the moist rays of the sun. When the King reaches out to grasp the trunk, it becomes cool and solid in his hand. He breaks the tree off—it's weightless!—and another flows up to take its place.

Rejoicing, the King carries the golden tree back to the hermit's hut. "But what good is it?" he asks when he arrives. "I have lost my dearest love!" When his wife sees the stricken look on his face, she steps out of the shadows and her veil falls to the ground. "You lost me," she says, "but now I am found."

Kneeling at his wife's feet, the King begs her forgiveness. She grants it and embraces him, then calls forth the son he never knew he had. When they return to the palace, the King divorces his other wives and sends them away without money or food. Then he and the Queen plant the golden tree outside their window and watch it grow as tall and as strong as their love, as tall and as strong as their son.

As the Jungian psychiatrist Allan Chinen points out in his interpretation of this fairy tale, many cultures have myths about a tree that is the source of life. The Garden of Eden has its Tree of Life—eat from it and you will live forever, we read in the Book of Genesis. In "The Golden Tree" the connection of the tree with generativity is quickly apparent. Immediately after the young Queen makes contact with it, she discovers that she is pregnant. Immediately after the King does, he discovers that he has a son. What is instructive about the story are the different ways each makes contact.

To understand these differences, consider the blends of agency and communion with which the Queen and the King begin the story. The Queen lacks social power, but she does have personal power—a foundation of agency. She does not become desperate when the King casts her out, or beg to come back. She simply follows the path of development into the forest. There, on the first night, she is resourceful enough to find a place of safety and strong enough to climb into it.

The Queen is also a woman of communion. She knows herself, she understands human nature, and she is able to give love. She can pass easily into the forest that symbolizes her inner life; after some initial anxiety, she finds rest, nourishment, and guidance there. There are many other ways of saying this: her defenses are mature, her memories are coherent, she can speak the three languages, she is intimate with herself. As a result of her blend of agency and communion, the Queen comes quickly to the source of generativity, receiving it in a dream on only her second night away from the castle.

The King is another matter. He starts out with an abundance of agency but little communion. He rules over a kingdom but is intimate with no one. Ignorant of human nature, he is easy prey to the deceit and manipulation of the jealous wives. When crisis comes, his first response is to call out the troops and scour the land. Isn't it *his*? His second response is even more agentic: if he cannot find the golden tree (dammit) he'll make one himself! He is, after all, the *King*!

These responses are, of course, ineffective. To find the source of life, the King must complement his agency with communion. He must enter into his kingdom, not just rule over it. He must do what God does as His character develops in the Bible.

Finally, the King catches on. He strips down to his basic humanity, travels on foot throughout his kingdom, and gets to know it intimately. Then he enters the forest and gets to know himself intimately. At the end of the story the veil falls from the Queen's face, but in reality it falls from his eyes. For the first time he can see his wife for who she is. For the first time he can enter into her, not just rule over her. Now he can become a father.

The King takes longer than the Queen to find the source of life because he has to discover communion. That is one of the differences between their two journeys. Another is how each makes contact with the source. The Queen lets it come to her, and it does so when she is passive—sound asleep, in fact. The King searches actively for it, wearing shoes that emphasize the steps he must take. The source comes to her, but the King must go to it.

Because "The Golden Tree" had its origins in a patriarchal culture, it is not surprising that the King occupies the active role and the Queen the passive one. But we must not be misled by this historical circumstance, for both orientations are needed on the Generative Way, and by both sexes. Psychology has long been associated with the active role—with taking steps, with learning "how-to's," with working on self-improvement. But psychology, and indeed all of us, would do well to learn from a Queen who stays put for a while, who waits for a child to be born and waits for a husband to mature, who is able to surrender and receive. And if you think that her passivity is weakness, ask yourself a question: who has the greater power, one like the King who must go to a source, or one like the Queen to whom the source will come?

7

Selecting and Letting Go

BY NOW YOU understand that when I speak of the Generative Way, I'm really speaking of a number of ways, especially in generativity's technical and cultural domains. In these domains, which we usually consider "higher," diversity reigns. Many roads lead to Rome, many to the golden tree. Still, no matter which you travel, no matter what its length and how it leads you, you will at a certain point have to come to terms with your past and stop any damage. You will have to find a voice, get someone to hear it, and blend it with another's. And then you can create.

But more needs to be said. As your creation comes into being, you will have to choose between what in it shall live and what shall die, though in some cases the choice will be made for you. And once it is able to stand on its own, you will have to release it, even if it has been taken out of your hands. These two tasks—selecting and letting go—are the sixth and seventh steps on the Way, and the subject of this chapter.

Selecting

I know of no better source to illuminate dilemmas of selection in generativity than one we consulted in the previous chapter: the Book of Genesis. So let us go back in that book to the point where the Lord God completes the work of creation. (This is well before He adds a communal element to His personality.) God's first impulse at that point is to see His work as good. But it doesn't stay good for long. Adam and Eve sin; God cuts them off from the Tree of Life and drives them from the Garden of Eden; and soon the whole world is corrupt. Now the creator, seeing His creation in a different light, becomes a destroyer.

This turnabout is jarring to the readers of Genesis, or at least it ought to be, for it happens in just four short chapters. *Why* it happens is not that clear, in part because two versions of the story are woven into one; but in any event, some combination of sadness, regret, and anger leads God to flood the earth with torrential rains, declaring that the end has come for all living things. God's new role as a destroyer is so different from His role as creator that in a related Babylonian myth the two are embodied in separate characters. One of them, the dragon goddess Tiamat, starts the flood. The other, the immense, two-headed Marduk, overpowers Tiamat and stops it.

In the Genesis narrative, God's turnabout serves the end I am now addressing: selection. Before the deluge comes, He decides to spare the one upright man left on earth. His name is Noah, and God tells him to build an ark and take his family aboard, along with a male and a female of every living creature. God seals them in the ark, as someone in another story once sealed a djinni in a copper bottle, and casts them out to sea. In telling essentially the same story, the *Qur'an* (or *Koran*) adds a poignant element. Noah's son declines to come aboard, remaining instead with the unbelievers. As the ark drifts away, Noah shouts, "Come with us."

But the son says, "I will climb to the top of a mountain and be safe."

"No one will be safe from Allah," shouts Noah, and then a wave comes crashing between the two of them.

It takes a while for all the human and animal life on earth to be destroyed (including, in the *Qur'an*, Noah's son), and even longer for the killing waters to recede, but after about a year, when all lies bloated and dead, Noah and his kin emerge from their vessel to make a fresh start. The hard-shelled ark pours forth life as fertile as that in a hard-shelled seed, as powerful as that in the djinni's copper vessel.

Ten generations after Noah, God makes another selection, calling forth Abraham from the land of Ur. On a starry night he tells Abraham how numerous his progeny will be; and then, miraculously, He gives him a son,

Isaac. But in another jarring reversal, He orders Abraham to kill the boy. Abraham obediently takes Isaac to a place apart, where he binds him and lays him on a sacrificial altar. As he raises a knife over his son, God calls off the execution. Apparently it was enough that Abraham was *willing* to destroy what he had created.

Once again, the *Qur'an* adds a touching detail. In its rendition, Abraham tells his son quite directly what is about to happen (in Genesis, he evades Isaac's inquiry), and the boy replies, "My father, do what you are commanded to do. Allah willing, I shall be steadfast." The boy (it is not clear in the *Qur'an* whether he is Isaac or Ishmael) surrenders to Allah just as his father did. Here, not only is the creator willing to kill, but the creation is willing to be slain.

Later on (I'm back in Genesis now) the boy who once lay passively on the altar comes to the point where he himself selects. One of Isaac's two sons, Esau or Jacob, is to receive the blessing of his old age. This is not any blessing, but *the* blessing, the one from deep within his soul, the one that will ensure favor and fertility, and establish dominance, for life. Isaac wants to give this blessing to Esau, but Jacob deceives him and receives it instead. When Esau discovers the lie and tries to rectify matters, he cannot. The selection, even though gotten by fraud, even though contrary to Isaac's wishes, is final. It carries its own power. "I blessed him, and blessed he will remain," says Isaac.

"Then bless me too," says the wronged brother. But Isaac cannot, for the power lies in the blessing. It is the power of selection.

Moments of selection occur frequently in the stories of Genesis. Some of God's creations are cursed and die; some are blessed and live; and waste is the order of the day.

As with the "supernatural," so with the "natural"—so with reproduction in generativity's biological domain. The human female is born carrying about two million eggs, but only a few will ever create a baby. The rest are selected "out"—cursed, if you will—wasted. Hundreds of millions of sperm are released in every ejaculation of the human male, and an incalculable number over a lifetime. All but a few are wasted. Even when the rare egg and sperm unite to form a new creature, that creature will find survival difficult. Most pregnancies fail, many of the failures being due to chromosomal abnormalities—many, too, to the predicament of Esau and Jacob, one twin losing out to the other. (Recent research has shown that at least one in eight natural conceptions are of twins, but only one in eighty or ninety live births are.) *In utero,* just as in Genesis, destruction and selection follow upon creation.

Selection also marks the broad progression of life outside the womb, where a variety of ecological niches "choose" from among the genetic codes of their inhabitants. Charles Darwin called the process "natural" selection. Genes that make for reproductive success are favored by the niche; other sets of genes are not. When some codes change (they do so at random as well as through the mixing of genes), they may gain nature's blessing and survive. On the other hand, they may fall from favor—prove maladaptive—and ultimately become extinct. From its start in natural selection, life on our planet has continued to reached upward, producing creatures who now dominate the earth and explore the heavens. And there's more reaching to come.

Whether one looks at the matter "naturally" or "supernaturally," then, one finds selection following hard upon creation. Actually, selection has been required from the very beginning of the Generative Way, where we had to choose among legacies received, keeping some, throwing others back into the sea. Later, when gaining a voice, we had to select who we were and who we were not, discarding possible identities in the process. Then, when blending that voice, we had to decide who to be *with* and who not. Remember that the King in "The Golden Tree" divorced many wives to make the youngest his Queen.

To be generative we must also *surrender to* selection, even as Abraham's son does in the *Qur'an.* We must accept the fact that we will be heard by one audience and ignored by another, embraced by this lover and rejected by that one. And if the selecting we do seems like slaying, that done to us will often seem like being slain. But we cannot accept, and have faith in, half the generative process. We must acknowledge the whole of it, the rejecting as well as the accepting, the passive as well as the active.

Perhaps the most difficult selections, however, are the ones we actively make among our own creations. Because a young woman whose story I told in Chapter 4 wanted to stop the transmission of genetic damage in her family, she decided after amniocentesis to abort the abnormal fetus she was carrying. "I willfully went in and terminated a pregnancy," she said, "and it was hard for people to deal with it." Hard for her, we might add. When she became pregnant again, she had another amniocentesis, this time with good results. "We started planning and we started coming up with names. When he was born, they took a blood sample and double checked. He was perfectly normal."

History has witnessed situations far more extreme. In the concentration camps of World War II, where the very word "selection" sent inmates to the gas chambers, mothers were forced by the SS to choose from among their children: one must die so that another might live, which would it be? During the massacre of Armenians in 1915, mothers voluntarily killed some of their children to protect the lives of others. In his old age, a surviving son told me the story of one such episode. His mother, his sister, and he were fleeing the slaughter when his sister became sick with measles. His mother took her, as Abraham once took his son Isaac, to a place apart. Over sixty years later, the son had vivid memories of her return:

> I came, and I asked my mother, "Where's my sister?" She started crying. I said, "What happened?"
>
> "I drowned her."
>
> You haven't got medical care, so what the hell you gonna do? My sister, she had her eyes blind and filled with maggots. My mother couldn't help her. She said, "There was a little lake over there, and I took her there, and I took her clothes off and said, 'I'm gonna wash you a little bit.'" She took her in the water and got out about this far and dropped her. But when she dropped her, my sister came back up and said, "Ma-ma, what have I done to you? You gonna drown me." My mother went back and picked her up and "her flesh came all over me," so she couldn't do nothing. She took her back out again and dropped her. My sister, she came up once again, and that was it. And then my mother sat down under a tree for hours. And this old man came and said, "She's gone now, so forget it." He brought her back, and she told me all that story.

It was a terrible assault on her generativity, but it may have saved her son's life:

> My mother was in her nineties when she died, and she would always talk about my younger sister that she threw in the water. She always talked, and then the tears came out of her eyes. Probably she dreamed about her.

She closed her eyes, she thought that she's still over there. That voice coming from the water, that "Why do you do this to me?" She would hear that young girl crying all through her life. That's all written in her life.

Few of us will face circumstances so excruciating, but as parents we are bound to face tough choices—as did the moral exemplars studied by Anne Colby and William Damon. In order to work with Mexico's poor, one woman had to deny necessities to her own offspring. "My $35 that I got for working at the hospital I couldn't spend more of it on my children because it was going for the orphans." There were times when she gave her own children's shoes to others with bare feet. A white woman who became involved in the Southern civil rights movement had to watch her children become social isolates because of public stands she and her husband took. "It *did* hurt the children," she says. "They were perfectly miserable. And none of them wants to come back to Montgomery now. Not one of them will even come back for a visit. That is the most painful part of the whole thing." While the exemplars affirmed the choices they made, they deeply regretted the cost to their children, which was often very real.

As creators, citizens, and shapers of worlds, no matter how small, we also have to act like the God of Genesis, "killing" projects, abandoning efforts, "cutting bait," and moving on. As a writer, I must do the same thing. And I part very reluctantly with long sections I have crafted that are somehow off the mark. I create; I find the Noah in what I have created; I destroy the rest; I open the ark and begin afresh. Over and over again. And the book that results becomes itself an instrument of selection, pulling some readers in, pushing others away—a voice finding an audience.

There may be no other point in the generative process when our ethical sense must be more alert than during the time of selection. (Paradoxically, there may be no other point studied so little.) We cannot simply wipe out descendants who have, in our eyes, "gone bad," cannot be the God who sends the flood. But we do have to make choices as He did, rejecting some of our creations—or some things *in* our creations—in order to develop others.

If we are generative, a bias will naturally inform the selections we make. We will favor whatever is young and vulnerable, whatever is just coming into being—and not just in children, but in adults, and in ourselves as well. Each time we find that hint of life, we will bless it. From the standpoint of behavioristic psychology, a blessing is a "positive reinforcement," just as a curse is a "punishment." But a blessing is something more than reinforcement, for it connects the ritual involved to a progression of life that goes beyond the enacters of the ritual. (Thus, one calls down a blessing "from above.") To something just coming into being, a blessing is an acknowledgment of existence, an assurance of belonging, an offer of protection and sponsorship—a welcome. It is a promise to bring the newfound idea or impulse to maturity, the newly born child to adulthood.

Fortunately, when fulfilling that promise, we are rarely forced to be the Isaac who blesses one child at the expense of another. Usually we can select for blessing qualities *in* our Esaus and *in* our Jacobs, abandoning less desirable qualities to "extinction." Here is a father who took over the coaching of his son's football team because they hadn't won a game. The problem was selection, so the dad decided on some races and a game he called Suicide:

> I'd have them run around the park. Then I'd be watching to see who had the best speed. See, they were all playing the wrong positions, and that's why they lost all their games. I had to reposition everybody. I had to see who was aggressive and who was not aggressive. When you play the game of Suicide, you'd find out the aggressive person, because he would hold onto the ball and get tackled. The other one would throw it away. So it was simple. You didn't embarrass anybody in that sense. So then I rearranged the whole team, and they came up with a pretty good team. I think they won the rest of the year.

Letting Go

Another step in the generative sequence is nearly as difficult as selecting. How and when do we let go of our child, our idea, our program—whatever our creation has been? Even if that creation is taken out of our hands, we must at some point release it emotionally. "I feel separated from the wonderful thing that was created," said a woman of people who have entered her life. "I lose it because I can't hold on to it. It slips like water through my fingers."

Releases are required almost from the beginning of a creation's life—the very first time, for instance, that parents entrust their baby to someone else. Small releases become larger as children grow. When they set out for school, the children enter a world of unknown friends and unseen forces that no parent will ever be able to control. Demands for release never stop coming until the nest is empty, and perhaps not even then. And sometimes it is the parent who must force the adult child to leave home, not the other way around. It is the master who must push the disciple away.

Timing is critical in matters of release, and it is difficult to coordinate the clocks of parent and child. When a mother of three decided to divorce her husband, her children were on the verge of adolescence. The separation came too soon for them, and the mother will never forget the day she made her announcement:

> I sat the kids down on the couch and said, "I would like to talk to you. I am going to leave." My husband was silent. Paul said, "I understand." Anne started crying. And Marie looked at me with dark, deep brown eyes—I still remember her eyes piercing through me—and said, "I'm very angry at you."

Mothers are not supposed to leave their children; their children are supposed to leave them, and never before the "right" time.

But for every premature abandonment, there is a release that comes too late. Another mother told me on one occasion how hard it was to stop rescuing her adult children, even though she knew that doing things for them prevented them from becoming self-sufficient. I remember how her arms went out in an enveloping womb as she described a protective instinct that would always be with her. Yet another mother resonated with that; her arms had gone out too often and for too many years to her alcoholic son. He had not gotten better, she said, until she was willing to say to herself, "Let him die, if that's what it takes. I cannot continue to do this." Artists can exhibit the same refusal to release, clinging to their work, protecting it, trying to orchestrate every review and reaction to it. And so can those who set in motion waves of social change.

Why do people *not* release? Seeing flaws in their creation, they may try endlessly to fix what cannot be fixed and end up "throwing good money after bad." Parents may be terrified by a child's terror at the thought of separation; they may envision no role for themselves once the children are gone. Better, then, to keep them tied to the apron strings.

Martha Graham's "children" were the dances she choreographed for herself, and for many years she refused to let her favorite ones go. No one else was allowed to perform them. No one was allowed to preserve them on film. "As a mentor, she abandoned a whole generation of performers," writes Susan Lee, an authority on psychology and dance who has studied Graham's generativity. Graham could not imagine her creations "in" the body of another; better that they die when she did. Like many dancers, she was determined to defy aging; and so, as she got older, she designed roles for herself that minimized the demands on her body. Finally, someone told her, "Martha, you are not a goddess. You must admit your mortality." Members of her dance company demanded the right to perform without her. But she did not retire from the stage until the age of 74. Significantly, when she choreographed dances for others after that point, they were different from the kinds of dances she had choreographed for herself.

Why was it so hard for Martha Graham to release her work? She was a dancer, she said. She didn't choose to be one; it chose her. "It is a very terrible and deeply rewarding experience." To give up her dances was not only an admission that she could no longer perform them. It was the end of all she knew herself to be.

For those who fear to let go of their creations, a detail from "The Golden Tree" is worth remembering. When the King breaks the tree off from its fountainlike source, it solidifies in his hand. All the while he carries it, it remains frozen. Its growth is arrested. Only when he returns the tree to the ground and walks away does it spring back to life.

When something has just come into being, a blessing of welcome is called for; but when it reaches maturity, the time comes for a blessing of release. Now it is incumbent to acknowledge all the influences on a creation that are *not* our own. The marvelous thing is that when we release a person or a product, it releases us. We lose the burden of responsibility. We can care without carrying. We can take energy that would otherwise go into "saving" the creation—futilely so—and invest it in another. As a counselor said of people who come to her in crisis, "I never let them become overly dependent on me. I never let them hold on too long. . . . I try to hold them when they need to be held and give them the courage to go out and be free."

Letting Go of Seitech

Let us witness now a dilemma of release where we might not think to look for one—in the world of business. When a company you've founded becomes your "baby," and when your baby reaches "adulthood," you face some difficult decisions regarding its freedom and your own.

Ten years ago Peter Seidenberg found a better way of getting a sailboat in the water. His simple technical innovation—the classic "better mouse-trap"—was so precisely right that it has now spread to beaches around the world, sold by the company he and his wife Fran formed, Seitech Marine Products, Inc. But the Seidenbergs have come to a crossroads. Although their baby (for so they call Seitech) is only ten years old, it has become unwieldy. They have both passed 60 and would like, not to retire exactly, but to get some relief from a grinding, seven-day-a-week work schedule. "I hardly have time to go to the grocery store," says Fran. Selling the company is out of the question; it has become too much a part of their lives and they have too many ideas yet to realize. Besides, Seitech could not yet survive on its own, or so they believe. "We have a tiger by the tail," Fran adds. But how—and when—do you let go of the tail?

Peter Seidenberg got his first taste of sailing on the Elbe River in East Germany, where he grew up in the aftermath of World War II. When he was 25, he and a friend climbed one night into a kayak and paddled for eight hours across the Baltic Sea to Denmark. That is how he escaped communism. From Denmark he went by way of West Germany to Canada, which became his home. Fifteen years later he met Fran on a skiing trip, and they married when he was 42 and she 41—too old, they agreed, to have children. Their life was soon built around Peter's love of competitive sailing. On weekends they would go to local regattas; on vacations to international ones. Sailing a single-handed fourteen-foot Laser, Peter competed in Canada and the United States, as well as in Australia, Thailand, France, England, and Greece. He won a number of North American and two world championships.

Despite his success in racing, however, and despite a fulfilling marriage, Peter suffered from episodes of depression. He had little "pride" in his life, he says. He was "aimless, drifting around, not sure of my role."

Then came the mousetrap. To get a Laser into the water you can ask your friends to help you carry it or you can roll it in on a cart—a "dolly." There were dollies on the market, but all had problems of one kind or another. So Peter designed one for his own use. It was light and durable, resistant to corrosion, easy to handle, easy to assemble—so much of an improvement, in fact, that Peter began to think of selling it. Having competed all over the world, he knew what sailors wanted. He knew that if the top racers accepted his product (they already knew and accepted him), it would find its way to others.

There was a history behind Peter's creation, a love of sailing going back to his childhood; there was voice, both authentic and credible; and there was a decade of support—a blending—during his time of depression and doubt. But now a huge decision had to be made, a true selection. The Seidenbergs put all their financial eggs in one basket, withdrawing their retirement funds (they were in their early 50s at the time) and using their house as collateral to obtain a loan. Peter recalls the second-guessing: "When our financial counselor heard we had invested our life savings and put the house up for collateral, he said, 'How could you do that?' And he cited examples of people who had lost everything by going into a foolish venture with retirement money. We didn't have much to reply. We left his office and had to go to a restaurant to calm down. We didn't feel too good. But there was nothing we could do."

Peter's design called for four major components. For the dolly's frame, he would use anodized aluminum tubing which he would purchase cut to size. The wheels he would import from England, replacing steel bearings with corrosion-proof plastic ones. A sling to support the boat would be sewn from polyester webbing. The fourth component—plastic joints to hold everything together—would, in one moment of truth, make or break the project. Eleven were required; they had to be injection molded; and the molds for each would cost $10,000. If any aspect of Peter's design was off, and if the flaw affected all eleven molds, the Seidenbergs' life savings would be gone. They had one, and only one, crack at success.

The design proved to be flawless, so Peter quit his job as a design engineer and became a one-man production team. He cut the tubes, drilled the holes, replaced the wheel bearings, packed the parts, arranged for shipping. Fran kept the books in her spare time. The Seidenbergs sold thirty dollies in their first year, 167 in their second. Advertising was minimal.

Peter would take a dolly to a regatta, let other competitors see it and use it, and tell them about Seitech. It didn't hurt that he often won the race. Though spread around the world, Laser sailors are a tightly knit group, and word of an innovation spreads quickly among them.

At the end of 1991, the Seidenbergs moved from Canada to Rhode Island, a center of sailboat manufacturing and a huge potential customer base. A few months later, Fran stopped editing schoolbooks to become Peter's full-time partner in the business. She took care of the office, learning accounting in the process; he took care of the shop. Each year thereafter sales grew substantially. Seitech dollies were selected for the 1992 Olympics in Barcelona, Spain, the 1994 World Championships in LaRochelle, France, and the 1996 Olympics in Atlanta. By 1997 the Seidenbergs were selling dollies in eighteen configurations and 250 sizes for all kinds of watercraft. Their baby had hit its growth spurt. "Adolescence" was underway.

The problem is that the Seidenbergs are not ready—are *beyond* ready—to become parents of a teenager; and it's this mismatch in timing that makes an orderly release so difficult. Other family businesses do not typically face this problem. The founders may have started earlier in life. They may have adult children in a position to take over. Their business may have run its course, even profitably so—a one-generation phenomenon. But the Seidenbergs began their company relatively late in life; they have no children; and right now Seitech's future appears limitless.

Fran and Peter's future is quite limited, however; and so they struggle with matters of release. A few years ago, they decided to relinquish control of manufacturing. It was a difficult step for Peter because he was so meticulous in his work. Who could possibly do it as well? A part-timer was hired; although he made some errors in the beginning, he is now a full-time employee who supervises others with an eye as close as Peter's. Then the Seidenbergs hired a full-time salesman to handle orders and take a more proactive approach to marketing. After a good start, his relationships within the company deteriorated, and he had to be dismissed.

When the release of an operation is successful, the Seidenbergs reap the benefits. Peter finds more time for design, where his heart really lies. He and Fran look into the future of their company. But when a release is unsuccessful, the Seidenbergs have to retighten their grip. They lose freedom. It took an enormous amount of time and energy, for example, to deal with the problems created by the hiring and the firing of their salesman. And, in the long run, all of the effort was wasted.

Behind the successes and failures lurks the dominant issue of release: ultimately, who will take over Seitech? Fran and Peter hope to groom an heir, but right now there is no one in sight. They have received offers to purchase their company, and they have given them consideration. But they have discovered in themselves a deep aversion to selling.

"He hadn't even bought our company and he wanted to change the concept!" exclaimed Peter of one potential buyer. "That set me off immediately." The buyer wanted to limit the number of Seitech's models, but Peter customizes. "A dolly for any dinghy," says the ad. Fran comments: "Recently Peter built a dolly for a sailor in Michigan, and he called me up and then wrote a letter saying how wonderful a product it is. 'The engineering is perfect, it went together so easily, and it's changed my life.' So many people have told us, 'Now I use my boat.' We had a 70-year-old woman who sails her little boat now because she can get it in and out of the water so easily." These continued expressions of appreciation will be hard to part with.

The Seidenbergs are learning that their release will have to come in stages and that it must be selective: some things will go and some will stay. And they are becoming clearer about what they want to stay. Although a technical innovation launched the company, it is a value—an abstract but very real element of culture—that must sustain it. The *name* Seitech has to mean something, its founders say. It has to mean quality, integrity, being the top of the line. "It's a standard," says Fran. Right now the younger generation of sailors uses the word "Seitech" for "dolly" the way others use "Xerox" for "photocopy." "Grab a Seitech," they say on the beach. Ultimately, Peter and Fran will be releasing that name into another's hands, hoping a certain spirit will follow.

Whether that spirit does indeed follow, whether the final release is successful, cannot be foretold. Decades from now, Seitech may not mean customizing; it may not mean top of the line. But that will be out of the Seidenbergs' hands, and out of their sight as well.

All of these considerations have forced Peter and Fran to determine not just what Seitech means but how much it means. Their conversation is peppered with phrases like "it's become a part of us" and "we could never give the whole thing away." Peter goes further: "Since I started Seitech, my whole life has been turned around. I know what I have to do in life. I have a purpose and I feel good about it. If something would happen to me now, well, I have a legacy that I didn't have before."

The stage the Seidenbergs hope to reach next is that of "grand-generativity," one I will explore in a chapter to come. Neither Fran nor Peter wants to retire. They love the creative side of their work. They love the learning they are continually forced to do. But they want some freedom from the bottom line. They want some time to dance, to sail, to see their friends around the world. They want to maintain a watch over the company's standards; they want to coach, consult, even help out around the shop; but they want to leave the operational details to someone else.

Right now that possibility seems exceedingly remote. The Seidenbergs let go of an operation, then take it back again; consider selling the whole business, then put the thought out of their minds; spot a potential heir, then give up on him. They remember the land mines they have stepped on in the past and know there are more that lie ahead. Meanwhile, the orders keep coming in, the opportunities keep arising, and they must be dealt with. Something has to give at Seitech—or be let go of. Its owners are in the middle of a dilemma of release.

8

Responding to Outcome

AS PEOPLE STRUGGLE with matters of release in generativity, they are being affected by outcome. They are seeing their business take off or fail, their children sink or swim, their words being honored or put to uses not of their choosing. How they respond to what they see constitutes the eighth phase of the generative process, the final step on the Way.

Watching how our creations turn out is like looking in a mirror, for what leaves our hand does indeed reflect on us. (When creation is excessively agentic, the reflection is its only *raison d'être*.) One mother looks at her adult daughter's problems with anxiety and depression, thinks back to her own mental state at the time of her pregnancy, and wonders about the similarity. Can these things be passed on in the womb? Another mother feels responsible for the accident that permanently disabled her son. Couldn't she have done something, anything, to prevent it? Still another, one who witnessed her daughter's slow deterioration into the "living death" of schizophrenia, wonders what might have been different if she had recognized it sooner. "It is a darkness," she says simply. "I try to forget her. She was my favorite child." We can never escape the feeling that we are implicated in the fate of our creations, even when we have had little control over it.

If an outcome is negative—if children, for example, "go bad"—we may try to absolve ourselves and blame others, as did Jesus Sanchez, immortalized by Oscar Lewis in *The Children of Sanchez:*

> My body is becoming half-paralyzed from being so angry with these children of mine. I am ashamed to talk about it. It is hard for a father to have such sons. They turned out bad because of bad surroundings, bad companions. Their friends are doing these boys no good. It is a shame that I cannot do anything about it. In spite of my advice, they go the other way instead of taking the straight path. . . .
>
> Tell me, what more could they ask for? Other boys would have been only too glad to have the big help I gave these two. I've spent my life working for them. I never failed in my duty as a father. I never shirked my responsibilities, never put them aside. No matter what it was they could count on me, whether it's a doctor at midnight or at dawn, or money for this or money for that to pay for medicine.

Or we may blame ourselves, as did the mother who left her children prematurely:

> I wish to God I could get rid of the guilt. If someday—I don't want to start crying—if someday they all make it, I think it will go away. I have terrible fears because of my guilt. A year ago the kids went on the plane back to Arizona, and all of a sudden my life just went out of me. I stayed in bed for a week. I didn't cook or anything. I was aware of what was happening, but I wasn't able to control it. It scared the hell out of me. I cried, and I said I've ruined their lives. I've ruined everybody's life.

As with children, so with technical innovations. In 1938, the German chemist Otto Hahn discovered the principles of uranium fission. Seven years later, as a direct outcome of his work, Americans dropped an atomic bomb on Hiroshima. The physicist Werner Heisenberg recalls the moment when the news reached a gathering of German scientists:

> Worst hit of all was Otto Hahn. Uranium fission, his most important scientific discovery, had been the crucial step on the road toward atomic power. And this step had now led to the horrible destruction of a large city and its population, of a host of unarmed and mostly innocent people. Hahn withdrew to his room, visibly shaken and deeply disturbed, and all of us were afraid that he might do himself some injury.

In his memoir, Heisenberg rushed to Hahn's defense, trying to minimize his involvement. Hahn, he said, had had no influence on developments in America. He had been loud and clear in advocating the use of atomic energy for peaceful ends alone. Besides, if he had not discovered uranium fission, someone else would have. "The individual who makes a crucial discovery cannot be said to bear greater responsibility for its consequences than all the other individuals who might have made it. . . . He may possibly be able to exert just a little extra influence on the subsequent progress of his discovery, but that is all."

Cultural innovations can follow the same deadly course as technical ones, going in a direction abhorrent to their makers. After Martin Luther took his stand on religious reform, fellow friars disbanded, changed the Mass, destroyed sacred images, banned music from church, and married—none of which Luther wished to see, all of which he subsequently preached against. Peasants revolted against their overlords; and although Luther had once called for rebellion ("we would smile did it happen"), he later turned against the idea. Peasants needed spiritual freedom, he wrote, not political freedom; if they rebelled, they deserved "a fist that brings blood to the nose." Seeing what was happening, Luther began to hear a new voice: "What if you were wrong, and if you should lead all these people into error and into eternal damnation?" Whenever that voice came, he would ask friends to reaffirm his doctrine of justification by faith so he could still believe in it. "Luther could hardly recognize what he had generated," wrote Erik Erikson in his study of Luther's defining moment. "The universal reign of faith envisaged in [his] early teachings turned into an intolerant and cruel, Bible-quoting bigotry such as history had never seen." The momentum generated by Luther's creation had escaped his control.

When an outcome is positive, however, a creator's joy may know no bounds. A 40-year-old mother speaks for many: "I'm lucky to have two very open, sweet, good children, and I'm not just saying that because every other mother says that about her child. I think they are." A slightly older mother, damaged as a child, speaks for those who buffer: "When my daughter graduated co-valedictorian with a GPA of 3.987, it was one of my proudest moments! I had won the battle I vowed to win. I had eradicated the repetitious cycle of abuse!" Another mother, older still, is speechless with gratitude over what her adult son has become. She wonders, "Could this be attributed to me?" And a man near 70 takes deep satisfaction from work in a different sphere. A state legislator, he helped convert abandoned oil wells and strip mines into a public lake and park. "I was only a little cog in the wheel that made it possible, but I appreciate the part I was able to play," he says. In his old age, he knows that families will enjoy his efforts for generations:

> After I was elected to the legislature, one of the first bills that I prepared was for two million dollars to start that. We had to make sure that all those oil wells were perfectly sealed, so they could never come back and pollute. Had to refill a lot of those strip mines so that we'd keep the acid out. I think we must have done a pretty good job of it, because today it's one of the best fishing lakes in Western Pennsylvania. I don't think you're gonna go to a place that's more beautiful in the fall of the year, when the leaves are turning. Everybody should go up and just sit there. It's a good place to go to dream.

The Final Blending

As a "little cog in the wheel" that created a beautiful Pennsylvania lake, this former legislator understood the truth about fractional contributions to generativity. But others fail to understand; they want a legacy that is *all me*. In Shelley's well-known sonnet, a traveller sees what happens to a legacy like that:

> *I met a traveller from an antique land*
> *Who said: Two vast and trunkless legs of stone*
> *Stand in the desert. Near them, on the sand,*
> *Half sunk, a shattered visage lies, whose frown,*
> *And wrinkled lip, and sneer of cold command,*
> *Tell that its sculptor well those passions read*
> *Which yet survive, stamped on these lifeless things,*
> *The hand that mocked them, and the heart that fed;*
> *And on the pedestal these words appear:*
> *"My name is Ozymandias, king of kings;*
> *Look on my works, ye Mighty, and despair!"*
> *Nothing beside remains. Round the decay*
> *Of that colossal wreck, boundless and bare*
> *The lone and level sands stretch far away.*

Ozymandias was like many who think of legacies as statues to themselves, who hope to impose the meaning of their lives on future generations. There is one problem with such an approach: it doesn't work. The reason is that the next generation will determine for itself what our lives have meant, blending their ideas with our own. In Shelley's poem, the traveler, a symbol of posterity, did not see the "king of kings" that Ozymandias declared he should; he neither trembled nor despaired before a mighty presence. Instead, he saw the sad remnants of arrogance. The meaning that the traveler put into the statue was very different from the one that Ozymandias did. Never mind that Ozymandias, in an act of agency, had etched his meaning in stone.

All the travelers who come upon our creations—who come upon *us*—are the final blenders. When they read a book we have written, for example, they mingle their thoughts with its, changing the book as they "digest" it. How much they change the book depends on whether they "incorporate" it or "identify" with it. (Recall the *i*-processes of Chapter 3.) But unless some exchange takes place, some final blending, the book will not live on. It will gather dust on lone and level shelves like the statue of Ozymandias, a product of creativity but not of generativity.

Actually, if any part of us is to live on, it will go through a series of blendings, none of which is ever "final." Sociologist Barry Schwartz has shown as much by tracing the influence of Abraham Lincoln over the course of a century. Lincoln was assassinated on April 14, 1865, five days after the official end of the Civil War. At the time of his death, Schwartz points out, Lincoln was not that popular a president. Sermons delivered throughout the North looked back on him as honest and well meaning, but far too merciful in regard to the Southern traitors, and far too merciful for his own good. Some preachers even said that God allowed the assassination to happen so that a stronger, sterner man would see to the righteous punishment of the Confederacy. Lincoln, they claimed, was just too insensitive to the cost of the war he had waged.

Subsequent generation abandoned this interpretation of Lincoln and fashioned others. They became genuinely fond of him, naming towns, streets, and businesses in his honor. Postage stamps began to bear his image. The image created at this point was that of "common man." Lincoln was the rail-splitter, the man of the soil, the people's president. It was stressed that he had come from a background of poverty, that he was simple and unpretentious, even awkward and homely. He loved to joke and tell stories. At the beginning of the twentieth century, the United States experienced a wave of egalitarian feeling known as the Progressive Movement, and Lincoln became its symbol. Numerous reminiscences were published by men who were young contemporaries of his and who were now in old age. The titles stressed his closeness and accessibility: "An Audience with Lincoln," "Lincoln as I Knew Him," "A Boy at Lincoln's Feet."

In 1909, the centennial anniversary of Lincoln's birth, his likeness was stamped on the most common object imaginable, a penny. (It replaced the older Indian head.) A memorial to Lincoln was also commissioned, and its location showed a significant change in how he was remembered. "His monument should stand alone," said Congress, "remote from the common habitations of man, apart from the business and turmoil of the city; isolated, distinguished, and serene." A huge statue of Lincoln was to be placed behind the pillars of the memorial, in the way the ancient Greeks placed statues of their gods in enclosed temples. Lincoln was becoming something new: the Great Emancipator, the Savior of the Union, the Christ-like Man of Sorrows who sacrificed himself for his country. In addition to a man people were fond of, he became one they revered.

Little was subtracted from Lincoln's identity across a century of blendings, but a great deal was added to it. Indeed, the combination of simplicity and dignity, familiarity and remove, made Lincoln a powerful symbol for enduring aspects of the American psyche, more powerful even than the country's first president, George Washington. In 1865, one of Lincoln's eulogizers had asked, "Who shall deny that Lincoln dead may yet do more for America than Lincoln living?" The eulogizer knew well how the memory of a person lives on by blending with the needs of changing times.

The new creations that result from a succession of blendings are celebrated in myths about the world's beginnings. A sample comes from the northwest frontier of India:

At first Kujum-Chantu, the earth, was like a human being; she had a head, and arms and legs, and an enormous fat belly. The original human beings lived on the surface of her belly.

One day it occurred to Kujum-Chantu that if she ever got up and walked about, everyone would fall off and be killed, so she herself died of her own accord. Her head became the snow-covered mountains; the bones of her back turned into smaller hills. Her chest was the valley where the Apa-Tanis live. From her neck came the north country of the Tagins. Her buttocks turned into the Assam plain. For just as the buttocks are full of fat, Assam has fat rich soil. Kujum-Chantu's eyes became the Sun and Moon. From her mouth was born Kujum-Popi, who sent the Sun and Moon to shine in the sky.

Unlike Ozymandias, Kujum-Chantu anticipates the final blending. Indeed, in an act of communion, she surrenders to it. And once it's underway, a marvelous thing happens: as she turns into her creation (this is what occurs in identification), her offspring find a place in her. The latter detail is worth remembering, for generativity involves that same reciprocity and receptivity: allowing children and successors to find a place in you, letting them become a part of who you are. Kujum-Chantu represents generativity's final blending, and perhaps its most frightening one. But it is she, not Ozymandias, who lives on.

Classic Wisdom

The Christian Gospels abound in metaphors, many of them drawn from the Galilean countryside, that illuminate the sequence of generative tasks I have been describing in the last two chapters. "It is a narrow gate and a hard road that leads to life," Jesus says, pointing out the necessity of selection. He tells his listeners to prune the branches of the vine that bears no fruit, to cut down barren trees, to sell everything they have in order to purchase the one field that contains a treasure. He teaches about release too, reminding them that seeds grow on their own, even while their sowers sleep. "Of its own accord the land produces first the shoot, then the ear, then the full grain in the ear." Even the mustard seed, the tiniest of them all, grows into the largest of shrubs, with foliage so thick that birds take refuge there.

One of the best known of these metaphors depicts the variability of outcome. It is the parable of the sower, a brief tale about a man who walks a field, casting seed as he goes. The seeds fall to the ground, but by the time each finds its niche in the earth, the man has already moved on. He loses track of what he has sown because it always lies behind him. At some point, however, he returns to see the results:

> Behold a sower went out to sow. And as he sowed, some seed fell by the wayside; and the birds came and devoured them. Some fell on stony places, where they did not have much earth; and they immediately sprang up because they had no depth of earth. But when the sun was up they were scorched, and because they had no root, they withered away. And some fell among thorns, and the thorns sprang up and choked them. But others fell on good ground and yielded a crop: some a hundredfold, some sixty, some thirty.

In the Gospels, this parable is directed at the hearers of Jesus' message. Do not be the soil by the wayside, it says; do not be the stony place, do not be the thorns. Be the good ground that welcomes the word of God and remains loyal to it. These are the meanings I remember hearing as a child. But as an adult I am struck by a complementary set of meanings that address the sower himself. In fact, the story's images—snatching birds, impenetrable rocks, and choking thorns—depict the fears of anyone who would generate. Will my creations be stolen by those who take advantage of their vulnerability? Will they wither from apathy or inattention? Worse still, will they take root and grow, only to be strangled by forces beyond my control? The parable also conveys a harsh truth about generativity: most of our efforts will go to waste. Still, there is hope: only a few "hits" are needed to produce in superabundance.

All in all, the sower learns that outcome is mixed. Some things, and some people, turn out well. Others turn out poorly. But the mix is deeper than that, and more complex. In a follow-up parable, Jesus tells of a man who sowed wheat in a field, only to have an enemy sow weeds in its midst. The man's workers ask if they should pull the weeds out, but he says no, you'll uproot the wheat as well. "Let both grow together until the harvest." This gets closer to the truth of outcome: not good in one place and bad in another, but good and bad in the same, their roots in a common tangle. The mother of a 13-year-old cannot pull the weeds out of her son, but she can bless the wheat:

I guess that's what I'm trying to do with him, to let him see that I've passed things on to him—and his dad has too. He's got some pretty good stuff from both of us, but he's got some weaknesses too. . . . I feel I've got to teach him more. There are still some areas in his life that I feel I've got to impact.

At the very time that we are beginning to see outcome in our children, they are awakening to legacies received from us. Generational conflict may ensue. Or other eventualities: a recent study of outcome uncovered complex, even contradictory, reactions in parents. "Children who are accomplished and well-adjusted may occasion pride, and even vicarious enjoyment, among parents," said the researchers. "Yet, these same wonderful children may evoke envy and the sense of missed opportunities in parents' own lives." Children who turn out well may remind us that in some ways we have not.

Even with the best of outcomes, however, we will not escape the waste that is intrinsic to the generative process. When I wrote a book about the work of priest, sociologist, and later mystery writer Andrew Greeley, he responded this way:

> I found myself saying, "What a wasted life, what a tragic misuse of time and energy and ability." . . . I've worked very hard over the last quarter-century, frequently to the point of exhaustion, in the production of an inordinate amount of printed pages. I see it all neatly arranged in the Kotre monograph and realize how much the effort was a waste, how worthless the product. Better never to have started.

That may have been a momentary reaction, but not an uncommon one, and it illustrates an extreme of judgment we would do well to avoid: I was the perfect mother or a terrible one, a success or a failure in my work. The reality comes in finer shades of gray: I was good enough as a parent, but not perfect; I failed in some ways, but not in all. Researchers studying highly esteemed creators have found exactly what the sower did upon his return to the field. In their lifetime, these creators produce more "good" works than others do, but also more "bad" ones. Posterity, selecting for itself, simply remembers the good and forgets about the bad.

Understanding that waste is a part of generativity, we can draw enormous satisfaction from the one treasure of a child we raised, the one efficacious word we spoke, the one community service that grew in significance. We can return, if only in memory, to the scenes of our successes—to the good ground—like the man who loved to visit the lake he helped create. And because so much of generativity is "accidental" or "unconscious," we can also be surprised when those who have benefited from our presence make us aware of outcomes we may not have seen. A young college president was enlightened by someone he had guided:

> There's a very talented man who was in our admissions office who's just going on to Princeton as an assistant dean of students. I got a lovely letter from him as he left that made me realize we have had the same kind of mentoring relationship that others fulfilled for me.

In the same vein, Herb Robinson, Jr., recalled a sermon he had delivered two years before:

> I wasn't satisfied with what I had preached. I felt that I had let God down. Just this past Sunday somebody came up to me and said, "You're Herbert Robinson, aren't you?" And I said, "Yes, I am." He said, "You preached a sermon on such-and-such a date, and I was there, and you won't believe how it changed my life."

Whenever we are granted a vision of outcome, it helps to remember that our contributions to it have been fractional, and that forces beyond our control have had their influence too. Thirty years ago, a young couple adopted a daughter who carried a 25 percent risk of developing Huntington's disease. Then they saw their worst fears realized as she was debilitated by the illness in her mid-20s, even earlier than expected. When she gave birth to a daughter of her own, the couple adopted this little girl too— their granddaughter—knowing that she had a 50 percent chance of developing Huntington's. They will not be able to have a genetic test until she is 21 and may not do so even then. And so they await the outcome, surrendering to invisible forces.

When genes play such a critical role in how a child turns out, and especially when the genes are not your own, it is easy to recognize the role of forces beyond your control. But the parents of any child need to recognize those forces too, need to see the point at which their responsibility for an outcome ends. Many influences beside their own contribute to the eventual fate of their children.

Here, as elsewhere on the Generative Way, faith is required, faith in the resilience of the next generation. If that resilience helped us to recover from intergenerational damage, it will help our successors as well. We need faith to realize that no outcome is ever final, no matter how things seem at the moment. We also need faith because of all the results we will never see, because of all the sowing we do without knowing it, all the "accidental" and "unconscious" generativity. "I think I have seen just a very small part of the effects of what I have done in my life," said an older woman, demonstrating faith in the unseen. Sister Jo Biondi knew this faith too: "The articles that I write and whose effects I never see, the words I speak on the air that millions of people hear on a Sunday, I don't know where they go, but somewhere in there, there is another touching." She did not see the fruits of her labor, but then she didn't need to. She was beyond outcome.

Beyond Outcome

If the parable of the sower contains wisdom about what to expect when we sow, it also contains wisdom about what to do. We are to *keep on sowing* despite the inhospitality of the world to what is young and vulnerable, despite all the results we do not see. The *Bhagavad Gita* goes further: we are to practice "nonattachment" to the fruits of our actions. It is interesting advice: while we teach the young to be aware of the consequences of their actions, we are supposed to teach ourselves to be unaware. "You forget forever all proprietorship in your own works," said the writer C. S. Lewis. "You enjoy them just as if they were someone else's: without pride and without modesty." Speaking of images of the Grail and the inexhaustible fountain, mythologist Joseph Campbell put the matter this way: "The source doesn't care what happens once it gives into being. It's the giving and coming into being that counts." He explained with an agricultural metaphor of his own: "Think of grass—you know, every two weeks a chap comes out with a lawnmower and cuts it down. Suppose the grass were to say, 'Well, for Pete's sake, what's the use if you keep getting cut down this way?' Instead, it keeps on growing. That's the sense of the energy of the center."

Energy—and detachment—of this kind characterized the hermit in the story of the golden tree. "It's the creating that matters to me," he said. "Nothing else." It also characterized a number of individuals in the Parks Daloz study of committed lives, which I cited in Chapter 5. "Success is not the measure of a human being," said one of them, a legislator. "Effort is." Another, a woman working to reduce violence in public schools, said she had to be realistic about outcome: "I won't see peace in my time." But she kept on working. Both of these people practiced a kind of detachment that shielded them from discouragement and burnout. As the Buddhists say, "Act always as if the future of the universe depended on what you did, while laughing at yourself for thinking that whatever you do makes any difference."

People who become deep centers of generativity—mythology's inexhaustible fountains—have a different orientation from those just starting out on the Generative Way. Novices must learn to see that their actions—their inactions as well—do indeed have consequences. They must learn to peer down the generational chain and think of the links they are forging, become aware of the trail they are leaving. But at the end of the path, when generativity is mature, we are to do the reverse. We must free ourselves from concern about the future, surrender our children and our works to life, let another reap what we have sown. The teachings of the centuries tell us to concentrate on the integrity of the present moment. That is easy to do in old age, when we know we will not live long enough to see the fruit of our efforts. But this teaching is meant not just for the elderly, but for anyone who travels the Generative Way, at whatever age they do it.

In this book I have told stories that depict the energy of which myth speaks as a djinni or a golden tree. That energy is nothing other than life, generative life; and when you find it at the "center," you will have reached the "end" of the Way. For the Generative Way is not a road that exists in some far-off place but rather an approach to life, a way of seeing and thinking and doing that will make your life count—to you and to others. It is the "how," not the "where," of the traveling.

PART

III

REFLECTIONS

9

Never Too Soon, Never Too Late

NOW THAT WE HAVE come to the end of the Generative Way, something else must be said: you can travel it more than once. You can embark a second time, or a third, to enact a fresh commitment, resurrect an old one, make amends, or simply express a dream. And it's never too late: if a lengthy stage of generativity is out of the question, you are still capable of a brief moment that could write a surprising ending to the story of your life. Each trip will be different because each will be colored by the season of life in which you set out.

What is generativity like in each of adulthood's seasons—in its early, middle, and late years? In this chapter I will sketch a kind of map, describing some typical journeys, taking note of some common experiences and some uncommon possibilities. These days, the journeys of late adulthood are becoming especially intriguing, for they are redefining, recoloring even, the very season of their occurrence. That season—retirement—did not even exist in 1900. But it does now, the creation of a century that saw life expectancy increase by over twenty-five years. Retirement is a wonderful gift of the twentieth century, but those of us who enter it in the twenty-first will have an opportunity, a calling even, to turn it into something finer. We can make end-of-life leisure productive leisure, turn the generativity of that period into something "grand."

Early Adulthood: Never Too Soon

When in life does generativity begin? I had no reason to question Erikson's assignment of it to middle age until I thought back to a childhood game of "Statues." I'd forgotten what its rules were and even what its objective was, but I did remember green grass and summer evenings and gliding about in slow motion, then freezing, suddenly, and trying to hold perfectly still. Twenty-five years later, on another summer evening in another city, I watched the neighborhood kids play Statues, my own children among them. Neither I, nor any adult that I'm aware of, had taught them how. The rules of the game were being passed from one generation of children to another without ever entering the world of adults.

Generativity? Among children? For what may be purely arbitrary reasons, I think of such behaviors as forerunners to generativity, preferring to reserve the word itself for adult manifestations. But these precursors are reminders that it's never too soon to look in a life for harbingers of what is to come.

Adult signs of generativity can appear as early as the 20s, in the first season of adulthood. A few studies have measured its levels at this age and found them to be substantial, though not dominant, and short of what they will be later on. Generativity in the 20s often appears as the desire to make a difference with your life, whether inside or outside the family. It appears as bits and pieces in the mosaic of identity formation. Young adults with a distinctively *generative* identity anticipate the possession and blending of a voice. This is a 23-year-old woman struggling to find hers:

> I don't think one day goes by that I don't worry about what my path is going to be. I keep coming back to the idea that I want to somehow make my mark. I want to help a person who is struggling. If I can't do that as a therapist, I would like to reach people with my writing.
>
> I keep thinking about my grandpa who is 70 and suddenly concerned with exactly what I plan to do with my future. It makes me want to hurry up and do something important, so he can see it in his lifetime! I wonder if he thinks about his contribution.
>
> I'm not sure if I will have children, but I want to make a difference in a child's life even if he or she is not my own. Maybe, if I'm lucky, I can say that I changed someone's life for the better. Maybe there's a term for being my age and being concerned with the legacy that I hope to leave.

It is the desire to "reach people" and "do something important" and "make my mark" that renders this woman's identity-in-the-making generative. It will take time for her voice to mature and find its audience—think of all the young count went through in "The Three Languages"—but given the length of life we enjoy today, there is time enough. There is even time to find a succession of voices. This young woman can be generative first as a therapist, then as a writer, then in some other way she has not yet imagined. Should she choose, she can also become generative as a mother.

Though they have plenty of time ahead, young adults may experience just the opposite—a pressure to hurry up and get their independence established and the realization of their dreams underway. They may find it difficult to coordinate generativity's clocks. (You can picture each domain as having one.) Right at the start there will be problems getting biological and parental timing in synch, for our bodies become fertile long before we are ready to become mothers or fathers. (The lengthy period of mistiming is known as adolescence.) For some young people, it will be career first, then children; for others, the reverse; for still others, no children at all. At any point a person may feel on time or off, ahead of schedule or behind. Here is another woman of 23 for whom a pregnancy came too soon:

> When I got pregnant I was really upset. I remember crying all by myself when I came home from the doctor's, thinking, "I've not had a chance to really begin my life, and now I won't be able to do anything." Steve and my family and his family were delighted about the baby. It was pretty hard not to share their enthusiasm, but I just wasn't ready for this.

Another woman of the same age, however, found that her pregnancy was right on time:

> I had so many people say to me, "Don't have a baby right away. You'll be tied down. You won't be able to work. You won't get any sleep. You'll be miserable." My mind never changed or wavered about having a child right away. Something so beautiful, created out of two people's love, how could it be so terrible? And now after having her, I find I was right. The most joyous moment in our marriage was the birth of our child.

An older man was more than ready when his time came. A gay African-American, he was 33 when his cousin abandoned her two sons, aged two and three. He volunteered to adopt them:

> They fulfilled what had been a lifelong dream. I wanted to be somebody's father. I had a father and a grandfather, and all of those examples were part of my life, and I wanted to do that. . . . When I got them, I felt anchored in time and space, and there was a real serenity connected with that.

For most people, parenting will be the first major enactment of generativity—what Erikson called "the prime generative encounter." But others will find opportunities in their work as well. Those who teach the young surely will, and many creators will achieve their breakthrough in their 20s and 30s. Frank Lloyd Wright began working independently at 26. Pablo Picasso and Georges Braque began their collaboration when they were both in their late 20s. Martha Graham found her distinctive approach to dance in her early 30s. Research has revealed that the peak years for creative output are likely to be the late 30s—earlier for poets, mathematicians, and theoretical physicists, later for novelists, historians, philosophers, and those like Freud who need time to build up a larger base of knowledge. This creativity is not by itself generativity, but it is the source from which generativity flows.

In our 30s, we may also experience a threat to our generativity: the sense that time is running out on one of its clocks. A biologist set his deadline at 40:

> The only problem that interests me is the one which is going to topple the field, or not topple it, but, well—shake its foundations. We really have to begin at the fundamental level. . . . But going right along parallel with that feeling is also the feeling that: Jesus, you know, you're getting on and. . . . It's characteristic of the field, as we all know, it's not historically well documented, but by the time you're 40 you've blown it.

Forty also looms as a cut-off date for many women wishing to have children. Even before that time, a significant number (about 15 percent of married women) will experience an inability to conceive, at least temporarily. After two miscarriages, writer Diane Cole wandered in her 30s "through uncharted ground in the land of infertility":

The climate is unpredictable there. One day I would wake up and say, "Get rid of all that medication! Throw away the ovulation chemistry set! Just live your life as a middle-aged married couple and be content!" The next day, I would say, "What do you mean? Look at your nieces and nephew! How can you possibly give up?" The third day, I would say, "Let's think seriously about adoption. . . ." It was odd how lonely this land could feel.

And numbing. In early adulthood, threats to generativity may follow hard upon the emergence of generative desire and the establishment of a generative identity. The creative breakthrough may not come, nor the child; and in their absence we may be left with what psychologist John Snarey calls "generativity chill." Paradoxically, this chill can either dampen generativity or intensify it.

Snarey demonstrated both possibilities in the longitudinal sample of working-class men to which I have already referred. From that sample he and his colleagues extracted a subset of fifty-two men who had experienced biological infertility, their own or their wife's, sometime during early adulthood. The problem was not always permanent, but the men's initial reaction to it was telling. At one extreme were those who turned to a preoccupation with bodybuilding, health foods, or macho sexuality—to a preoccupation with themselves. In middle adulthood (age 47), they were the least generative of the entire group, even if they had eventually become fathers. At the other extreme were men whose immediate response to infertility was to become involved in youth groups, or teach a Sunday school class, or act as a "big brother" to a neighborhood child. At 47, they were among the most generative of the original fifty-two. They were also the most likely to have adopted a child and to have been deeply involved in that child's life. In them, generativity had been intensified.

As each of Diane Cole's efforts to become pregnant failed, her desire followed the latter course. It intensified. Eventually she and her husband arranged to adopt a son from Korea. "Even as he was placed in my arms, I felt surge through me an urgent sensation of love, infatuation, and responsibility," she wrote. "I knew he was the child I had yearned for all those years."

Diane's chill was followed by a "thrill," and it illustrates another force that amplifies generativity in early adulthood: having an outlet. Ethologists observe that a baby's face is a powerful stimulus that instinctively "releases" an adult's tendency to care. Physical anthropologists add that as human children grow, they retain their baby face longer than any other mammalian species. Children, it seems, have been designed by evolution not only to receive care from their parents but also to actively solicit it, like an audience does a voice.

Remarkable new evidence is showing that, in the case of fathers at least, the generativity which children call forth spreads to other areas of life. When adults from 19 to 68 were tested for broad generative concern, those who had children scored higher than those who did not, even though only one of the twenty items on the test even mentioned the word "children." The presence of children effected a slight increase in the generative concern of women (it was higher to start with), but a large increase in that of men, the wild cards in the enterprise of parenting.

An even clearer demonstration of generativity's spread comes from Snarey's sample of working-class men. Here it was found that fathers who invested in their children as young adults tended in their middle years to invest in their communities as well. Because of concern for their children, the fathers had become scout leaders or baseball coaches or members of the school board. They had anchored themselves in their communities, taking parenthood, in Snarey's words, as "a moral metaphor and model for good citizenry." Though comparable data are lacking for women, one study suggests that generativity spreads in the same way for them, moving from "proximal" to "distal" roles.

Because of the presence of children—and sometimes because of their absence—the typical pattern for generativity is to rise during adulthood's first season, even though it may never dominate a personality. During the 20s and 30s, time is on our side. We can maintain a faith that in one way or another, in one domain or another, our generative identity will find expression. But as we enter the 40s, time ceases to be an ally, and that faith may be called into doubt.

Middle Adulthood: Second Chances

Middle age brings with it an end to certain kinds of generativity—biological expressions, first of all. In women, the ability to have children drops dramatically in the 40s and then stops altogether around 50. In men, its decline is more gradual. A few people try to delay the end through extraordinary medical means. In 1994, an Italian woman used "egg donor" technology to give birth to a son at the age of 62—a world record. She had lost her only son in an accident and was considered too old to adopt another, so she had eggs "recruited" from a younger woman, fertilized by her husband, and implanted in her own womb. In 1996, an American woman used the same technology to break her record by a year.

Most people respond to the approaching end of fertility in the opposite way, however, choosing to stop the biological clock well in advance of its scheduled time. In the United States, they have chosen surgical sterilization so frequently (whether through tubal ligation, hysterectomy, or vasectomy of their partner) that it is now the number one form of birth control for women over 30. Infertility may chill in early adulthood, but in the middle years it is far more likely to bring relief. The *fear* of pregnancy is gone.

Another kind of ending takes place when grown children leave home. The emptying of the nest is not a discrete event but rather a gradual process that can take ten or more years. As it begins, some mothers may be "out" of generativity:

> Two summers ago I realized that I was constantly being called upon to do things for others. Nothing was coming in to replace all that was going out. I just started crying and couldn't stop. The cry was coming from deep down within me. My husband said, "What's wrong? Why don't you take a nap?" But it wasn't a nap I needed; I wasn't that kind of tired. . . . I was tired of giving. I felt like an octopus, overextended.

A father can feel empty, too, especially when he is taking care of aging parents as well as growing children. This is the gay man twelve years after adopting his cousin's two sons:

> I had no idea that it would take this long. . . . I always wanted to be a father, but the children were unexpected, and so I never got a chance to prepare for leading, you know, my life, where I was the main focus, and taking on all of these other responsibilities, so I have a lot of deferred stuff.

Another kind of emptiness stems from the inability to provide for one's children. Here is a steelworker who was laid off in his late 40s:

I'm to the point now that when I go into town and I buy myself something, I feel guilty that I'm hurting the kids. They're the ones, you know. . . . I even had a time I was thinkin' of suicide. I did one time, I did. I told my wife, and she says, "Ahh, what would that prove?" I figured that's a coward's way. Many a time I was thinking if God would take me in my sleep, but then I figured, "Hey, I still want to see these kids." And I want to see them get to the regular age when they can take care of themselves.

In our 40s and 50s we see for the first time the outcome of generative efforts—the results, if you will, of our first trip down the Way. Along with the good that we did, we see the bad, and all that went to waste. Now comes the need for a new kind of release, a letting go of earlier dreams and of longings for what might have been. If we desired children and are childless, we accept that outcome. If we have not been creative in the way we wished, if our contributions have not been recognized, we yield to those eventualities. Whatever our complicity in how things turned out, there is nothing more to fix. What is imperfect will stay that way; what turned out well will be a treasure. We release it—and ourselves.

A respite might be needed following such a release, an escape from any concern about generativity. Following a divorce, another woman who was "out" of generativity (she had little to begin with) accompanied her new husband on a temporary assignment to Hawaii. For the first time in a long time, she could focus on herself:

I got a library card, and I walked around, and I just loved it. All my life I had dreamed that I would have a nice place around me, and everybody would just leave me alone, and I could have books and music. In Hawaii, all this selfishness came to the surface, and I didn't have to feel bad about it. Every hour of every day I was able to enjoy. Every hour I was aware of things. It was hitting me that life was fantastic. Why would anyone want to step out of it?

Carefully negotiated, a passage of release and acceptance will return us to the beginning of the Way, nourished and ready to start afresh. Once again, we will have to confront legacies from the past. This time, however, they will come not from previous generations, but from the first half of our lives. Once again, we will have to discard what is dead, burdensome, and broken, and keep what contains the djinni. In middle age, we may become generative for the first time; or, after an early adulthood blessed with positive outcomes, we may move on to new domains. A woman who had an "accidental" pregnancy at 35 saw it as an opportunity to make amends:

> Since I screwed up on the other three, I thought here's another chance. My whole feeling through the pregnancy, the delivery, and when she was an infant was different. I felt calm. I felt nurturing. I was getting another shot at being a mother and not messing up.

Another shot: this woman was far from unique in sensing a *second chance* coming her way as middle age approached, though certainly in the minority in experiencing it as the result of a pregnancy. Far more parents experience a second chance when their children grow up and become independent adults. After her respite in Hawaii and a few years in a new marriage, the woman I mentioned above began to feel very differently about her offspring:

> I like my kids much more now that they're becoming adults. I enjoy Marie tremendously. I still can't handle Anne and Paul, but I enjoy them when we're alone, one to one. When Anne plays the violin, tears come to my eyes, and it hurts because I try to control it. I say, Oh, my God, I wish my mother were alive and could see this! And I feel an anger that my father never saw the kids. If only he could see them now!

In middle age, one moves toward relationships with children that are mutual and symmetrical, one adult to another. And yet this second way of relating carries memories of the first. To some extent an adult child will always be one's "little" girl or boy, and a middle-aged parent one's "mom" or "dad." The challenge is to integrate memories of the first way of being a parent with the realities of the second.

Another kind of second chance, still in the realm of parenting, comes with the arrival of grandchildren. Typically, this is a happy occasion; research indicates that grandparents will enjoy their grandchildren's preschool years more than any other. "It was like a second time around," said one grandfather, remembering an afternoon of tobogganing with his grandchildren, "because we did all these things with our daughter." His joy was unmistakable. But he also learned quickly of another role that grandparents are called upon to play. In middle age especially, they are the family's insurance policy, the backup parents. When this man's daughter divorced, he and his wife had to step in and help:

> My daughter would call us quite often and tell us that she didn't have any food in the house. And payday was a distance away. She had so many bills to pay and so she was without food. We'd bring sacks of groceries over. Hardly a weekend went by that we didn't go to visit our daughter. We'd have barbecues and cookouts outdoors, and I even planted a huge garden in back of their place, eighty-foot square. And that garden kept them with food all summer long.

The second chances that come in middle age might mean repeating a past success, but they might also mean making up for a past failure. And while a making up—a redemption—may not eradicate guilt, it can channel that guilt into productive ends.

For one middle-aged couple, it was not guilt, but pain, that was turned to such an end—the pain of losing their teen-aged daughter to cancer. Most parents leave a legacy for their children, but this child left one for her parents. Impelled by her daughter's "need to leave some sort of mark," the mother took up full-time work in the worldwide peace mission of her church. After thirty-four years as a commercial banker, her husband became director of a community food bank that collects surpluses and distributes them to the needy. Why? "She was the kind of young woman who cared about people," he says. Their generativity—a second and very different trip down the Way—carried their daughter's influence far outside the family.

Psychologists who measure generativity find that it typically reaches a peak in the middle years. According to several pieces of research, people expect to be more generative in their 40s and 50s and in the main they actually are. In a single-case study, psychologists Bill Peterson and Abigail Stewart combed through the diaries of British author, feminist, and mother Vera Brittain, looking for references to identity ("why I became a Socialist"), intimacy ("I can always say that I love you"), and generativity ("I don't want that account of myself to go down unchallenged to posterity"). They found that intimacy references outnumbered generativity references by about five to one in Brittain's early twenties. By her late 40s, however, the balance had shifted: now there were nearly five generativity references for every one of intimacy. True to Brittain's artistic nature, however—or perhaps true to contemporary human nature—issues of identity predominated at both times.

One reason for generativity's "normal" rise during middle adulthood is that this is the time when agency and communion come into a better balance. As their obsession with power and achievement wanes, men typically work a communal element into their personality. They are less threatened by competition, more concerned about relationships. "You get into the nurturing business," a Hollywood talent agent told journalist Gail Sheehy as he took some younger agents out to lunch. "I feel I really have a sense of the past and a connection to the present and maybe to the future more than almost anybody else. If I can communicate a little of that, I think that's important for them, and it makes me feel good."

The addition of agency makes women effective mentors as well. "When I'm in my territory, I feel like I'm really in charge," said one in her mid-50s who had lived a difficult and fearful life. "I know what to do. I know how to do it well." The mother of four adult daughters, she was director of student development at a small college and an advocate for middle-aged women returning to school. She was beginning to see herself as a "repository" for all that women had been through:

> It's like you can see people on a journey. And the ones that are farther along can talk to the ones who aren't so far along. . . . I can say, "I've felt things like that. Let me tell you. Let me tell you when I was so scared. I've been alone. I've been frightened to be alone. I've been a woman who didn't have any way to earn money. I went to school and didn't make it once." Those things are very effective. It's as though my failures are more important than my successes.

Like some of the working-class fathers studied by John Snarey, this woman used parenthood as a moral metaphor for relating to the larger world. She believed in the solidarity of women and was a kind of mother to those under her care:

> I was thinking the other day about the business of a chain only being as strong as its weakest link. And I thought that was stupid, because a lot of us in my group are weak right now. What it should be is: the individual

woman is only as strong as the collective woman. It's like a net. You may get a little hole in it here, but it's still a powerful net. And we're all as strong as we are collected together."

Another impetus to middle-aged generativity is a new chill—the fear of death. Research has shown consistently that this fear (call it the Big Chill) is greater in middle age than it will be later on, when the end is actually nearer. In fact, the study which in 1965 coined the term "midlife crisis" (it involved some three hundred artists) suggested that the core of the crisis was a deeper experience of one's mortality, a finding that may be true of men more than it is of women. Awareness of death stimulates generativity in a very concrete way: it necessitates the writing of a will. But it also turns one's thoughts to legacies of a less material kind.

Perhaps the dominant reason for generativity's increase in middle age, however, is that this is the season in which we are responsible for the running of society. We are members of the "command" generation—the public officials, the owners of businesses, the administrators and managers, the union leaders, the members of school boards and church councils and neighborhood organizations. As creators, we are producing the mature works that require an accumulation of knowledge and experience. Whatever our particular role, we are in a position to teach, coach, mentor, and sponsor the young. In middle age the demand for generativity is great, and the targets that elicit it are numerous.

Responsibility—for younger generations, for families, for society's institutions—is a major feature of generativity in the 40s and 50s. It's the kind of responsibility felt on a daily basis by a dairy farmer who runs an operation that's been in his family for 165 years. He is the middle link in the chain of generations. His father, 69, is still healthy and helps out when he can; his oldest son, 22, is still learning the role into which he will step; his first grandson, just born, is the promise of further continuance. But it is *he*, the 45-year-old, the man in the middle, who bears the brunt of keeping the enterprise going. Each day is different, he says. Each presents a new emergency. Each requires split-second decisions.

His father once carried that kind of responsibility, but now he's in another season of life. "When Dad doesn't feel like doin' something, he doesn't do it, and I respect him for that," says the farmer. His son, just beginning early adulthood, "hasn't come to the bottom line yet. At this point in his life, he can be easygoing. 'Hey, let somebody else make the decision. I can live with it.' "

But the man in the middle cannot afford either luxury. "If the tractor's broken down, or the tank didn't cool right, it's comin' on my shoulders. Maybe the input's there by my father or my sons, but the decision is made by myself. I am the bottom line."

The generativity of adulthood's second season is typically bottom-line generativity. Even as this farmer embraces it, he looks forward to the day when it will end—the day, still in the future, when he and his wife say good-bye to their position of command and turn the farm over to their children.

The Wisdom of a Conjure Woman

Saying good-bye is the subject of a story that depicts the end of adulthood's second season and sets the stage for the third. It is one of many "conjure tales" that its author, William Hooks, heard growing up in the Carolina Low Country, tales of men and women who could cast and remove powerful spells. Its heroine is a slave woman in whom agency and communion unite, making for an abundance of generativity. She wants one thing above all: to set her adult daughter free.

The woman's name is Mama Marina, and she is the most respected and feared woman on the entire plantation. One senses this from the very beginning of the story, when the master of the plantation comes to her with a problem. Every fall, it seems, when the grapes ripen, the slaves eat the best of them before they are picked for wine. Every year he threatens the slaves, and every year the grapes still disappear. Now, in the heat of summer, the master wants Mama Marina to cast a spell, so that anyone who eats a grape will die. The master doesn't believe in Mama Marina's conjuring, but he knows the slaves do. If she casts a spell, those grapes *will* stay on the vine.

"I need one ingredient to make it work," she tells the master.

"What's that?" he asks.

"A piece of gold."

The master digs one out of his pocket and gives it to Mama Marina. Then she asks, "How many of these I need to buy my daughter's freedom?"

The master laughs. "A fine strong slave like Sheba? I'd say a hundred."

Now Mama Marina has been hiding coins in a pouch for many years, but the one she gets from the master makes only twenty. Still, she conjures the grapes.

A few days later Sheba comes in from the fields and asks if all the grumbling is true. Has her mother cast a spell on the grapes? Why would she do such a thing?

"I done it for a few more miles on your road to freedom," replies Mama Marina.

Sheba is with Joe Nathan, the young man she loves and the best leather-worker in the county. "I'll take no freedom without him," she declares. "We go together, or we stay as slaves."

Mama Marina knows that Sheba means what she says, and that of course makes matters worse. How can she buy the release of two slaves, not one? And Joe Nathan, the best leatherworker in the county, will cost far more than one hundred pieces of gold. As the summer draws on, Mama Marina grows more and more troubled.

Then, in the darkness of one fateful night, she goes to the vineyard and walks up and down the rows of grapes. In the distance it begins to thunder, and as a storm comes closer, she raises her hands and summons the spirits, asking to be shown a way. A bolt of lightning hits the vineyard with a snapping explosion. For a split second, the land is as bright as day, and then darkness and stillness return.

Now Mama Marina knows what she has to do.

The very next night she brings Sheba and Joe into the vineyard. She picks two bunches of green grapes and tells them to eat. Holding the conjured fruit, they begin to tremble. "Eat!" demands Mama Marina. "You'll go down through the valley of death, but you won't die."

They eat.

That fall the slaves harvest the master's grapes without eating a single one. But on the morning of the first frost, as the grape leaves shrivel up, so do Sheba and Joe Nathan. Sheba's hair turns gray and she starts to walk hunched over like an old woman. Joe's fingers become so stiff and bent that he can no longer work leather. A month later the two of them are as gnarled and twisted as the vines in the wintry field. Everyone can tell they are dying, and everyone knows why: they have eaten the conjured grapes.

On February's coldest day, Mama Marina goes to see the master. "I want to buy those dying slaves," she says. "How much they be worth?"

"Worth?" he laughs. "Who would buy a dying slave?"

"I would, sir. Would you consider twenty gold pieces?"

"You're a fool," he says, but he takes her money.

"Yes, sir," answers Mama Marina, "but don't forget the papers of freedom." And the master writes them for her.

Throughout the rest of the winter Mama Marina brings Sheba and Joe Nathan a strong tea of St. John's weed and rabbit tobacco. She seeks out the old man who drives the supply wagon to Charleston and whispers that she needs a favor. "Name it," he says. In March, just as the buds start to appear on the grapevines, she feeds Sheba and Joe a bowl of cornmeal gruel, and they take a turn for the better. A week later she hides them under a blanket in the wagon that is heading for Charleston. "Hold on to your freedom papers," she says, "and go straight to the Quaker meeting-house."

Once the wagon carrying her children disappears over a distant hill, Mama Marina returns to the vineyard. In the bright sun, she notices how the leaves are coming out on the vines, and she knows the grapes will soon follow. Then she will remove the spell, she thinks as the story ends. Then Sheba and Joe Nathan will be free.

As Mama Marina stands in the springtime vineyard, she can rejoice in the conclusion of adulthood's second season. She has raised a child to maturity and released her into freedom—at great cost to herself, I might add, for she may never see her again. Throughout her middle age she has mothered an entire community, using her gift of conjuring to its benefit. Agency and communion have united in her. She is a woman of great power who knows human nature well enough to outwit the master of the plantation. She is willing to bring the children she loves to the edge of death, no matter what they suffer. She feeds them poisoned grapes with one hand and a healing tea with another, comforting them through the sickness she has caused. She is both a rock and a deep source of love.

Mama Marina's power comes from a connection with the mysterious world of spirits. A young woman told me of a power like hers in her great-grandmother, an old Polish immigrant who spoke in broken English. "She knows things," said the great-granddaughter. "Lillian knows who will die and speaks with the spirits of the dead." The great-granddaughter wasn't superstitious, but she could not explain her forebear's power:

> She has many stories of family members visiting her at the time of their death. She has stories of premonitory dreams and intuitions that almost always come true. She tells the stories with no mysteriousness at all. She tells them as if it were something that makes her just a little different from the rest of her family. Her brothers and sisters say, "Lillian knows things." My grandmother calls it a gift. My mother is not interested. I am afraid Lillian will leave this gift with me.

In *The Tempest* William Shakespeare connects generativity in the second half of life to this same kind of familiarity with the spirit world: there Prospero uses his magic to do for his daughter what Mama Marina did for hers. In the *Arabian Nights* collection, the narrator Scheherazade makes the same connection in sequels to the story of the fisherman and the djinni. This is how the story continues: after releasing the djinni for good, the fisherman is led by him to a magic lake high in the mountains, where he casts his net once again. This time he catches fish who are really people in bondage, placed there by an evil sorceress. Following the djinni's instructions, the old man takes the fish to a young sultan and leads him to the magic lake. There the sultan, assuming the bottom line, takes over. He explores the surrounding area, unravels the mystery of the sorceress, tricks her into releasing her spell, and finally kills her. When the people are liberated, they pay homage to the sultan, but the sultan honors the old man. Everything has been initiated by his ability to talk to the djinni and deal in the stuff of the spirits.

What is this stuff—this connection to the spirit world that seems so important to mature generativity? It is, I think, an understanding of the mysterious forces that shape human destiny—natural forces, supernatural forces, conscious forces, unconscious forces, higher forces, lower forces: however you think of them. It is an ability to move those forces toward benevolent ends, through insight or prayer, for example. In another context, it might be called wisdom: *"rerum divinarum et humanarum scientia,"* as Cicero defined the concept: "a knowledge of affairs divine and human."

Throughout the ages, wisdom has meant knowing *more* than the ordinary person and also knowing *deeper*—this, according to Aleida Assmann, who has studied the history of the concept. Assmann notes that wisdom, as opposed to the utopian spirit, does not seek to change the world or alter the fundamental conditions of life. It is more practical and immediate than that. It "suggest[s] new options at a moment when life is paralyzed. 'Solomonic solutions' and 'paradoxical interventions' break up the paralysis and restore lost balance." Life was paralyzed for Sheba and Joe Nathan until Mama Marina went to the vineyard, contacted the spirits on a stormy night, and walked away with a plan for a paradoxical intervention: she would give Sheba and Joe life by bringing them to the edge of death.

It is psychological rather than technological knowledge that makes for wisdom, adds psychiatrist Allan Chinen. An engineer he interviewed became president of a multibillion-dollar company in his early 60s. In that role he focused on being a good judge of people. "I can't follow the technical details anymore," he said, "but I'm pretty good at judging who to trust when they recommend a project, and who not to trust. That's my responsibility now, figuring people out, not projects."

Psychological research on wisdom has shown quite clearly that it is not restricted to late adulthood. The story of Mama Marina is not inaccurate, then, in attributing it to someone in middle age. But late adulthood can add something—a knowledge of forces so long in range that they become invisible, the lore and common sense and even the factual information of a bygone era. For wisdom to operate in old age, however, it must blend with the world of youth. It must be open to the knowledge and innovations of succeeding generations, especially in the realm of technology, and especially today, when change is so rapid. Grandparents who learn about computers from their grandchildren, in other words, have a far better chance of imparting wisdom to them than those who do not—something a conjure woman, living in a different era, did not need to know.

Retirement?

As the second season of her adulthood comes to an end, there is a thought that never occurs to Mama Marina. Her lifelong goal achieved, her bottom-line generativity done with, Mama Marina does *not* say to herself as she heads back to her cabin, "Now I can retire." The thought is absent not because she is a slave but because her story is set in the nineteenth century.

A remarkable thing happened in the hundred years following Mama Marina's fictional death. A new and very powerful belief took root about the normal course of life and in particular about what was supposed to happen at the end of it. The belief spread so far and so fast that it now seems native to the life cycle. In 1900, people believed that they were to work until they died. But now they believe that they are owed ten, twenty, or even more years of leisure before they die. For many today, the purpose of the working years is to accumulate the resources to enjoy the end-of-life leisure to which they are "entitled."

It was Otto von Bismarck, the first chancellor of the German Empire, who came up with the idea of retirement in 1889. Legend has it that he picked age 65 as the starting point because it enabled him to get rid of political rivals older than himself. In 1935, when the Social Security system was established in the United States, the same age was settled on, but it could just as easily have been 60 or 70. In the decades that followed, the average retirement age dropped to 62 and life expectancy increased to over 75. The proportion of a lifetime devoted to work reached its lowest point ever. Today, if we were to offer retirees the same number of leisure years that Bismarck did a century ago, we would not set the retirement age at 65, but rather at 80.

One cannot even begin to think about the generativity of adulthood's third season—its new season—without first considering Bismarck's remarkable invention. Nor without considering the Age Wave that followed in the wake of that invention and is now bearing down upon us.

Recall the dimensions of that enormous tide: in 1900, one in twenty-five Americans was over the age of 65; today one in eight or nine are. By 2030, it will be one in five and building toward one in four. These figures are for the United States, but similar demographic transitions are taking place around the world. Nor have they bypassed the poorer, developing countries, where average life expectancy has risen from about 40 in the early 1950s to over 60 today. China's shift is extraordinary: between 1982 and 2000, its over-60 population will increase by 72 percent, while its population at large grows by only 19 percent.

The human population is aging—dramatically so—around the world. And the question of the moment is whether this aging population will create generative, nongenerative, or even antigenerative, societies. Take the

United States: its federal government is currently spending eleven dollars on every citizen over 65 for every single dollar it spends on one under 18. If you factor in what state and local governments do, especially in the area of education, that discrepancy is significantly reduced; but still, a direct correlation exists throughout the country's fifty states between an increasing elderly population and decreasing per-pupil spending, especially in areas where the students involved are children of color (and they will increasingly be children of color). Put the matter another way: thirty years ago, 35 percent of the elderly were living below the poverty line; today, only 12 percent are. In contrast, 20 percent of U.S. children are living in poverty—the highest figure for any age group. Look at it a third way: in 1950, 16.5 workers in the United States supported each Social Security beneficiary; today only 3.3 do, even though beneficiaries are getting back far more from the fund than they ever put into it.

The numbers are relentless and the conclusion inescapable: if we in the Age Wave are going to pay our own way, and not burden younger generations, we will have to work more years (and, incidentally, do a better job of saving for our eventual retirement).

It is not such a dire prospect. In his search for the optimal experience he called "flow," psychologist Mihaly Csikszentmihalyi was drawn to the research of Italian psychologists who had studied some of the oldest residents of a tiny village in the Alps. These people worked sixteen hours a day—and wouldn't have it any other way. None drew a line between work and leisure. One of them was Serafina Vinon, 76:

> When Serafina was asked what she enjoys doing most in life, she had no trouble answering: milking the cows, taking them to pasture, pruning the orchard, carding wool. . . . When she was asked what she would do if she had all the time and money in the world, Serafina laughed—and repeated the same list of activities: she would milk the cows, take them to pasture, tend the orchard, card wool.

None of the old people in this village would choose to work less if given the opportunity. But their grandchildren, aged 20 to 33, felt differently. And so do we, according to Csikszentmihalyi's research. If you ask people directly, he reports, they say they want less work and more leisure. But if you catch them unawares, if you give them beepers that go off at random intervals and ask them to record what they are doing at the moment and how they are feeling about it, you'll find they are happiest when they are at work. Csikszentmihalyi was surprised by "how frequently people reported flow situations at work, and how rarely in leisure. . . . When supposedly enjoying their hard-earned leisure, people generally report surprisingly low moods; yet they keep on wishing for more leisure."

In the century to come, generativity will require that we relinquish the belief that we are owed extensive leisure at the end of life—leisure that is less than pleasurable anyhow. "We seek satisfying love and sex after sixty," writes former U.S. Commerce Secretary Peter Peterson. "Why not satisfying work as well?" Not paid work necessarily, if we are well pensioned. Nor physically demanding work, if we can no longer perform it. Nor work with the burden of the bottom line. (Actually, it can be a generative act to step aside from the bottom line and make way for the next generation.) Nor even work that rules out the time to enjoy this earth more than we have before. But work nonetheless, and as long as we are able: full- and part-time service jobs in health care, child care, and various education and training efforts, suggests Peterson for a start.

For those who have found their work satisfying, retirement is a chance to continue plying their trade on a different basis, one that is commensurate with their present energy level. "I want to keep moving as I've moved all my life—at a slower pace, but independent," said a 61-year-old owner of a family butcher shop. For those whose work has been tedious, even brutal, retirement is a chance to get (or create) a satisfying job, to work in ways they may never have dreamed of when they were dependent on a boss and a paycheck.

By 1997, Americans were getting the idea, if only because economics were forcing them to. In that year the trend toward early retirement was finally reversed, as labor force participation rates increased at all ages from 62 to 70. Only time will tell whether beliefs were reversing too, whether Americans were beginning to see retirement not as an end in itself but as a stepping-stone to something finer.

Late Adulthood: "Grand" Generativity

The work one undertakes in one's 60s, whether paid or voluntary, whether in partial or full retirement (or in no retirement at all), may very well carry over characteristics of adulthood's second season. It may very well extend middle age. At some point, however, if generativity is to continue, it will have to take on a look all its own. It will have to become "grand" generativity—"grand" because it is like grandparenting, "grand" also because it is tied to the grand scheme of things.

Erik Erikson coined the term "grand-generativity" late in his life, in a book published in 1986. He wanted it to cover the roles of "aging parent, grandparent, old friend, consultant, adviser, and mentor," describing a kind of care that relinquishes the direct responsibility of middle age. But one can develop the idea further than Erikson did and use it to point out a way through adulthood's final season.

Grand-generativity takes into account the losses that inevitably come with aging: a decline in physical strength and energy, problems in vision and hearing, aches and pains in the joints, and finally, the inability to get around on one's own and even to take care of oneself. It acknowledges the economic and social losses too: reduced income and status, the end of relationships with co-workers, the death of friends and loved ones. "I feel more constricted, hemmed in by my finitude," wrote a woman of 67. It's no wonder that tales of late adulthood—ones that reveal a developmental path yet to take—often begin with a man, a woman, or a couple living alone in a small and deteriorating hut.

One cannot be "grand" by denying such losses. A student of mine once completed an exercise that simulated the physical losses of old age and then wrote that she would do all she could to "prevent the inevitable" in her own life. Now the inevitable is awfully hard to prevent, but there is more than enough writing on late adulthood to suggest that it can be done. If you look inside the cover of Gail Sheehy's *New Passages,* for example, you will see a map of adulthood in which there is not a hint of decline from the 60s onward, only a vision of endless frontier. The Serene Sixties give way to the Sage Seventies, then to the Uninhibited Eighties, and then to the Nobility of the Nineties. At the end of the map come Celebratory Centenarians, one on the bow of a ship looking through a telescope at an unlimited future, the other riding a dolphin into it. Beside the dolphin is the phrase "active risk taking." For a 100-year-old!

Not only will that map become useless as you age, it will lead you away from generativity, for it removes the chills that stimulate it. Without decline and death, without limits on our individual existence, what need is there to concern ourselves with those who follow? What need, even, to reproduce?

The time for unlimited frontiers is young adulthood. It is then that one hopes *to do* something grand, to be the hero or heroine of ancient tales, the Luke Skywalker or Princess Leia of a modern one. In late adulthood, however, one knows the limits of one's place and how immense the universe truly is. And so, instead of doing something grand, one hopes *to do a small bit within* the grand scheme, and connected to that scheme. One hopes to be the Yoda living in his tiny dwelling. As a 64-year-old postal worker said upon his retirement, "I have no more mountains to climb. I've achieved what I wanted to achieve. Now it's time to do some of the things that give you a kinda personal satisfaction, you know?" Or a 74-year-old astrophysicist, "I still enjoy science, but I don't have the ambition to write the most brilliant paper ever written."

Research is showing that generativity typically declines in late adulthood, as one steps out of positions of command. But that does not mean you cannot do your bit. "It is a very small niche," said one retiree of a project she had just begun, "but one I can handle with my heart and soul." One of the committed people studied by Laurent Parks Daloz (Chapter 5) described himself as a "grain of sand" on the beach, but noted, "without my grain, it would not be the same beach." Another was a "little speck in a huge, huge universe" but nevertheless "related to that universe in some way." A third was "a flea on the tail of a dog, but at least I'm on the dog biting strategically." It took faith to believe that one's bit had some bite—a faith not limited to the elderly but especially apt for them.

At the end of life, such bits might be called "swan songs." Looking at the music of classical composers, psychologist Dean Keith Simonton found that work written shortly before their death was briefer, simpler in structure, less original and yet more profound than work written earlier. It also proved to be more popular. Sensing the end, the composers had distilled the essence of their works-in-progress, creating a "swan song effect" discoverable only by counting years from the end of a life, not from its beginning.

Swan songs are not only distillations of work but also distillations of identity—a matter of getting *me* down to my essence, a statement about *who I am* in the end. After suffering a creative block for nearly sixty years, writer Henry Roth decided that he must be a transmitter. Nearing death, he saw himself hanging on to a high-voltage wire:

> The current is killing you, but you can't get rid of it—except by converting yourself, figuratively speaking, into a vehicle for discharging the immense store of static electricity you've accumulated over the years. . . . Don't let the high voltage kill you if you can still convert it into a conduit for communication with your fellow humans.

A well-publicized professor of sociology, Morrie Schwartz, chose in this spirit to be a conduit to the last. As he was dying, he made his final course a personal seminar on how to die. Likewise, a woman in failing health began to close every phone conversation with, "I love you," and to give everyone a hug when she left them. How she would leave this life mattered, she thought; she knew her final acts would have the testimony of a lifetime behind them.

Who knows what a swan song might set in motion? Once, when the philosopher and psychologist William James was offered a drink, he was reported to have said, "If I slake my thirst in this way, how goes it for the rest of the cosmos?" It was not a prideful remark but one that showed an awareness of the interconnectedness of life and thus of the far-reaching effects of even the slightest gesture. Had James known of chaos theory, he might have subscribed to what it calls the "butterfly effect"—the notion that the flap of a wing in Beijing today will affect the weather in New York a month from now, that "tiny differences in input [can] quickly become overwhelming differences in output." Bits, in other words, can multiply in significance. And doing yours is one of the characteristics of grand-generativity.

A second characteristic of grand-generativity is *emancipated innocence* or, in everyday terms, "being a kid again." At the outset of adulthood we must suppress our naivete as we become responsible citizens and followers of social convention, work long and hard to hone our skills, and, not incidentally, encounter some of the worst in human nature. When a man turns 60 in Japan, psychiatrist Allan Chinen observes, he dons a red garment that signifies his return to childhood. Now he can recover the sense of wonder, spontaneity, and play that he had long ago. "At my age, I can do anything and say anything I want! I don't worry about what other people think, the way I used to," says a 72-year-old American woman. This second innocence is not "regression," however. It does not replace the mature judgment of earlier years; it complements it. One becomes as wise as a serpent *and* as simple as a dove—and in the process acquires a new basis on which to relate to children.

Yet another characteristic of grand-generativity is a willingness to *step aside,* to make way for the next generation. At the end of middle age, stepping aside might mean leaving positions of command in the world of work. Near the end of life, however, it is likely to mean refusing extraordinary medical treatment whose only goal is to add an extra year or two of life. (The cost of those extra years may very well compromise medical care for the young: nearly a third of U.S. Medicare spending in 1998 was for patients in their last year of life.) A recent survey found that 89 percent of Americans supported the idea of a living will that would preclude such treatment; it also found that only 9 percent actually had such a will. Drafting one can be generative in the most profound sense of all. As Erikson wrote long ago, "Healthy children will not fear life if their elders have integrity enough not to fear death."

The passage to grand-generativity is depicted in a number of elder tales, one of which, from Italy, is called "The Shining Fish." This story begins with an old man and woman living alone in a tiny hut near the sea, barely eking out an existence. One day, while gathering wood in the forest, the old man meets a stranger who gives him a bag full of gold. The man hurries home and hides it under a pile of manure so his wife won't fritter it away. But the wife sells the manure to a farmer and the gold is lost. The sequence repeats itself a second time—the stranger gives the old man more gold, the man hides it, this time under some ashes, and the wife unwittingly gets rid of it. The third time around, the stranger offers the old man a bag of frogs which he is to take to town and exchange for the largest fish he can find. It's only frogs, not gold, so the man does just as he is told, but he returns home so late that he cannot clean the fish. He hangs it high on some rafters outside the house.

That night there is a terrible storm, and in the middle of it the old man and his wife are awakened by a knock on the door. They open it to find a group of exultant young fisherman thanking them for guiding them safely to shore. "How?" the old fisherman asks, and they point to the fish hanging from the rafters. The man looks up to see it shining with an intense light that can be seen for miles. From then on the old man hangs out the fish every night, and every night it guides the fishermen home. And the fishermen see to it the old man and his wife have all that they need to survive.

This story tells us about possibilities for change at the very end of life, about moving up to higher and more encompassing forms of generativity. Twice the man is given a treasure; twice he decides to hoard it; and he ends up losing it both times. But he is given a third chance, and with it some very specific directions. Now he is able to overcome his greed, which is actually a greed for life. His inner transformation, symbolized by frogs becoming fish becoming beacon, enables him to make the developmental leap to grand-generativity. He becomes a light to others when he can no longer go out to sea himself.

Take It from the End

Having followed the life course of generativity, we might now ask whether the end of the journey is predictable from the beginning. Today, scientists can launch a hundred different missiles in a hundred different directions and predict with great (though not unerring) accuracy which stages each will go through and where each will land. But can psychologists, scientists of another kind, do anything similar with lives? Can they take a hundred people at birth and forecast the stages of their life and the place they will occupy at death? Can they tell where they will end up on the map of generativity?

Coming out of the psychoanalytic tradition, Erik Erikson—an artist, not a scientist—painted a picture of the life cycle that said yes. Each of the stages of life he delineated had to go well if subsequent development was to go well—much like an eight-stage rocket launched into space. Thus, trust established in the first year of life led to autonomy in the second, a sense of initiative after that, and feelings of industry and competence during the school years. Those were the first four stages. Industry set the stage for the creation of identity in adolescence, and so in turn for intimacy in early adulthood, generativity (stage seven) in middle adulthood, and integrity in old age. Erikson never said that the connections between his eight stages were inevitable—he was too aware of the complexity of life— but he left the clear impression that the outcome of later stages was highly dependent on the outcome of earlier ones. If you didn't have trust, autonomy, initiative, and industry early in life, there was little chance you would have generativity later on.

What is the empirical verdict on Erikson? The only way to render one is to track lives from beginning to end. But this tracking—longitudinal research—is very difficult to do. Generativity is a notoriously nebulous concept; testing it "scientifically" is like staking a cloud to the earth and keeping it pinned down for half a century. In practice, the cloudkeepers retire or die; others take their place; questions and approaches change; patches of cloud drift away. Still, researchers do what they can.

When George Vaillant inherited a study begun *before* the word "generativity" had even been coined, he looked long and hard at the question of predictability. The study (which I have cited before) was begun in the early 1940s. At that time researchers assessed the home environment of some five hundred working-class boys around the age of 12. In the late 1970s, Vaillant and his colleagues, working now with Erikson's model (it wasn't published until 1950), reviewed the reports and reinterviewed most of the subjects, who were now 47. Did the boys who had gotten off to the best start in life end up being the ones who had attained the stage of generativity?

Yes—and no. Childhood experiences did predict outcome thirty-five years later but at a very low level. The researchers determined that 31 percent of the entire sample had reached the stage of generativity. But of the men who had gotten off to the *worst* start in life (the bottom fourth in that category), 23 percent achieved generativity. The difference was enough to produce a level of predictability that in the eyes of the researchers supported Erikson. But the researchers missed the dominant story: a bad start in life reduced the odds that a boy would become generative, *but it didn't reduce them by very much*. Findings like this ought to occasion hope. Who becomes generative? The conventional answer has been those who get off to a good start in life. And this is true, but only to a very slight extent. Lives are more like mysteries than missiles, more like good page-turning novels that are full of surprises right up to the end.

The fact of the matter is that, when it comes to most any life outcome, prediction has been very difficult for psychology. Early on, the reason given was that our science was in its infancy, that human behavior was complex, and that it takes time to discover all the forces that bear upon a life's trajectory. In other words, we couldn't predict *yet*. But we've been a science for over a century now and must surely be past our infancy, not to say our childhood and even adolescence. We've completed our first great waves of longitudinal research, and we have yet to find a way of forecasting how lives will turn out.

Few if any psychologists are saying today that the levels of predictability in their longitudinal research are going to get higher "once we know more." We've gained a certain wisdom, and I would hope a certain humility, from decades and decades of trying. Even more, we've begun to appreciate how malleable and resilient members of the human species really are. In the language of science, our life course has proven to be "plastic"; in that of religion, capable of "redemption" and "transformation." It is so much easier to anticipate the flight of a missile.

Psychology's failure to predict the course of lives is really a discovery, the negative results of a well-designed and well-executed experiment. The discovery has major implications for the Generative Way. For one thing, we can no longer explain lives simply by taking them "from the beginning," interpreting their present condition in terms of what did or did not happen early on. Even Erikson questioned this practice. In the course of studying the life of Mahatma Gandhi, he wrote that "beginnings do not explain complex developments much better than do ends, and originology can be as great a fallacy as teleology." For one thing, you can never know all the forces that are present at the beginning of a development (say, in an acorn) until you see the end (the fully grown tree). And any sporting enthusiast knows that a last-second score can change the meaning of an entire game. Try watching a game "live," then view it again on videotape when you know the final score. Even its opening will seem different.

Teaching tales help us to "take it from the end," which is especially important along the Generative Way. You never know what's going to happen in these stories. Their heroes and heroines are as unpredictable as subjects in longitudinal research. Their lives are not determined by their beginnings, nor are they rendered helpless because of them. They are faced with choice after choice and receive chance after chance. Most important, you never know a person's true character until the story is over. You never know the meaning of a life until you see its fruit.

10

The Corruption of Generativity

SHE WAS A LITTLE GIRL in tattered clothes, about 9 or 10 years old, and after church she made her way up to the young student minister. Fighting through a terrible stutter, she said, "I l-l-love you," and gave him a handful of violets. The young man was captivated. He and his wife inquired about the girl, found out who her mother was, then asked to adopt her. Her mother, admittedly not the best of parents, agreed. In her new home, and with the help of a speech therapist, the little girl flourished and eventually lost her stutter.

Her name was Agnes, a word that means the "pure one."

Agnes was not the first child the minister-to-be had taken under his care. At the age of 19, he had rushed his wife's 10-year-old cousin to the hospital for an emergency appendectomy that probably saved the boy's life; the couple then provided him a home for over a year, since his own father had died and his mother was incapacitated. The new parents went on to adopt six more children of different races and to have one of their own, creating what they called a "rainbow" family.

When he was 25, this same minister founded an interracial church at a time and in a place where mixed congregations were not only a rarity but a target of violence. He set up a recreation center for children of different faiths. He established soup kitchens and nursing homes, a job placement center, even an animal shelter. He conducted healing services for the sick and had a knack of making people who were nobody feel like somebody. "We surrounded him with our reverence," recalls one of his followers. Indeed, thousands referred to him as "Father" or simply "Dad."

But on November 18, 1978, in the obscure South American country of Guyana, this father, the Reverend Jim Jones, coaxed 913 of his "children" to take their own lives. "They started with the babies," said a surviving witness. Mothers would give a drink of Kool-Aid mixed with cyanide to their own children before taking the poison themselves. Among those found dead in the days that followed were Jones's wife and three of his adopted children, now adults. One of them was Agnes. "What a legacy," Jones was heard to say as he began the call to self-immolation. "What a legacy!" He himself was found shot in the head.

Here is a life whose meaning must be taken from the end, one in which generativity went horribly, incomprehensibly, awry. Jim Jones lost the Way, and in the final act of his life became the antithesis of generativity, the epitome of the dark side. It *must* end with me, he said; my progeny must die when I do. How, in retrospect, can we understand the corruption of his generativity? More important, what can we learn from it?

"How Much I Have Loved You"

"Alone. Always was alone." Those words, coming from the 46-year-old Jim Jones, were found on a tape recording made in Guyana a year before his death. Jones had been born in 1931 in a small town northeast of Indianapolis, Indiana, in the midst of the Great Depression. His father was a veteran of World War I whose lungs had been rendered useless by mustard gas. Too weak to work, he said little because he had little breath to say it with. Jones's mother, on the other hand, had words and breath to spare. Sixteen years younger than her husband, she was educated and independent, in some respects the town eccentric. Though she worked in canneries and factories (the only jobs available) she found the time to read, to write, and to pass on her verbal gifts to her son. "Don't be nothing like your dad," she would tell him within earshot of her husband.

Isolation is a characteristic of that orientation psychologists call agency, and in the life of Jim Jones the course of agency is worth following. "Jimmy" was the only child of an uninvolved father and a mother who spent most of her time working. He was, as he says on his late-life recording, "the trash of the neighborhood, because in those days they referred to you as white trash." Jim's mother would let him wander through the town dirty and unkempt, much like little Agnes. To counter his loneliness, he collected stray animals, picked up sacks of kittens thrown out of cars, kept rabbits, chickens, ducks, pigeons, and a goat in a small pen in the back of the house. Those who knew him remember that he talked to his menagerie of animals and tried to train them. They also remember that he talked other children into the dirty work of caring for them.

It was a neighbor who introduced the young Jim Jones to religion. She took him to services at her church, and then he started visiting others on his own—the Quakers, the Methodists, then the Pentecostals in the Gospel Tabernacle on the edge of town. There, for a while, a woman minister took him under her wing, put him in a pulpit, and began to groom him as a child evangelist. About the same time, he set up a little church for neighborhood kids in the loft of a small barn behind his house. Occasionally the church became a classroom—or a laboratory where Jim conducted "scientific" experiments on animals, even attempting on one occasion to graft the leg of a chicken onto a duck. When an animal died, he would preside over a ceremony in which the remains were wrapped solemnly in a shroud, anointed with oil, placed in a cardboard box, and carried outside to a grave.

Knowing how Jones's life ended, it is easy to pick out the "predictors." There were omens in the barn loft: the chair where Jim, and only Jim, could sit; the lock on the outside of the trapdoor (once he imprisoned two children there for the better part of a night); the fact that he, and he alone, made the rules; and, of course, the odd mix of preaching, biological experimentation, and death rituals. In the loft Jim could have chosen to *be with* other children, but he decided instead to *be over* them. He liked the feeling of power. In psychological terms, he chose agency when he could have had communion.

There was probably more to his agency—a deep and dangerous anger related to being trash. Full of rage at 46, Jones remembered rage in his childhood:

> I was ready to kill by the end of the third grade. I mean, I was so fucking aggressive and hostile, I was ready to kill. Nobody give me any love, any

understanding. In those days a parent was supposed to go with a child to school functions. . . . There was some kind of school performance, and everybody's fucking parent was there but mine. I'm standing there. Alone.

Toward the end of junior high school, when other Indiana boys were caught up in "Hoosier hysteria" on makeshift basketball courts, Jim began to wear white robes and evangelize his neighbors, preaching to them on the street corners. They paid little attention. After school he read about religion, medicine, and world events at the public library; he studied powerful figures like Gandhi, Marx, Stalin, and Hitler. He took his preaching to Richmond, an industrial city to the south, hitchhiking to get there. He talked about poverty and brotherhood to street corner crowds, black and white, who were also society's trash. Jim Jones was only a teenager, but in terms of the Generative Way he was finding a voice and finding someone to hear it.

He was also finding someone with whom to blend it. Marceline Baldwin was a student nurse whom Jones met while working as an orderly at a hospital. An idealistic young woman, she was attracted by his good looks, his energy, the compassion he showed toward patients. She discovered that they shared a Christian outlook and a dream of making the world a better place. She believed in him. (She also believed his fiction about being the star of his high school basketball team and quitting because the coach made racial slurs.) Jim Jones and Marceline Baldwin were married in 1949, when Jim had just turned 18. Marceline was 22.

Three years into their marriage, Jones decided to enter the ministry. He became a student pastor at a Methodist church in a poor white section of Indianapolis—the place where he first met Agnes. He studied the techniques of tent evangelists, wanting to emulate their healing. In 1953, when he was 22, a small white-haired minister—another woman in his life—introduced him to an assembly in Columbus, Indiana. "I perceive that you are a Prophet that shall go around the world," she said. "And tonight you shall begin your ministry." Watching her husband ascend the pulpit, Marceline was terrified. Jim himself froze, lost for words. Then something happened: the words came. In an instant, the people came as well, streaming up to the altar, praising the Lord, falling at Jim's touch. Marceline was filled with awe. This was the man she loved, and now his time had come.

In 1956, at the age of 25, the Reverend Jim Jones founded his own church, first called Wings of Deliverance, then People's Temple. It was located in a racially mixed neighborhood in Indianapolis. Here he conducted healings, phony ones and genuine ones. He set up the soup kitchens and nursing homes I mentioned earlier. People's Temple provided free clothing for the indigent, sometimes paid their rent, sometimes delivered coal so they could heat their homes. Jones raised the money for a Sunday night radio program and traveled far and wide, even to Cuba, to recruit members. He recruited a family too. He and Marceline adopted three Korean war orphans (one died in a car accident), had a child of their own, then adopted a black child who was given Jim's name—apparently the first interracial adoption in Indianapolis.

But Marceline was torn. She admired her husband's concern for the downtrodden, but it cost her the dream of having a normal family. She craved privacy, but there were times when her husband had a dozen extra people, including his mother, living in her house. Honest by nature, she was often forced to help in the deception at healings. Once, when she was pregnant, Jim lost his temper and kicked her in the stomach. And yet she defended him to the outside world and tried to conceal his shortcomings.

Perhaps Jim was torn too, for in his late 20s he seemed to be on the verge of a nervous breakdown. He would break out in hives or literally collapse. In the fall of 1961, he told an associate that he had been hearing voices from extraterrestrial beings. Then he had a vision of an impending nuclear blast and was so terrified that he moved his family to Brazil, ostensibly to find a new site for People's Temple. He became a preacher in a land where he didn't know the language.

By December of 1963, the Brazilian venture had failed, and Jones returned to Indianapolis. Now he began to attack the Bible in front of his congregation. Many of his fundamentalist listeners deserted, and his radio program was taken off the air. But those who stayed with Jones, having severed a deep connection to what they considered the Word of God, became ever more connected to him. In 1965, he took 140 of them to a region of northern California that *Esquire* magazine had declared the safest in the United States from nuclear attack. Jim Jones was leading his children to a place apart.

In California, membership in People's Temple grew to thousands. On the outside the church was as civic minded as it had been in Indianapolis. It operated nursing homes for the elderly, foster homes for children, a day-care center, and a ranch for mentally handicapped boys. But on the inside Jones's control was growing more insidious. Somewhere along the line it became sexual. Once an advocate of celibacy (he had not practiced it), Jones started to expound on the virtues of "open" sexuality. Desiring the wife of one Temple member, he talked the man into divorcing her, then sent him a mistress. When the man married the mistress, Jones became involved with her as well, and spread the rumor that her husband was a homosexual. To make Temple members "better socialists," he forced them to talk openly in meetings about their sex lives. On questionnaires he included items about the sexual feelings of young boys for himself. He had sex with men as well as women, enjoying in particular the domination of "macho" types.

Jones fathered a son by one of his mistresses and, curiously, claimed paternity of another. In a document written shortly after the latter's birth, the father (or at least the man whose name was on the birth certificate) made a startling revelation:

> I, Timothy Oliver Stoen, hereby acknowledge that in April 1971, I entreated my beloved pastor, James W. Jones, to sire a child by my wife, Grace Lucy (Grech) Stoen, who had previously, at my insistence, reluctantly but graciously consented thereto. James W. Jones agreed to do so, reluctantly, after I explained that I very much wished to raise a child, but was unable after extensive attempts, to sire one myself. My reason for requesting James W. Jones to do this is that I wanted my child to be fathered, if not by me, by the most compassionate, honest, and courageous human being the world contains.

The boy's father or not, the writer of this document was not, like most of Jones's recruits, a person of little education. He was a lawyer and the local county's assistant district attorney. Marceline Jones, also intelligent and educated, was a signed witness to the document. She said later that she had given her husband permission to impregnate the boy's mother. The truth of the matter has never been established.

In California, too, Jones's paranoia grew more extreme. He had his inner circle, the Temple's "planning committee," raid garbage cans to gather intelligence on church members. He built a watchtower, surrounded himself with armed bodyguards, and disguised some of them to look like him. More than once, he staged his own assassination. In 1971, he told a woman he had met in Brazil that he was the reincarnation of the Egyptian Pharaoh Ikhnaton, and that she was his daughter. Jones, it seems, had also been the Buddha, Jesus Christ, and Lenin. He was making it clearer to his congregation that he was the only God they needed. This is from a sermon at 40:

> When you came to your socialist worker father, some of you never knew the fulfillment of happiness, you never knew that anyone cared. Your children were in difficulties. No one came to the jails. You prayed to your sky God and he never heard your prayers. You asked and begged and pleaded in your suffering, and he never gave you any food. He never gave you a bed, and he never provided a *home*. But *I, your socialist worker God,* have given you *all* these things.

In 1972, Jones moved the headquarters of his growing congregation to San Francisco. There, disturbing rumors began to spread about People's Temple and about Jones's extravagant claims. His fears mounting, he began to make arrangements with the Guyanese government to lease 3,824 acres in the rain forest for an "agricultural project." The project would be called Jonestown, and it would be located thirty-six hours by boat from the coastal capital of Georgetown—truly a place apart.

Over the summer of 1977 nearly one thousand Temple members emigrated to Jonestown. Roughly 70 percent were black; almost that many were female; nearly three hundred were under 18. Three of Jones's children came, including Agnes. So did the little boy whose paternity was in dispute.

To most of the immigrants, the jungle settlement was a Promised Land. One of Jones's mistresses wrote to her father about "acres and acres" of new kinds of crops, about a medical clinic that was already benefiting the local population: "gastroentronitis (if that's how you spell it—which I'm sure it's not) has been virtually wiped out in this area." A visiting minister declared, "I thought of Israel's understanding of herself, and later, the Church's self-understanding: 'We who were nobody are now God's people.'" A 15-year-old wrote her grandmother, "I am sorry to hear that you called the radio station but since you did I will not be writing to you any more. I don't know what you think—all I know is that I *love* it in *Guyana* and I *truly* am *happy!*"

To a few who got out, however, Jonestown was anything but a Promised Land. People were overworked and poorly fed, they said; they suffered from fever and diarrhea; many lost weight. Medical treatment was practically nonexistent. Jones confiscated passports and Social Security checks, censored mail, forbade telephone calls to the outside, and threatened to kill anyone who tried to escape. He used his "Extended Care Unit" to drug those who misbehaved—a young man who ran off into the bush, a 19-year-old mistress who wanted to leave Jones for someone else. He himself was taking Valium, Quaaludes, amphetamines, barbiturates, whatever he wanted. A public address system transmitted his harangues for much of the day. It carried the screams of those being punished by electric shocks from a machine known as Big Foot. Or the screams of children being punished: "I'm sorry, Father. I'm sorry, Father." They had been tossed in a well and pulled underwater by people already there.

In the fall of 1977, Jones conducted the first of what he called "white nights." "Alert, alert, alert," he would shout over the loudspeaker, summoning everyone to the settlement's central pavilion. Security guards would appear. Jones would then talk about all of Jonestown's enemies and the need for self-defense. As the white nights became more common, he began to talk about self-destruction. (He himself had been losing weight and looking like he might die.) "We're going to drink poison and kill ourselves." A batch of fruit punch would arrive and the people would drink. A loyalty test, Jones would then say, and reveal the drink was harmless. But if they ever *really* killed themselves, he would add, "it would go down in history as great act," for it would show the world the evil nature of the U.S. government. One white-night participant left a written record: "If the potion we drank had been the real thing, then it would have been the end of Dad's pain. He would not have to suffer for us anymore. . . . Thank you Dad for the test and not letting us suffer."

In the United States, relatives of Temple members in Jonestown were becoming concerned. The parents of the boy whose paternity Jones claimed, having left the Temple, were trying every means possible of getting their son back. Finally, in November of 1978, Congressman Leo Ryan led a delegation to Guyana to investigate conditions and give those who wanted to leave the chance to do so. After a tense night and day, Ryan's delegation left with fourteen defectors. But as they were boarding planes at a nearby airstrip, the party was ambushed by Jones's security squad. Five were killed, including Ryan and one of the defectors. A dozen others were wounded. Meanwhile, in Jonestown, Jones was calling his people together.

"How much I have loved you," he began. "How much I have tried to give you a good life."

As his followers gathered at the pavilion, a woman cried out that the children deserved to live.

No, said Jones, they deserved peace. They should be the first to die. And so they were.

Satan: Agency Amok

Three years before the Guyana massacre, a psychiatrist whom Jim Jones had consulted diagnosed him as "paranoid with delusions of grandeur." (After the diagnosis Jones said that his mind had been found to be "in perfect working order.") Some two decades after his death, another psychiatrist concluded from studying his life that he was "demonstrably psychotic." There is no doubt that Jones was a con artist, an abuser of drugs, a cult leader in the most dangerous sense. And yet he was a father to thousands, most of whom put their complete trust in him and would not leave him. If he was indeed mad, it was with a madness that played itself out under the guise of generativity.

Such madness is difficult to explain, and it is not my intention to make yet another attempt. Rather, I hope to draw a lesson from it. I hope to illustrate one of the ways in which generativity can be corrupted—through the unchecked growth of agency.

Agency, you recall, is a term coined by the psychologist David Bakan, to represent the self-asserting, self-protecting, self-expanding existence of the individual. It manifests itself in the quest for power, in repression and control, in the formation of separations within and between persons. In the right amount, agency is not evil. It is in fact an essential ingredient of generativity—or so the research is indicating. Evil arises when agency, in the absence of communion, is free to roam. Then it runs amok, like a cancer.

Or like Satan (Bakan makes the comparison): the prince of darkness, the seducer, the sower of dissension, the lion who prowls about seeking whom he can devour. Satan tempts by offering dominion. He performs signs and miracles; people fall down and pay him homage.

The story of Satan begins when he is cast out of heaven and forced into a separate existence. The story of Jim Jones begins the same way. As a child, he is expelled by circumstances from his home and called the "white trash" of his neighborhood. He becomes an outcast. In his isolation, Satan seeks to become master of the world; in his, Jones tries to find a world to master. He does so by forming separations. He collects followers, removes them from their environment, places them in an enclosure, and tries to exert power over them—to become their God.

Some interpreters in the early centuries of Christianity claimed that Satan's original sin consisted of trying to convince his fellow angels that he had created himself. "Creating himself" may be an apt description of Jones, who was never fathered in the psychological sense of the word, never nurtured or mentored by a person of his own sex. (It was older women who were present at key developmental moments.) Jones's father was powerless, barely able to breathe, almost nonexistent. When Jones rejected his "sky God," it was for the same reason of impotence. As he told his congregation in California, "You prayed to your sky God and he never heard your prayers. You asked and begged and pleaded in your suffering, and he never gave you any food. He never gave you a bed, and he never provided a *home.*" Like his father, this God just wasn't "there."

And so Jones sought to fill the void. All the things that the sky God had not given his congregation, he said, "I, *your socialist worker God,* have given you." In contrast to the generative men studied by criminologist Shadd Maruna (Chapter 5)—men who talked of *surrendering* to a "higher power"—Jones sought to *become* a higher power, indeed to become the very highest one.

If one is to draw a lesson from the life of Jim Jones, a place to start is his forming of enclosures. The pattern began with the pets that he caged and the playmates that he took to the barn loft behind his house. It continued in his adulthood when he led his family to Brazil and, later, his flock to rural California. Jones broke the pattern when he moved the headquarters of People's Temple to San Francisco, but reestablished it when he found the most remote place imaginable for his final move. Generative adults create enclosures too, and they too exercise control over them. But they know the day will come when they open the gate and release their creations, and from the beginning they prepare for that day.

Not only did Jones separate his congregation from the world, he separated its members from one another. Though People's Temple gave the impression of being a single organism at peace with itself, it was as divided internally as it was cut off externally. Jones broke up natural family units and played one member off against another. He divided in order to conquer. In the aftermath of Guyana, one of the survivors described the results: "The last person you felt like trusting was somebody else from Jonestown."

Once people were in an enclosure, Jones would not let them go. He never released his adult children; he sought rather to bring them to Guyana. Nor did he let go of those who left the Temple. He stalked them, manipulated their guilt, threatened to kill them. When a member of the Temple's planning committee broke away, he ranted, "How can she do this to me after all I have done for her?" When her husband also left, Jones suffered a "heart attack" almost every night—and made sure the man knew of his condition. (These were the parents of the child Jones claimed as his.) For Jones, losing followers was like losing a piece of himself. A defection was a personal betrayal.

Approaching 40, a time when many men moderate agency with communion, Jones became even more repressive and controlling. Feeling his "children" slipping away (that feeling is inevitable as agency becomes corrupt), he tightened his grip even more. In California, he penetrated their bodies, claimed their children, appointed guards whose job it was to keep "family" in as well as "enemies" out. In Guyana, he confiscated passports, cut off telephone lines, terrified with punishments, drugged malcontents. On Jonestown's last day, he controlled the "voluntary" drinking of cyanide. No one was to decline the poison.

The repression and control of agency also characterized the way Jones *knew*, just as it has the depictions of Satan's knowledge. Throughout history, in fact, great knowledge has been attributed to Satan, much of it psychological in nature. The knowledge gives him the ability to prey on the minds of others, to be a tempter and a deceiver. With his legions of demons, the stories say, he can be anywhere and everywhere in a single instant. Jim Jones also tried to be anywhere and everywhere. He established interrogation committees, built a watchtower, ordered the sifting of garbage, censored mail, and forced the public revelation of private feelings. This was not the empathic knowing of communion, but the divisive knowing of agency. It was a declaration that Jones owned everyone's thoughts.

Jones knew *himself* in the same agentic way. In terms I have used earlier, he was full of immature defense mechanisms—denial, for example (the darkness of the Satan image), and certainly projection (Satan as father of lies). Jones saw his own homosexual impulses as residing in everyone else, declaring himself on one occasion to be the Temple's only heterosexual. He saw his own internal fears as the Temple's external enemies and at one point the Bomb. He turned his own suicidal tendencies into the wish of his followers to die. Full of inner division, Jones could not "talk" to his inner places, could not open the secret ones to contact. He lacked the intimacy within.

From the life of Jim Jones we can learn much about unrestrained agency, and especially about its warning signs: The sense of being an outcast. The lust for power and the desire to master. The gathering of followers, the separating and enclosing of them, the desire to control their every move. The sowing of division under the appearance of unity. The mental manipulation, the deception (including self-deception), and the drawing of veneration to oneself. Finally, the "wages of sin": death.

Without using the terms "agency" and "communion," and without using the imagery of Satan, psychiatrist Anthony Storr observed the pattern I've described not only in Jim Jones, but in another "father," David Koresh, who in 1993 led a mass suicide, this time by fire, in Waco, Texas. Eighty-six perished on that occasion, twenty-two of them children. Agency also had its way with the twentieth century's dictators, who were ruthless in their pursuit of power. According to Storr:

> Dictators cannot afford the luxury of friends. Although they may marry and rear families, they depend primarily upon the plaudits of the unknown multitude rather than on true affection from intimates to maintain their self-esteem. It is not surprising that leaders of this type become suspicious, often to the point of paranoia. . . .

If a dictator is to hold on to power even when the country is in trouble, he must ensure that he is totally in control and that no rival has a chance of supplanting him. To do so requires the apparatus of informers, secret police, and spies which is so characteristic of dictatorial regimes. . . . Paradoxically, the "friends" and allies on whom a normal leader might depend for advice and support during crises, often constitute the greatest threat.

Like Jim Jones, dictators often perpetrate their evils under the guise of generativity. Adolf Hitler saw the Third Reich as his gift to downtrodden generations of Germans, the legacy the young would inherit. In 1942, a German officer executing gypsies, Jews, partisans, and "other such riff-raff" on a daily basis wrote to his commander about building "a more beautiful and eternal Germany for our children and our children's children." Another officer wrote to his children directly, "You can trust your Daddy. He thinks about you all the time and is not shooting immoderately." Decent men are not immune to this kind of thinking. Trying in 1953 to comprehend a world in which two superpowers suddenly possessed the hydrogen bomb, United States President Dwight Eisenhower wrote a memo describing circumstances in which "we would be forced to consider whether or not our duty to future generations did not require us to initiate war at the most propitious moment that we could designate."

Rarely in history does the figure of Satan appear as a father. We hear of "God the Father" but not "Satan the Father"—except as the father of lies. Jim Jones appeared to be a father, but in the end he was not a father at all. His generativity was a lie. Despite his preaching about socialism, he never decentralized authority in People's Temple, never created the kind of organization that could survive his death. He never groomed successors; he had them practice suicide. I had always thought of cloning as the ultimate form of agentic reproduction, but what Jones did went beyond cloning. His "children" were not *copies* of him; they *were* him, and they were never released. From the standpoint of reproduction, this was not reproduction at all. It was a fulfillment of the ominous words of David Bakan, "When the agentic is unmitigated by the communion feature, the tendency toward infanticide arises."

The life of Jim Jones tells us in an unforgettable way about the deception and delusion that can be involved in generativity. In the absence of communion, agency ran amok in his life—a corruption of fatherhood, a tragedy for children, a cautionary tale on the Generative Way.

The Lack of Agency

A list of generativity's corruptions could easily fill a book the size of this one. They occur in all the domains of generativity and at every step of the Way. At the very outset, a meeting with the past can be compliant when it ought to be resistant. The voice that comes further on can beckon from where Jim Jones's did and lead in the same direction. Blending can be as manipulative as Frank Lloyd Wright's was at Taliesin: "A perfect democracy flourishes here at the Fellowship. When I'm hungry, we all eat." Selection can turn into eugenics, compulsory sterilization, euthanasia, the Final Solution. Release can be corrupted too, as when a teacher clings to students in order to steal their energy and skills. And so can outcome: not liking how their children turn out, parents write wills to punish them, even control them from the grave. There is no stretch of the Generative Way, no phase of the generative process, immune to the possibility of corruption.

Not all of generativity's corruptions, of course, fit the description of agency amok. Sometimes a *lack* of agency allows evil to flourish. (Remember that buffers express agency.) For generations in one family—no one knows how many—fathers abused their daughters. A granddaughter in her early 20s speaks of the "deafening silence" that covered "years and years of rape":

> My family acted as if nothing ever happened. It was as if no one knew how to end the madness. He was just dear old Grandpa. We all got together on holidays. He was at my graduation. We were a normal, happy family on the outside. We just didn't talk about all the divorces, the alcohol and drug problems, the grandchildren that didn't finish high school or ended up in a psychiatric facility. I believe everyone knew of the horrors in that house, but no one stopped the pain. That silence tied everyone to the crime. That silence keeps everyone quiet still today.

A similar silence occurred among Holocaust bystanders, write Ernst Klee and his colleagues:

Many were only small cogs in the overall murder machinery, for example people who assisted in transporting the victims or cordoning off the execution areas. . . . Think of the army chaplains who looked on while children died in the Byelaya-Tserkov region of the Ukraine and merely compiled reports "so that no more would be said about the situation." . . . To say nothing of those who gawped [*sic*] at the murder of the Jews out of curiosity or watched stunned.

How do people become cogs in a murder machine? Often participation begins with an insignificant gesture, a small bit that multiplies in significance—the dark side's butterfly effect. Participation continues because cogs are prevented from seeing what the entire machine is doing. Or they undergo psychological change and choose not to see. According to Ervin Staub, a psychologist who has studied genocide:

Small, seemingly insignificant acts can involve a person with a destructive system: for example, accepting benefits provided by the system or even using a required greeting, such as "Heil Hitler." Initial acts that cause limited harm result in psychological changes that make further destructive actions possible. . . . In the end people develop powerful commitment to genocide or to an ideology that supports it.

Seemingly insignificant acts play a role in the buffering of evil as well—bits of agency that throw a monkey wrench into the machine of destruction. In his studies Staub was impressed by how often heroic resistance to genocide began with a small initial act. People who intended to hide a family for just a few days remained committed to their protection for years. Rescuers who started out by helping a friend ended by helping strangers. The movie *Schindler's List* tells the true story of a Nazi whose small acts of kindness on behalf of Jews working in his factory escalated into the risking of his life and the sacrifice of all his possessions to save more than a thousand of them. Especially if it comes in the beginning of a destructive sequence, resistance breaks a momentum, says Staub. It forces perpetrators to look at their actions from a different perspective, to have some doubts about what they are doing, to worry, even, about retaliation.

In Le Chambon, France, villagers saved the lives of several thousand Jews, most of them children, by hiding them in their homes and sending them into a nearby forest when a raid was coming. Their willingness to sacrifice their lives impressed would-be perpetrators. Staub cites P. P. Hallie:

> As the Resistance in Le Chambon developed, a curious phenomenon was taking place there: many of the Vichy police were being "converted." . . . Even as the official policy of the Vichy toward Le Chambon and the Jews was hardening, *individuals* among the police and the bureaucrats of Vichy were more and more frequently resisting their orders to catch or hurt people who had done no visible harm to anyone. They found themselves helping those who were trying to save these innocent, driven creatures. Caring was infectious.

Not only did the evil of genocide begin with bits, so did resistance to it. In the end, the villagers of Le Chambon stood up when they could have stood by. They had no lack of agency.

11

Of Skin and Spirit

LET US GO now to the top of a mountain, there to gain the sweeping perspective to which the subject of this book impels us. I want to tell the story of generativity on our planet, and gather from it a sense of where we have been as a species and where we might be going. The mountain I have in mind happens to be on the moon, for it is only from far away that we can see the earth as a single entity. And there it is: set against the blackness of outer space, a perfect sphere of blue covered by streaks and swirls of white. Beneath the white, broad splotches of reddish gray—the continents. Four and a half billion years ago, that earth was nothing more than a fiery mass being formed out of debris from the original Big Bang. And the moon on which we stand had just crashed into it and fallen into orbit.

Half a billion years after the moon's impact, a tiny patch of life came into being near the earth's surface, and in no time at all it was spreading rapidly. Eventually it took the form of animals that swam in the sea and walked on the land and flew in the air—and bore offspring. It took the form of plants that stood and swayed in the same media—and dropped seeds. All of these creatures, all of life in fact, occupied a narrow band between the bottom of the earth's oceans and the underside of its atmosphere. That band was like a membrane covering the blue sphere. It was a skin, a thin skin—the earth's "biosphere."

Had we been on our mountain one fine lunar day just a few years ago, we would have witnessed something extraordinary. We would have seen a small object come from the direction of the earth and land on the plain beneath our feet. We would have watched a two-footed creature step out of the object, putter around a bit, and then leave. Several more visits would have followed; and then, mysteriously, they would have ceased. Perhaps we would have climbed down from our mountain and gone through the debris left by the earthlings. But even had we not, we would have come to an inescapable conclusion: there was not only life on the planet out there, but intelligent life. Not only had the planet grown a skin; it had developed a mind. And we would have wondered: how could a big round rock, half covered with water, produce first one and then the other?

No one on the moon could have answered that question, and no one on earth could have either. We do not yet understand the origin of life and the emergence of thought, and perhaps we never will, but we live every day with the result of those two remarkable births. We *are* the result of those two remarkable births. The second is particularly intriguing, for it's becoming independent of the first. By that I mean that we humans now use our minds to do things that are biologically useless. We drink in beauty, we make music and dance, we piece together the story of our origins, we determine what is good and evil, we weave electronic internets, we send probes into the universe, and we call the earth with its sensitive skin our Mother. Other living creatures have a kind of consciousness—even plants "know" where the sun is—but only we humans puzzle over the meaning of consciousness. We do not need to do these things to stay alive, yet we do them anyway. Somewhere along the line, in other words, we developed an interior life, a subjectivity; we became the planet's "noosphere"—its mind, its soul, its spirit. And in life of its collective spirit there was the same pattern as in the life of its collective skin. Both skin and spirit stayed alive through the birth, growth, reproduction, and death of individuals. That, in essence, is the story of generativity on our planet.

The Earth's Skin

But let us look more closely. Among the oldest rocks on earth are some from Greenland that are nearly four billion years old and some from Australia that are close to three and a half billion. Both contain evidence of life. Where that life came from, and how it got there, no one can say. No one has been able, at least not yet, to start life in a laboratory. But we can be quite certain that life has been present on our planet for most of its existence, and that in the beginning it encountered some very extreme conditions, whether of heat or of cold.

The Australian rocks contain fossils of different types of bacteria. Descendants of these one-celled creatures survive yet today, and some in fact live within our bodies, helping *us* to live. Studying these descendants, we can imagine what the earth's skin was like in the beginning, when it was almost entirely bacteria. Those were wild, promiscuous times, at least in the thinking of some biologists. Bacteria penetrated each others' membranes and transferred genes with abandon. Some water-using bacteria created the atmosphere of blue and white we see from the moon today, the one that earthlings breathe so readily, craving the oxygen the bacteria put there. About two billion years ago (a very rough estimate), bacteria spun off a new kind of cell, one with vestiges of other cells inside. This new kind of cell sequestered its genes in a kind of inner sanctum known as a nucleus. The results were staggering. Programmed death entered the biosphere, as did sex, and the stage was set for the kind of reproduction we know today—set, in other words, for *biological* generativity. "Old" life continued to perpetuate itself the bacterial way, but "new" life adopted a different strategy. It built individual creatures to be temporary carriers of itself and focal points of replication. It built these creatures the way an egg builds a chicken, the point of the chicken being to make more eggs and then die.

Chickens, of course, were a long time coming. In the fossil record we find the first evidence of animals a little over half a billion years ago. They were small, sea-dwelling creatures who eventually took to the land and evolved into dinosaurs and mammals and a whole host of other creatures. Sixty-five million years ago, perhaps after the impact of a massive asteroid, the dinosaurs became extinct and the mammals became more numerous. Our immediate mammalian ancestors appeared about four million years ago in the form of little apelike hominids that trotted around on their hind legs. It took them about two million years to evolve into the first members of the *Homo* genus, and roughly another two to become *Homo sapiens*—human beings, us. The last transition occurred in Africa about 200,000 years ago.

By the time of the dinosaurs and the mammals, *parental* generativity had come into being. A block of sandstone from 75 million years ago contains the fossils of a nine-foot dinosaur sitting on a nest of eggs. Reluctant to leave the nest, the mother—or father—may have been engulfed in a sudden, giant sandstorm. Fossilized mud over three and a half million years old contains a tale just as extraordinary—two sets of hominid footprints, one larger and one smaller, proceeding side by side. The larger may have been left by an adult and the smaller by a juvenile walking next to the adult.

After that history-making walk, some hominids went on to develop intense parental commitments. Instead of leaving children they had weaned from the breast to fend for themselves—the way baboons do, for example—humans kept them and provided food for them. From the dawn of our species, it seems, we've had protective adults, male and female, walking next to their children and feeding them long after weaning.

As parental generativity was developing, so too was *technical.* Our hominid ancestors probably used sticks to unearth edible roots, as well as rocks to crack nuts and hard-shelled fruits. They also *made* tools: stones that were split and used for cutting and scraping have been dated as far back as two and a half million years.

Over time, these early tools (or pre-tools) turned into others. An excavation in Kenya suggests that 700,000 years ago, a precursor to *Homo sapiens* was using a kind of template to make axes of the same length but of different breadths—an early attempt at mass production. These technicians belonged to a species called *Homo erectus,* and although they must have done some teaching (or pre-teaching), they did not talk. Pointing and gesturing were the most likely form of communication.

As the making of tools became more complicated, however, hand signaling must have become more cumbersome, for it interfered with the work that was literally *at* hand. Some teachers must have tried something different. They must have tried to communicate with mouth noises—the "sounds of apprenticeship," say James Burke and Robert Ornstein, who have written extensively on the history of technology and consciousness. Slowly, very slowly, the shape of the head and mouth changed to accommodate these sounds. The tongue became more flexible. The bones of the skull got lighter and opened up space for the expansion of the brain. Our ancestors developed the capacity for speech.

These developments, let us remember, took place over hundreds of thousands of years, the time frame required by natural selection. Once humans became facile with their tools and their tongues, however, once crafts were being passed from one generation to the next, the pace of change quickened. Years of evolution were no longer counted in the hundreds of thousands, but in the tens, and then in the *tenths.* But then this was a new kind of evolution. It was no longer biological. It was technical.

As humans moved out of Africa, they brought their tools and their teaching with them. Sometime around the end of the last Ice Age, having trekked all over the earth, they turned from a nomadic existence to a settled one. Instead of looking for food, they started to grow it. Instead of chasing animals, they began to domesticate them. Towns and cities sprang up. Commerce developed, and with it ever more technologies. "The town now included herdsmen, ploughmen, oxmen, fishermen, butchers, brewers, bakers, boatmen, farmers, gardeners, builders, carpenters, potters, and weavers, as well as those dedicated to the production of luxury items, like jewelry and oil lamps," write Burke and Ornstein. Some of the artifacts survive to this day, and some of the tools that made them. But the words of the teachers, the sounds of apprenticeship, do not. Their preservation would await the most incredible tool of all: writing.

Writing may have originated some ten to twelve thousand years ago with small clay tokens that stood for particular commodities—a cylinder for an animal, a sphere for a bushel of grain, and so on. To keep track of their possessions, the Sumerians (living in what is now Iraq) placed such tokens inside sealed "envelopes" of clay. Then someone started pressing the tokens against the wet clay on the outside of the container to indicate what was inside. It was a short step to the realization that the tokens on the inside were no longer needed.

Transitions followed that made writing more manageable, first to simpler kinds of picture notation, then to symbols based on the sounds of words, not what they represented. The earliest writing based on sounds is found on rock faces outside an ancient turquoise mine in Sinai, and is thought to be thirty-six hundred years old. Sound-writing also appeared in Phoenicia (modern Lebanon) about three thousand years ago, or roughly 1000 B.C.E. The Phoenicians were probably the ones who brought it to the Greeks, who created letters for vowels as well as consonants and strung them together from left to right, making processing easier for the left hemisphere of the brain (so we know today). The Greeks named their letters *alpha, beta,* and so on. As far as we can tell, their invention of the alpha-bet was unique; all subsequent ones are derived from theirs.

Imagine what happened to technical generativity once teaching was preserved in writing, and imagine what happened two thousand years later (earlier in China and Korea) when writing was preserved in printing. In 1450, when Johannes Gutenberg made an alphabet out of interchangeable pieces of metal and inserted them into a converted winepress, there were no printed texts in Europe. By 1500 there were twenty million books in thirty-five thousand editions. No innovation in history had spread so far and so fast. Now teachers could extend their reach farther than ever before. Now learners could absorb instruction on their own, reading—even as you are now—in private, at a distance from their instructor.

It would take a library of books (or a small box of compact discs) to contain the whole story of humans' technical ingenuity. One section of the library (or one disc) would tell of arches and domes and columns and buttresses—and the wonderful cantilevers of Frank Lloyd Wright. Another would display finger drawings on cave walls and brush strokes on canvas—and the little cubes with which Georges Braque and Pablo Picasso launched modern art. Yet another would portray the swaying of bodies, the tapping of feet, the movement of hands—and the powerful contortions of Martha Graham. The library would speak of mental tools as well, such as the statistics that came into being during Florence Nightingale's time and helped her wage war on the conditions that bred disease, or the free association and dream analysis that formed the basis of Sigmund Freud's psychoanalysis. Nor would the instruments of evil be ignored, neither the weapons nor the strategies of destruction, for they too have resulted from the technical ingenuity of *Homo sapiens.* The library would follow innovation down to the present day, when physical and mental tools, when "hardware" and "software," have combined once again, this time to create an electronic "web" for the worldwide communication of thought.

A special place in this library of technology would have to be reserved for the Dutch toolmakers of the seventeenth century, the ones who crafted the optical instruments that enabled us to know the earth as we do today. One of their creations, a spyglass, inspired Galileo to make a telescope for the heavens; it gave him a close-up of the very moon from which the perspective of this chapter is taken. Galileo learned that its surface was not smooth, as had been thought, but craggy and mountainous, as we know now. The same instrument showed him a transit of Venus, proving that the planets did indeed orbit the sun, as Copernicus had said. It showed him more stars than anyone had imagined, revealing a whole new setting for planet earth. Later, Leeuwenhoek's microscope revealed the subtleties of its skin. For the very first time, a human being saw bacteria, one of the biosphere's earliest life-forms.

Its Spirit

Libraries, of course, contain much more than the story of humanity's toolmaking. They devote entire wings to history and literature, to art and music, to law and morality, to philosophy and religion, to "pure" science and "pure" mathematics. This is the stuff of the earth's noosphere, its spirit, the milieu in which *cultural* generativity takes place.

And tools were instrumental in its creation. According to Burke and Ornstein, the Greeks could conceive of "atoms," elementary particles that combine and recombine to form the material world, because they had the alphabet, whose elementary letters combine and recombine to form a written language. And it must be more than coincidence that figures like Moses, the Buddha, Confucius, Aristotle, Jesus, and Muhammad appeared all over the world within the same narrow band of time—the very time when the technologies of trade and travel, and especially of written communication, were beginning to spread like wildfire. Think of the ideas that were then introduced: justice, enlightenment, wisdom, truth, redemption, transcendence, and in many places the metaphor of the Way. Some of these ideas came before the technologies of communication, some came after, but all came in the same great wave. The ideas had an impact on earth as great as the moon's original one, or that of the asteroid that may have wiped out dinosaurs sixty-five million years ago. All of a sudden the earth had inner experience, subjectivity, self-consciousness. At least in one place, the universe had thought within itself.

When did the impact that created the noosphere come? *Very* recently. If the earth's existence were collapsed into a single year, it would have been born on January 1. Signs of a biosphere would have appeared around the first of March, just in time for spring. But dinosaurs would not have been sitting on their eggs until the middle of December, and hominids would not have been fashioning tools until New Year's Eve, just a few hours before midnight. And if you were looking for "pure" thought, and if you wanted your proof for its existence in writing, you would have to wait until 11:59.

Thought has gone on quite a journey in that last cosmic minute, and so has inner experience, although it is very difficult to follow the path they took, even with the trail left by writing. To *remember* the path is what I really mean to say, for early ways of thinking are nearly impossible to reexperience. The reason is that they become incorporated into later ones, like the waters of a stream that flow into a river, or the ideas of a child that become adult. In their new milieu, the original water, or the "child within," become lost. So a "paleontology of consciousness" (a term of the psychologist Julian Jaynes) is far more difficult to accomplish than a paleontology of bones and tools. Can we in the West, for example, really imagine a consciousness before it had ideas like self and identity?

Some of the earliest Western thinkers talked as if life had crossed a great divide when the noosphere appeared. Plato was so impressed by the world of ideas that he said it existed in its own right, eternal, unchanging, and more real than the world we see. Plato was a dualist; he saw mind and body as two separate things. Today, more thinkers are likely to be monists, seeing mind and body as two aspects of the same thing. Monist or dualist, one can be equally awestruck by the emergence of thought on earth, by the epiphany of all that I am referring to as "mind," "soul," and "spirit."

Monist or dualist, one can also marvel at how intricately body and mind dovetail, especially when it comes to culture. Frank Lloyd Wright designs cantilevers, then talks about "truth" in architecture, about materials representing themselves and nothing else. Pablo Picasso and Georges Braque paint with little cubes, and in so doing give birth to "abstract" art. Martha Graham creates a new repertoire of movement, then reflects that performing it requires "vision" and "faith" and "desire." Florence Nightingale invents the bar graph, spells out nursing procedures in intricate detail, then describes the character of the "ideal" nurse. And as he develops techniques like free association and dream analysis, Freud releases into the noosphere ideas such as "ego" and "id," "conscious" and "unconscious"— concepts as real as any oxygen released by the earth's earliest organisms.

We live at a fascinating point in the history of our planet because its newly arrived noosphere is becoming independent of its biosphere, and cultural evolution independent of biological. We still need the bacteria that were there at the beginning; without them we would not *be,* much less *be thinking.* The earth's spirit still needs its skin. But the propagation of spirit—its birth, growth, reproduction, and death—proceeds in a different way from the propagation of skin. (Or, as Plato said, pregnancy of the soul is different from pregnancy of the body.) Darwin's *idea* did not spread because he sired more children. It spread in some of the ways I have tried to describe in this book.

This spreading, which I have called cultural generativity, would astonish us were we not so accustomed to it. Today, we are able to "take in" presences from the distant past, to "ingest" and "digest" them—and create our very selves in the process. We are also able to *be* a presence that is taken in (incorporated, identified with) by others far into the future. Not very long ago, this kind of transmission was unknown to this planet. Without writing, it might be unknown today. But it is more than known today; it is happening all around us, and all the time. We move about in the noosphere as comfortably as we do in the biosphere. And we breathe in its influence as easily as we do oxygen.

The Secret of Infertility

There is a detail in the story of generativity that is easily overlooked when standing on the moon. It is a particular pattern: the curtailing of biological generativity as parental, technical, and cultural generativity come into existence. Somewhere along the line, for example, a biological mechanism arose that suppressed ovulation in nursing mothers. Biological generativity was held in check "so that" (a storyteller's phrase) parental generativity could come along. Call it the human *secret of infertility:* it is seen most clearly in the way our genes time the sequence of birth, growth, reproduction, and death. No other species allots its years the way we do. None devotes so much biological time to infertility.

During the course of life, our bodies go through three major periods, two of which are sterile. The first stretches from conception to the time when we become sexually mature and able to reproduce. The second covers the adult years in which we are biologically fertile. And the third spans the "postreproductive" years, the time when childbearing is over. Biologically, that final period is as distinctive to humans as their upright posture and their big brains. It's an odd appendage to the life cycle, something like a third leg growing out of the trunk of our bodies. And, in one sense, that's exactly what the postreproductive years are—a third leg on the journey through life.

Humans have the capacity to live an astounding number of years after they stop having children. The pattern is clearest in women: they are about 50 when they experience menopause, yet they live close to 30 years after that. (The program for men calls for them to lose their fertility more gradually.) Our closest living relatives are the chimpanzees, yet their biological plan is quite different. Female chimpanzees appear to be fertile almost to the end of life. Some who reach their 40s experience the same hormonal change as human women in the midst of menopause, but this chimpanzee menopause comes at the equivalent of 80 or 90 human years. Since the biological goal of any species is to reproduce, it seems odd for humans to "waste" so many years on nonreproductive activities. Why the extra leg?

Some anthropologists speculate that because childbirth became increasingly hazardous as women grew older, there was evolutionary pressure for fertility to end. That way mothers could take care of the children they already had and bring them to reproductive age. They could also take care of their children's children. Among macaque monkeys, a grandmother high on the dominance ladder is often able to obtain for her grandchildren a higher position than they would otherwise have. Among langurs, grandmothers will defend a young grandchild against the attacks of a new dominant male even though the infant's own mother will not. If having grandmothers is adaptive for monkeys, it was probably even more so for humans, whose young need protection for many more years.

Other anthropologists emphasize the development of technical generativity. As hominid brains became larger, they say, parents became smarter. They had more to teach their children. Gradually, the length of childhood increased, giving the young more time to learn. Adulthood lengthened too, giving the old more time to teach them: where dependable fruit trees were located, where birds' nests and small game could be found, where streams ran, how to respond to natural disasters that occurred once in a lifetime, all the things that made a difference between living and dying. However it happened, *Homo sapiens* seems to have discovered that when children have the time to develop the potential in their brains, and when grandparents have the time to help them do it, the species gains a competitive edge.

Infertile years, in other words, give humans the opportunity to use the brain intergenerationally. It's not that we teach, learn, and create only outside the reproductive years; history says otherwise. But think of how much would never have come to pass, and how much would have been lost between the generations, if humans were having their first child at 5 and no one were surviving beyond 50—if the earth, in other words, had not discovered the secret of infertility.

A Generative Ethic

The story of generativity is not one we can take "from the beginning." We cannot, that is, explain the emergence of later forms ("higher" forms) in terms of genetic dispositions inherited from earlier forms ("lower" forms). The reason is that our ideas of what the beginnings are change constantly, not only because of new discoveries, but also because of changes in our present mood, changes which are then projected back in time. Simply put, we can imagine our origins, but we were not there to witness them.

Nor can we take the story of generativity "from the end," as we can the story of individual lives, because we do not yet know what the end will be. Life on our planet might well be snuffed out by a cosmic event totally beyond our control. It might well end through a miscalculation on our part. It might go on indefinitely. We have no way of knowing because we are still in the *middle* of the story. There are surprises yet to come.

As we live through our chapter of the story, however, we can do our bit to shape its outcome. At various times and places Erik Erikson spoke of generativity as an ethical orientation, and scholars have since drawn sweeping pictures of "generative man" or "generative humanity" as ethical ideals. A few are now saying very specifically, as John Snarey does, that generativity entails "sociomoral commitments that are freely made, but ethically binding." Generativity may fill a void in us, in other words, but that is not the point. It may enhance our self-esteem or psychological "well-being" (research has consistently shown that it does), but neither is that the point. The point is that, self-esteem or not, psychological well-being or not, we who inhabit the earth have a moral obligation to act on behalf of future generations.

Some psychologists are now bringing this conviction to their counseling. Struck by the fact that generative concerns have been "almost dormant" in family therapy, David Dollahite, Brent Slife, and Alan Hawkins propose an approach that bypasses today's medical model for a moral model. "Generative counseling," they say, encourages choice on behalf of the next generation. It reinforces convictions in that regard and offers reminders of responsibility. "One does not care for the next generation because one is attempting to benefit oneself; one cares for another because one *ought* to care for another, even if that caring entails self-sacrifice or suffering."

If we can approach psychotherapy with a generative ethic, so can we the many dilemmas facing humanity today. We have in the twentieth century opened the atom as the fisherman did the copper bottle: how do we now reap the benefits of nuclear energy while making the world safe for the nuclear family? We have opened the gene as well, and we can ask a similar question: how can we learn to control it, to rework it even, while respecting its power? In that effort we will need to realize, as the great moral teachers have done, that we have the ability to rise above the genetic nudges that evolutionary psychologists and sociobiologists tell us about, that we are indeed working with a new (and, yes, "higher") form of generativity.

Already we have taken the secret of infertility into our own hands with a conscious and very deliberate attempt at birth control. But we must not forget that the secret offers biological infertility *in exchange for* better parenting. And there is no reason why that parenting cannot include the children of others, cannot involve adopting them in every sense of the term, not only as mothers and fathers, but also as teachers, mentors, and guides. We need to put to good use those very "postreproductive" years that are now creating the world's Age Wave. And we need to address on behalf of children all the problems of the earth as a whole: global warming, deforestation, the taxing of resources, the loss of biodiversity, overpopulation, the quality of air and water.

The thinking we bring to these issues will have to be complex, for the issues involved are many, and their unraveling will require far more books than this one, and far more competence than its author's. What I can do is suggest that the work be done in the spirit of a generative ethic, one that flows from the astounding story of life on our planet.

12

The Gift

THERE IS A FAIRY TALE from India that sums up the message of this book. Like other stories I have passed on in these pages, it is not a tale for children, but rather for adults, especially those in the long, final leg of life's journey. An old grasscutter named Wali Dad comes to the point where he must do something with the pot of pennies he's been accumulating all his life. A simple man, content with his tiny hut, he can think of nothing that he wants for himself, so he goes to a jeweler and buys a golden bracelet. Then he asks a friend who is a merchant, "Who is the most beautiful and virtuous woman in the world?"

"The Princess of the East," says the merchant.

"Then take this bracelet to her. But do not reveal who has sent it." Now the land of the East is far away, but the merchant agrees to deliver the bracelet on his next trip there. When he arrives and gives the gift to the Princess, she is intrigued. Who is her secret admirer, and what sort of man is he? She decides to send a gift in return—some beautiful and expensive rolls of silk. The merchant brings them back to Wali Dad.

"And what am I to do with these?" the old grasscutter asks, for he has no need of them. He thinks about the matter for a while, and then he says, "Who is the most handsome and virtuous man in the world?"

"That would be the Prince of the West."

"Then take these silks to him."

So the merchant sets off in the opposite direction, travels a great distance, and eventually comes to the land of the West. Naturally, the Prince is surprised by the gift and curious about its sender. So he reciprocates with something finer.

"A dozen stallions?" asks Wali Dad when the merchant returns. "What am I to do with a dozen stallions? Take them to the Princess of the East!"

When the horses come prancing into her palace, the Princess is at a loss for a response. The King suggests that she end the affair by sending back a gift so magnificent that it will put her secret admirer to shame. They send off twenty mules loaded with silver.

But Wali Dad has no desire for wealth. "Take some of the mules for your trouble," he tells his merchant friend, "and deliver the rest to the Prince of the West!"

And the Prince refuses to be outdone. Soon a caravan of camels and elephants weighed down with precious gifts is headed back to Wali Dad's hut. No sooner does it arrive than Wali Dad sends it on to the Princess of the East.

At this point the King and Queen can come to only one conclusion: the mysterious admirer wants to marry their daughter. So they set out with the merchant to find him. As they draw near to Wali Dad's village, the merchant grows troubled. What will this procession of royalty think when they are led at last to a little hut and a withered old man within? He rides ahead and warns Wali Dad of what is imminent. Fearing humiliation, unable to accept what may be required of him, Wali Dad heads that night for a cliff, but cannot even bring himself to jump. He collapses on the ground, enveloped in darkness and despair.

Suddenly, there is a great halo of light that grows brighter and brighter. Two angelic beings appear. One touches Wali Dad's clothes, and they turn into elegant robes. The other touches his hut, and it turns into a palace. The next morning Wali Dad receives the King and Queen, the Princess, and their entire entourage. In the middle of a sumptuous feast, the King gives his enthusiastic consent to his daughter's marriage.

"Alas," says Wali Dad, "as you can see, I am too old to marry. But I know someone who would make a perfect husband for your daughter." He summons the Prince of the West, and soon the Prince and Princess fall in love. They marry in Wali Dad's palace and the families celebrate for days and days. When it's time for everyone to return home, the King and Queen, the Prince and the Princess, and thousands of their flag bearers salute Wali Dad, who salutes them back with a handful of grass he has cut that very morning. It is the sweetest and freshest grass he has ever smelled.

And so the tale ends. It's a story with a familiar ring: a man does his bit in the grand scheme of things, and in no time at all his tiny gesture multiplies in significance. It happens the way a butterfly's wings change the weather, or the way the Gospel's mustard seed grows: "It is the smallest of all the seeds, but when it has grown it is the biggest of shrubs and becomes a tree, so that the birds of the air can come and shelter in its branches." Wali Dad's golden bracelet, the fruit of his life, grows like that mustard seed. Sown in just the right place, it becomes rolls of silk, then a dozen horses, then twenty mules loaded with silver, then a caravan of camels and elephants bearing precious gifts. It leads to the union of a Princess and a Prince, of the far ends of the earth. The story of Wali Dad expresses a hope—and an imperative—for those of us who would travel the Generative Way. The hope is that something of value will emanate from our lives; the imperative, that we invest it wisely in future generations.

Let us look at the story in greater detail. The royal procession—King and Queen, Prince and Princess, thousands and thousands of attendants —is symbolic of the grand Procession of Life in which we all momentarily take part. Wali Dad is near the end of his individual life, and he reflects: What have all my pennies and all my years added up to? What difference have they made? How much have they counted? Now he selects, distilling the essence of who he has been. All that cannot be refined into gold is forgotten—all the guilt, all the regret, all the waste, all the anger and bitterness, all the lingering pain. And the resulting bracelet is invested wisely, at that point in Life where it will bear the most fruit. It is given to the Prince and Princess, who stand for the power of Life yet to be. But they cannot activate that power on their own. It takes someone who has gone before to provide a spark, and the spark that Wali Dad provides is nothing more nor less than the substance of his life.

Wali Dad's wisdom about where to invest stems from his acceptance of his own place in the life cycle, an acceptance Erik Erikson called "ego-integrity." Wali Dad is content with his life's work and with the house he has lived in. He does not wish to be young again. When he despairs, it is because he fears that he will have to step out of his place in the Procession of Life, lose the simplicity of his station, and be something he is not—a husband to a young Princess. When the angels touch and transform him, they do not give him a new nature but rather reveal his true nature. His virtue is indeed royal, his home a castle, and now it is clear to everyone, Wali Dad included. At the end of the story Wali Dad is what he has always been, a humble grasscutter, but that identity seems sweeter and fresher than ever. His acceptance of his place in Life is the source of his wisdom and generativity; and Life, which is about to leave him, pays him tribute for it.

What is the moral of Wali Dad's story? The lesson to be drawn from it? Actually, there are many. To be generative, "The Gift" suggests, we have to think and act in certain ways. We have to answer a call. We have to give away our pot of pennies. We have to unite the ends of the earth. We have to step aside. And through it all we must have faith in the great Procession of Life.

Answer the Call

The story of Wali Dad is set in motion when he takes his life savings and buys a golden bracelet. It begins with an initiative of his. But the critical point occurs when the initiative is with someone else. King, Queen, and Princess come with their entourage to his doorstep. They call, and he must respond.

Throughout this book I have tried to validate the scene at Wali Dad's door, to reestablish the authenticity of demands "from the outside," to resurrect the idea of identity as a calling, to bring out the receptive side of the Way. I would like to add here that "answering a call" is not the same as being "on call," a phrase that describes the state of bottom-line responsibility that is left as one moves on to grand-generativity. "Answering a call" refers to what a 60-year-old woman, just retired, said of the volunteer work she was beginning to do at a hospice: "There are so many needs, you see? I could very well join a bridge club, but I feel that this is what God wants me to do." It refers to what an 82-year-old woodworker meant when he said there were "things to do in this world that are necessary." To him, creating beauty—the kind only *he* could create—was necessary. In these cases, there is identity in generativity, which one does not experience when merely being "on call."

When Wali Dad received his call, he was terrified, and there is a message here as well. Like him, we may feel inadequate to our summons. But what happened to Wali Dad on the edge of a dark precipice can happen to us too. Our "higher" nature, symbolized by the angels in Wali Dad's story, can take over. We can rise to the occasion, discovering within ourselves resources we never knew we possessed, bringing about what we could not have dreamed of had we simply been mere seekers of self-fulfillment. A call can get us up in the morning when self-fulfillment lets us sleep as late as we like.

Give Away the Pennies

A second moral may be drawn from the story of Wali Dad by looking into the nature of the wealth he gives away. In most tales of this type, the hero finds a treasure ready-made or receives it from a mysterious stranger. But Wali Dad comes by his wealth "the old-fashioned way," as the television commercial says. He earns it, each and every penny. What does this kind of treasure represent?

Let us begin literally, interpreting the money as . . . money. This interpretation is especially relevant today, when many in the forefront of the Age Wave are doing so well financially, and when children, as we have seen, are not. Wali Dad may have been saving his money for a rainy day, but that day never came, and now there is nothing he wants to buy. He does not believe he is "entitled" to what he has earned, nor does he feel guilty about having it when others do not. The point is that he does not cling to it. He invests it in people and in Life. Most of us would dispose of such resources in a will, but Wali Dad gives his gift well before a will would take effect. That enables him to see the outcome of his actions and to reap the inner benefits of the giving.

Wali Dad is selective, very selective, about where to invest his small fortune. He seeks out two people among all the earth's inhabitants who possess special qualities. They are *virtuous,* and if this story provides guidelines for our giving, it tells us to seek the good ground in the parable of the sower. It tells us not be taken in by appearances in the young but rather to see through their deceptions. The people Wali Dad chooses are also *virginal,* a Prince and Princess, not a King and Queen. So if our giving is to be generative, and not merely altruistic, it will bypass what is well established for what is coming into being. The Prince and Princess are likewise *vigorous.* They have energy as well as potential. They possess the power to multiply Wali Dad's investment. Not all of our giving, financial or otherwise, will follow this model, but that which is "generative" would do well to consider it.

But Wali Dad has accumulated more than material wealth, and so we must look deeper into his pot of pennies. In one sense, the pennies represent his hard-earned experiences, and in the story every one of them bears fruit. Wali Dad's treasure was collected in *his* hut, it reveals *his* history, it reflects *his* identity. So all of *him* becomes gold. This is the ideal that inspires generativity, especially near the end of life, though we know that the generative process entails far more waste than this fairy tale acknowledges.

In another sense, and at its deepest level, Wali Dad's action contains a moral for people of every age. "Give away the treasure" is not an ethical command but rather a formula for the regulation of the life we feel within us. If we try to cap that life, the story tells us, we will get no more. If we are afraid the golden tree will stop flowing, it will. So we are not to hide our treasure under manure or ashes—remember the hero of "The Shining Fish"?—and we are not to put our lamp under a basket. "You've got to give it away to keep it," says a motto from Alcoholics Anonymous. "The more you give, the more you've got to give." Even though Wali Dad earned every one of his pennies, he treated them as if he had received them from a stranger. By emptying himself, he created the space to receive more.

Unite the Ends of the Earth

Wali Dad's generativity is clearly "grand." He has come to the point in life where he no longer wants bottom-line responsibility, so he puts it in the hands of someone else, a younger man who travels from East to West and handles the increasingly complex process of gift giving. In this regard, Wali Dad acts more like a grandparent than a parent.

But Wali Dad's generativity is "grand" in another and more important sense. It is global in scope, uniting the far ends of the earth. The Princess of the East and the Prince of the West could not have been more different, coming from the distances they did. They must have been of different "races," but they were essentially alike, both virtuous. It is interesting that we hear nothing of Wali Dad's own children in the story. Was he married? Did he have any? The questions are irrelevant because he has overridden his "selfish" genes, overcome the "pseudo-speciation" that Erikson warned against, and identified with humanity as a whole. It's a realistic identification: in the midst of controversies about genetic differences, it is well to remember that over 99 percent of human DNA is identical. Not similar, but identical—exact copies carried by you and me and anyone on earth we can think of.

Early in the twenty-first century, when the human genome is completely mapped, we will know in finer detail just how identical we all are. We may realize that we are all descended from a few common ancestors. Scientists will be starting on similar maps of other species, both plants and animals. When we lay the maps side by side, we will see a new story emerge about the interconnectedness of all life-forms. We will be able to compare the genetic record, the one we carry in our bodies, with the fossil record, the one the earth carries in its. Then we shall see more clearly and "remember" more accurately the history of the planet's biosphere, that thin skin that supports its spirit, and we shall unite the ends of the earth in a far different way.

As the world gets smaller, its economies more interdependent, its communication faster and farther-reaching, the far ends of the earth are coming to our doorstep, as they did to Wali Dad's. Generativity cannot ignore their arrival. When you choose your generative acts, "The Gift" says, keep the global dimension in mind. Be highly selective, but make at least one of your efforts "grand."

Step Aside

Did you notice what Wali Dad did on the story's final morning? When the wedding and celebration were over, when everything was said and done, he went back to work. He cut some grass, plying his trade to the very end. No "retirement" for him.

But that detail is incidental to the story as a whole. In "The Gift," Wali Dad's crisis comes when he thinks he will have to marry the Princess and become a King, for he is clearly too old to do either. His crisis is resolved when he gains the resources to rise to one great generative moment. Once that moment has passed, however, Wali Dad's natural instincts take over. He steps aside, saying good-bye to the royal Procession of Life.

Stepping aside was not difficult for Wali Dad—he feared, in fact, that he would have to return to the mainstream—but it may be for us. We fear being *overthrown* by the next generation, being *put aside* in a corporate downsizing, say, before we are ready. We fear not being cared for in our waning years. Greed, too, is involved, not only the financial greed that makes us overstay our years in a high-paying job or resist a reconsideration of government entitlements, but also the greed for life, for the extra year or two that extraordinary medicine might bestow.

This book has not been the place to discuss the complex ethical issues involved in making way for the next generation, whether at the time of leaving a job or the time of dying, but it is the place to suggest that Wali Dad's is the spirit in which any decision about stepping aside should be made. The point of his story is that clinging to life will keep us from Life. This is true all along the Generative Way, but especially at its end, when one must finally yield to the inevitable succession of generations.

Have Faith in the Procession of Life

All of these difficult requirements of generativity—answering the call, giving away our treasure, uniting the ends of the earth, stepping aside—make no sense unless one trusts in the Procession of Life that is symbolized in "The Gift" by the royal entourage. For a few decisive moments, Wali Dad takes part in this procession, and then it leaves him behind. But his faith in it never wavers. How else could he give his gift with anonymity? How else could he be so peaceful at story's end? When Erikson speculated on reasons for adult failures in generativity, he included "the lack of some faith, some 'belief in the species,' which would make a child appear to be a welcome trust of the community." While it takes great faith to bring a child into the world, Wali Dad's faith is greater, for he puts his resources into someone else's children and through them into something as broad and communal as Life itself.

The faith that underwrites generativity is faith in Life, and not in any individual life. It's Life with a capital L, because it transcends particular life-forms. To one person that Life may be God, to another it may be Nature, to a third it may be the enduring value of Science, to a fourth it may be something else again. But unless our object of faith is transcendent, unless it came before us and survives our death, it cannot support generativity. Without such an object of faith, you cannot commit years of your life to an uncertain project or even complete the small piece of it that must be done each day. Nor can you release it into a threatening world or trust in its unseen fate.

Is this faith a "requirement" for generativity? Even though I have been speaking of it as such, it is more a description of the kind of thoughts that generative people have quite naturally. It is the conscious side of their unconscious life. It is what happens in their heads when life flows in and out of their hearts. Is the faith illusory? If it is, I have but one reply: put it in the drinking water. It's what enables people to make the transition from Me to Beyond Me.

Will the growing number of people in the second half of life—will any sizable number of us?—be able to make this transition? Be able to see our moral status as more than bearers of entitlements? I have no way of anticipating what will happen in the future; but if this book has a message, it is this: Wali Dad's pot of pennies was never his in the first place. Nor was ours ours. We received those resources from Life; and, one way or another, we must return them to Life. That is the meaning of Wali Dad's story, and that is the meaning of generativity—a word whose time has come.

Notes

Chapter One. The Idea Whose Time Has Come

Page

4   *"or win a race.":* B. Wischmeyer, *A Kid from Cleveland . . . in Ann Arbor* (Ann Arbor: Annen Press, 1996), p. 42.

4   *"and guiding the next generation":* E. Erikson, *Childhood and Society* (New York: Norton, 1950/1963), p. 267.

5   Two of my early critiques of self-fulfillment and self-actualization: J. Kotre, "Generative Humanity," *America,* December 20, 1975, pp. 434–437; J. Kotre, "Religion, Psychology, and the Sterile Self," *Commonweal,* May 12, 1978, pp. 295–300. Previously, Don Browning had analyzed concepts of the "good man" in psychoanalytic writings, including those of Erikson; see D. Browning, *Generative Man* (Philadelphia: Westminster, 1973).

5   J. Kotre, *Outliving the Self* (Baltimore: Johns Hopkins University Press, 1984; New York: Norton, 1996).

6   Aging of the population in Italy: A. Cowell, "Affluent Europe's Plight: Graying," *The New York Times,* September 7, 1994.

7   *"dead before birth.":* D. Cole, *After Great Pain* (New York: Summit, 1992), pp. 13 and 153.

7   *"no good to anybody.":* O. Lewis, *The Children of Sanchez* (New York: Random House, 1961), p. 370.

8   A recent therapeutic approach that is mindful of generative outlets: D. Dollahite, B. Slife, and A. Hawkins, "Family Generativity and Generative Counseling: Helping Families Keep Faith with the Next Generation," in D. McAdams and E. de St. Aubin (eds.), *Generativity and Adult Development* (Washington, DC: American Psychological Association, 1998).

8   *"It was all from me.":* Kotre, *Outliving the Self,* p. 43.

8   The United States secretary of defense is Robert McNamara. See R. McNamara, *In Retrospect* (New York: Times Books, 1995).

8   The scientist quoting the *Bhagavad Gita* is J. Robert Oppenheimer.

9   *"are reproduced in the baby.":* E. Erikson, *Gandhi's Truth* (New York: Norton, 1970), p. 193.

9   *"the part I was able to play.":* J. Kotre, "Late Adulthood," *Seasons of Life Television Series,* Program 5 (Ann Arbor: The University of Michigan; Pittsburgh, PA:

WQED; and Washington, DC: The Corporation for Public Broadcasting; 1990).

10   *"to be a part of life itself."*: The woodworker, George Nakashima, is quoted in J. Kotre and E. Hall, *Seasons of Life* (Boston: Little, Brown, 1990; Ann Arbor: University of Michigan Press, 1997), p. 385.

10   *"can a woman expect?"*: R. Coles, *The Old Ones of New Mexico* (Albuquerque: University of New Mexico Press, 1973), p. 59.

Chapter Two. What Is Generativity?

Page

11   *"providing for the next generation"*: D. McAdams and E. de St. Aubin, "A Theory of Generativity and Its Assessment Through Self-Report, Behavioral Acts, and Narrative Themes in Autobiography," *Journal of Personality and Social Psychology,* 1992, *62,* 1003–1015. Professional readers will also want to review D. McAdams, H. Hart, and S. Maruna, "The Anatomy of Generativity," in D. McAdams and E. de St. Aubin (eds.), *Generativity and Adult Development* (Washington, DC: American Psychological Association, 1998). *Generativity and Adult Development* is a superb collection of research on generativity, much of it interdisciplinary in nature.

11   *"responsibility for others."*: G. Vaillant and E. Milofsky, "Natural History of Male Psychological Health: IX. Empirical Evidence for Erikson's Model of the Life Cycle," *American Journal of Psychiatry,* 1980, *137,* 1348–1359.

11   *"outlive the self."*: J. Kotre, *Outliving the Self* (Baltimore: Johns Hopkins University Press, 1984; New York: Norton, 1996), p. 10. My description of generativity's four types first appeared in this book, and I have carried some of that description over into the present one.

Jerome Wakefield has identified *Outliving the Self*'s four types in Plato's *Symposium,* which postulates a "pregnancy of the body" (biological generativity), tending that which one brings forth (parental generativity), inventing and passing on skills (technical generativity), and creating wisdom, beauty, and virtue (cultural generativity). The latter two constitute "pregnancy of the soul." See J. Wakefield, "Immortality and the Externalization of the Self: Plato's Unrecognized Theory of Generativity," in McAdams and de St. Aubin, *Generativity and Adult Development.*

Researchers might also consult S. MacDermid, C. Franz, and L. De Reus, "Generativity: At the Crossroads of Social Roles and Personality," in McAdams and de St. Aubin, *Generativity and Adult Development.* MacDermid and her colleagues discuss the expressions of generativity in various roles and present data, mostly on women, that show the expressions vary. Their concept of "roles" is roughly equivalent to what I call "kinds," "types," or "domains."

12   *"He was perfectly normal."*: J. Kotre and S. Millett, "And Then We Knew," *Seasons of Life Audiotapes,* Program 3 (Ann Arbor and Washington, DC: The University of Michigan and the Corporation for Public Broadcasting, 1990).

13   *"any place prettier or nicer anywhere."*: R. Coles, *Migrants, Sharecroppers, Mountaineers* (Boston: Little, Brown, 1971), pp. 204–205.

14 *"was the truth.":* Kotre, *Outliving the Self,* p. 234.

14 *"he's going to be happy.":* Kotre, *Outliving the Self,* p. 245.

15 *"then you sleep well.":* Kotre, *Outliving the Self,* p. 245.

How should one classify material legacies, such as those commonly conveyed in wills? To determine what kind of generativity is involved in a particular gift, I would look at its beneficiary. If the legacy stays in the family, parental generativity is at work. If it goes beyond, the legacy enters the domain of cultural generativity.

16 *"stifled his generative potential.":* E. de St. Aubin, "Truth Against the World: A Psychobiographical Exploration of Generativity in the Life of Frank Lloyd Wright," in McAdams and de St. Aubin, *Generativity and Adult Development.* Except where noted, quotations from Wright and others come from B. Gill, *Many Masks* (New York: Ballantine, 1987).

19 Wright's "watch the genius" method: Gill, *Many Masks.*

20 *"What is immortal will survive.":* D. Hoppen, *The Seven Ages of Frank Lloyd Wright* (Santa Barbara: Capra Press, 1993), p. 37.

20 *"a full-fledged genius.":* M. Secrest, *Frank Lloyd Wright* (New York: Knopf, 1992), p. 83.

21 On Copernicus in relation to Ptolemy see H. Butterfield, *The Origins of Modern Science* (New York: Macmillan, 1956).

21 *"in the broadest sense.":* G. Sheehy, *New Passages* (New York: Random House, 1995), p. 412.

22 On feelings of immortality, see R. J. Lifton, "The Sense of Immortality: On Death and the Continuity of Life," in R. J. Lifton, (ed.), *Explorations in Psychohistory* (New York: Simon & Schuster, 1974), pp. 275–276.

On the relationship of generativity to immortality, see H. J. Berman, "Generativity and Transference Heroics," *Journal of Aging Studies,* 1995, 9, 5–11, and L. E. Thomas, "Transcending, Not Outliving the Self," *Journal of Aging Studies,* 1995, 9, 21–31. My reply to Berman and Thomas, entitled "Generative Outcome," appears in the same issue of the *Journal of Aging Studies,* pp. 33–41. There is also a Japanese story entitled "The Man Who Did Not Wish to Die" about a man who learns the wisdom of generativity only when he gives up the desire for immortality. The story is contained in A. Chinen, *Once Upon a Midlife* (New York: G. P. Putnam's Sons, 1992). Another treatment of generativity in relation to immortality appears in Jerome Wakefield's "Immortality and the Externalization of the Self," which I have already cited.

22 *"something I did on earth.":* S. Terkel, *Working* (New York: Pantheon, 1972), p. 589.

23 Generativity as a *stage:* An interview method has recently been devised for identifying ways of "resolving the crisis" of Erikson's seventh stage. On the basis of the interview, people are assigned to one of five generativity "statuses." See C. Bradley and J. Marcia, "Generativity-Stagnation: A Five-Category Model," *Journal of Personality,* 1998, 66, 39–64.

Generativity as a *relationship:* McAdams and de St. Aubin, "A Theory of Generativity."

24 Studies of men reaching a *stage* of generativity: Vaillant and Milofsky, "Natural History of Male Psychological Health." In this research, a man was determined

to have reached the stage of generativity if his interview protocol showed that he had assumed "sustained responsibility for the growth, well-being, and leadership of others." When the Harvard-educated men reached 60, somewhat different criteria for stage attainment were used by the researchers. See G. Vaillant, *The Wisdom of the Ego* (Cambridge: Harvard University Press, 1993).

24   Men and women with a generative *motive:* D. McAdams, *Power, Intimacy, and the Life Story* (Homewood, IL: Dorsey, 1985), pp. 269–272. Researchers measured generativity by scoring written accounts of future plans or "scripts." A high score was given to accounts "which evidenced a strong concern for establishing and guiding the next generation either directly (via caregiving, teaching, leading, mentoring, etc.) or indirectly (via contributing something that one has created to others or to a community at large, as in the case of literary, scientific, artistic, or altruistic contributions)."

24   G. Moran, "Cares for the Rising Generation: Generativity in American History 1607–1900," in McAdams and de St. Aubin, *Generativity and Adult Development.*

25   *"the colony's 'present state.'":* T. Breen, *Puritans and Adventurers* (New York: Oxford University Press, 1980), pp. 165 and 169.

25   *"generativity in that society.":* Moran, "Cares for the Rising Generation," p. 315.

26   *"in terms of scale—grandparents.":* Moran, "Cares for the Rising Generation," pp. 318–319. The historian Moran cites is J. Murrin, "Review Essay," *History and Theory,* 1972, 21, 226–272.

27   *"and impossible for many.":* Murrin, "Review Essay," p. 239, cited in Moran, "Cares for the Rising Generation," p. 322.

27   *"it leaves to its children.":* Bonhoeffer is quoted in Peterson, "Will America Grow Up Before It Grows Old?" *The Atlantic Monthly,* May 1996, 277, 55–86. Readers looking for more on the generativity of societies would do well to consider R. Bellah, R. Madsen, W. Sullivan, A. Swidler, and S. Tipton, *The Good Society* (New York: Knopf, 1991). Bellah and his colleagues call for a "politics of generativity" that is "concerned about the common good and the long run" (p. 279).

Chapter Three. Talking to Your Past

Page

31   My rendition of "The Fisherman and the Djinni" is drawn from several sources. John Payne's translation of the story, originally published in 1881, can be found in J. Campbell (ed.), *The Portable Arabian Nights* (New York: Viking, 1952). Sir Richard Burton's translation, a modification of Payne's, appeared in 1885; see R. Burton, *The Book of the Thousand Nights and a Night* (privately printed by the Burton Club, 1885). I also consulted N. Dawood (trans.), *The Thousand and One Nights* (New York: Penguin, 1954).

When Bruno Bettelheim interpreted "The Fisherman and the Djinni" in *The Uses of Enchantment* (New York: Knopf, 1976), he treated it as a fairy tale for children. He also changed the ending, having the fisherman toss the djinni back into the sea. In a deceptively simple and very wise book called *In the Ever After* (Wilmette, IL: Chiron, 1989), Allan Chinen stressed the age of the fisherman, considering the story an "elder tale" and drawing quite a different lesson from it. My interpretation, meant to bring out facets of generativity, is intended for adults of all ages.

34 *"means something in my future.":* J. Kotre, *Outliving the Self* (Baltimore: Johns Hopkins University Press, 1984; New York: Norton, 1996), pp. 66 and 80.

38 *"I can do it too.":* G. Vaillant, *The Wisdom of the Ego* (Cambridge: Harvard University Press, 1993), pp. 353 and 351. Vaillant observes that there are at least eighteen different definitions of the word *identification* alone and then goes on to present a lucid description of it and the other five *i*-words.

38 Readers familiar with the work of Daniel Levinson will recognize the changes in Herb Robinson's 28th year as an example of the Age 30 Transition. See D. Levinson, *The Seasons of a Man's Life* (New York: Knopf, 1978).

40 *"so much of him is me!"* J. Kotre, *Simple Gifts* (Kansas City: Andrews and McMeel, 1979), pp. 182–183.

41 "Robert Creighton" is a pseudonym. The first version of his life story, which appeared in *Outliving the Self*, was based on interviews conducted when he was 33 and 35. The present version incorporates an interview of Robert and his two sons that took place when he was 42.

47 *"creates a pearl.":* G. Vaillant, *Adaptation to Life* (Boston: Little, Brown, 1977), p. 7. Vaillant's work on defense mechanisms can be found in this book as well as in G. Vaillant, and E. Milofsky, "Natural History of Male Psychological Health: IX. Empirical Evidence for Erikson's Model of the Life Cycle," *American Journal of Psychiatry*, 1980, *137*, 1348–1359. Vaillant now believes that as a general rule defenses mature until about the age of 30; after that there is no consistent pattern. See *The Wisdom of the Ego*, p. 172.

48 Defense mechanisms as "handles" and "grips": There is a story called "The Tree of Sorrow" (I cannot remember where I first heard it) that illustrates what it's like to have mature defenses. In the story, everyone in the world is given the chance to pass by a certain tree, take one sorrow from their life, and hang it on a branch. One by one they file by, removing their deepest pain. But once the last has passed and all the sorrows of the world are hanging open to view, an unexpected announcement is made. Now everyone must pass the tree again, this time taking up one of the sorrows. All choose their own. They do so because their own sorrow is the one they can handle, the one on which they can get a grip, the one around which their defenses have matured.

49 The London attachment research: F. Fonagy, H. Steele, and M. Steele, "Maternal Representations of Attachment During Pregnancy Predict the Organization of Infant-Mother Attachment at One Year of Age," *Child Development*, 1991, *62*, 891–905.

51 Replications of attachment findings: M. van IJzendoorn, "Adult Attachment Representations, Parental Responsiveness, and Infant Attachment: A Meta-Analysis on the Predictive Validity of the Adult Attachment Interview," *Psychological Bulletin*, 1995, *117*, 387–403.

51 *"are reproduced in the baby.":* E. Erikson, *Gandhi's Truth* (New York: Norton, 1970), p. 193.

52 *"in their own childrearing behavior."*: J. Snarey, *How Fathers Care for the Next Generation* (Cambridge: Harvard University Press, 1993), p. 278. Snarey's book contains excellent summaries of research on positive modeling, negative modeling, and reworking.

52 Regarding child abuse: J. Kaufman and E. Zigler, "Do Abused Children Become Abusive Parents?" *American Journal of Orthopsychiatry,* 1987, *57,* 186–192; C. Widom, "Does Violence Beget Violence? A Critical Examination of the Literature," *Psychological Bulletin,* 1989, *106,* 3–28.

Chapter Four. Stopping the Damage

Page

54 Substantial portions of this chapter were excerpted and adapted from J. Kotre and K. Kotre, "Intergenerational Buffers: The Damage Stops Here," in D. McAdams and E. de St. Aubin (eds.), *Generativity and Adult Development* (Washington, DC: American Psychological Association, 1998).

54 My source for the story of Orestes and the house of Atreus is E. Hamilton, *Mythology* (New York: New American Library, 1958). It was originally called to my attention by Scott Peck in *The Road Not Traveled* (New York: Simon & Schuster, 1978). Peck, in turn, learned of it through the writings of Rollo May and T. S. Eliot.

56 Karen and Don's story was first told in J. Kotre and S. Millett, "And Then We Knew," *Seasons of Life Audiotapes,* Program 3 (Ann Arbor and Washington, DC: The University of Michigan and the Corporation for Public Broadcasting, 1990).

58 Buffering vs. reworking: In practice, the three responses to legacies received— repeating, reworking, and buffering—are not totally distinct. Indeed, I know of no "pure" cases of repeating or buffering, which is another way of saying that all legacies are, to a greater or lesser degree, reworked.

67 My account of Patty Crowley's role in the birth control commission is drawn from J. Kotre, *Simple Gifts* (Kansas City: Andrews and McMeel, 1979), and R. McClory, *Turning Point* (New York: Crossroads, 1995). Quotations come from both sources.

73 S. Bolkosky, "Interviewing Victims Who Survived: Listening for the Silences That Strike," *Annals of Scholarship,* 1987, *4,* 33–51. My other source for Bolkosky's views is personal communication.

74 *"Nothing to say. Sad."*: L. Langer, *Holocaust Testimonies* (New Haven: Yale University Press, 1991). The quotations I have used from this book come from pp. 63, 59, and ix.

75 *"a future to look for."*: A. Kay, "Generativity in the Shadow of Genocide: The Holocaust Experience and Generativity," in McAdams and de St. Aubin, *Generativity and Adult Development,* p. 343. The next quotation from Kay comes from p. 346.

76 *"and gave chase."*: This quotation, and those that follow from Clarissa Pinkola Estes, come from *The Faithful Gardener* (San Francisco: Harper, 1995), pp. 16–23 and 74.

Chapter Five. Finding a Voice of Your Own

Page

78 The radio series on the human life cycle was entitled *Seasons of Life* (Ann Arbor and Washington, DC: The University of Michigan and the Corporation for Public Broadcasting, 1990).

79 *"into German hearts."*: E. Erikson, *Young Man Luther* (New York: Norton, 1958), p. 233.

80 *"and psychological awareness."*: Erikson, *Young Man Luther,* pp. 47–48.

80 *"prick up both ears."*: Erikson, *Young Man Luther,* p. 244.

80 *"speak to him."*: Erikson, *Young Man Luther,* p. 207.

80 *"demand for commitment."*: E. Erikson, *Gandhi's Truth* (New York: Norton, 1969), p. 412.

81 *"and are used."*: S. Lee, "Generativity and the Life Course of Martha Graham," in D. McAdams and E. de St. Aubin (eds.), *Generativity and Adult Development* (Washington, DC: American Psychological Association, 1998), p. 444.

81 *"I'm like a boy."*: A. Miller, *Death of a Salesman* (New York: Viking, 1958), p. 23.

81 *"of some kind of life."*: Miller, *Death of a Salesman,* p. 58.

81 *"than a cliff."*: R. Bolt, *A Man for All Seasons* (New York: Random House, 1962), p. xii.

82 *"I do—I"* and *"to find himself again."*: Bolt, *A Man For All Seasons,* pp. 123 and 140.

82 *"and to act accordingly."*: E. Erikson, *Childhood and Society* (New York: Norton, 1963), p. 42.

82 More on durable identities: In 1980, George Vaillant looked at the longitudinal samples I have referred to earlier and found that "career consolidation" often preceded the attainment of generativity. Career consolidation is a kind of job stability that gives workers "an integrated self from which they can speak with authority" (*The Wisdom of the Ego* [Cambridge: Harvard University Press, 1993], p. 190). Vaillant's research was originally reported in G. Vaillant and E. Milofsky, "Natural History of Male Psychological Health: IX. Empirical Evidence for Erikson's Model of the Life Cycle," *American Journal of Psychiatry,* 1980, *137,* 1348–1359.

   More on the sense of being called: G. LeVoy, *Callings* (New York: Harmony Books, 1997).

83 *"a contrary course"* and *"at frequent intervals."*: A. Colby and W. Damon, *Some Do Care* (New York: Free Press, 1992), pp. 72 and 184.

84 *"'always doing ministry.'"*: D. McAdams, H. Hart, and S. Maruna, "The Anatomy of Generativity," in D. McAdams and E. de St. Aubin (eds.), *Generativity and Adult Development* (Washington, DC: American Psychological Association, 1998), pp. 31–32. See also D. McAdams, A. Diamond, E. de St. Aubin, and E. Mansfield, "Stories of Commitment: The Psychosocial Construction of Generative Lives," *Journal of Personality and Social Psychology,* 1997, *72,* 678–694. The research subjects in these studies were in their 30s, 40s, and 50s.

84 *"I am asked to do."*: Colby and Damon, *Some Do Care,* p. 73.

85 *"more fully through them."*: L. Daloz, C. Keen, J. Keen, and S. Parks, *Common Fire* (Boston: Beacon, 1996), p. 197. Other quoted material comes from p. 198.

85 The modern concept of identity: R. Baumeister, *Identity: Cultural Change and the Struggle for Self* (New York: Oxford University Press, 1986); D. McAdams, "Personality, Modernity, and the Storied Self: A Contemporary Framework for Studying Persons," *Psychological Inquiry*, 1996, *7*, 295–321.

86 I tell the story of my grandfather's gloves in the opening of *White Gloves* (New York: Free Press, 1995; New York: Norton, 1996).

86 A. Toffler, *Future Shock* (New York: Random House, 1970).

86 *"recedes from view."*: K. Gergen, *The Saturated Self* (New York: Basic, 1991), p. 7. See also R. Lifton, *The Protean Self* (New York: Basic 1993).

86 Self-as-story: D. McAdams, *Power, Intimacy, and the Life Story* (Homewood, IL: Dorsey, 1985); McAdams, D., *The Stories We Live By* (New York: Morrow, 1993).

87 *"I always felt sorry for him"* and *"to other people in life."*: McAdams, Hart, and Maruna, "The Anatomy of Generativity," p. 31.

87 Early memories and current identities: Kotre, *White Gloves*.

88 *"belief in the species."*: Erikson, *Childhood and Society*, p. 267. One questionnaire study found "modest support" for Erikson's notion that belief in the species and generativity are linked. See D. Van de Water and D. McAdams, "Generativity and Erikson's 'Belief in the Species,' " *Journal of Research in Personality*, 1989, *23*, 435–449.

89 *"the dragon doesn't win all the time."*: Colby and Damon, *Some Do Care*, p. 89.

89 Stories of reform: S. Maruna, "Going Straight: Desistance from Crime and Life Narratives of Reform," in R. Josselson and A. Lieblich (eds.), *The Narrative Study of Lives*, vol. 5 (Newbury Park, CA: Sage, 1997).

90 *"molding plastic, young life."*: Maruna cites J. Brown, *Monkey Off My Back* (Grand Rapids, MI: Zondervan), p. 146.

91 *"a slight variation in wording."*: C. Woodham-Smith, *Florence Nightingale, 1820–1910* (New York: McGraw-Hill, 1951), p. 12. Except where otherwise indicated, quotations from Florence Nightingale are taken from Woodham-Smith or from George Vaillant's treatment of her life in *The Wisdom of the Ego*.

Miss Nightingale also carried on a vast correspondence. Over 13,000 letters survive, some of them twenty to thirty pages in length. All were handwritten; some were preceded by a rough draft; and some were followed by the making of a copy. Thus, some of the 13,000 were actually written three times, with abbreviations, in Nightingale's own hand. See M. Vicinus and B. Nergaard (eds.), *Ever Yours, Florence Nightingale* (Cambridge: Harvard University Press, 1989).

95 *"she was set apart."*: Woodham-Smith, *Florence Nightingale*, p. 180.

97 *"cup dry underneath."*: F. Nightingale, *Notes on Nursing* (Princeton: Brandon, 1970), pp. 47, 25, and 39.

97 *"of delicate and decent feeling."*: Nightingale, *Notes on Nursing*, p. 71.

97 *"due an oracle."*: Woodham-Smith, *Florence Nightingale*, p. 355.

98 *"it's going to pass."*: J. Kotre, *Outliving the Self* (Baltimore: Johns Hopkins University Press, 1984; New York, Norton, 1996), p. 199.

98 *"the opinions of certain others.":* Colby and Damon, *Some Do Care,* p. 172.

98 *"to do something else.":* Colby and Damon, *Some Do Care,* p. 12.

100 *"of General Motors"* and *"more than any other.":* H. Gardner, *Leading Minds* (New York: Basic, 1995), pp. 132 and 142.

100 *"an audience ready to hear it.":* Gardner, *Leading Minds,* p. 291.

101 One version of "The Three Languages" appears in *The Complete Grimm's Fairy Tales* (New York: Pantheon, 1944). Another can be found in *Grimm's Complete Fairy Tales* (New York: Doubleday, no date).

103 "Down below" and "up above" in "The Three Languages": Erik Erikson's studies of Luther and Gandhi are remarkable precisely because they give both the frogs and the doves their due. He addresses both the lower and the higher nature of his subjects without turning one into the other.

Chapter Six. Blending Your Voice and Creating

Page

104 The New Zealand snail *Potamopyrgus antipodarum:* J. Gutin, "Why Bother?" *Discover,* 1992 (June), *13,* 32–39.

105 The malarial parasite: I. Sherman, "Membrane Structure and Function of Malaria Parasites and the Infected Erythrocyte," *Parasitology,* 1985, *91,* 609–645.

105 The version of "The Three Languages" that includes marriage to the lord's daughter appears in *Grimm's Complete Fairy Tales* (New York: Doubleday, no date).

106 *"into his own self.":* The tale of Prajapati can be found in C. Long, *Alpha: The Myths of Creation* (New York: Braziller, 1963). The brief quotation is from p. 131.

106 *"and meditating upon it.":* Long, *Alpha,* p. 171.

106 *"to nourish our children.":* The quotations in this paragraph come from Long, *Alpha,* pp. 103 and 104.

107 *"of the other sex.":* E. Erikson, *Childhood and Society* (New York: Norton, 1963), p. 266.

107 *"in joint inspiration.":* E. Erikson, *Identity: Youth and Crisis* (New York: Norton, 1968), p. 135.

107 *"sacrifices and compromises.":* Erikson, *Childhood and Society,* p. 263.

107 *"mutual satisfaction?":* G. Vaillant, *The Wisdom of the Ego* (Cambridge: Harvard University Press, 1993), p. 149.

108 Married subjects in McAdams's research: D. McAdams, A. Diamond, E. de St. Aubin, and E. Mansfield, "Stories of Commitment: The Psychosocial Construction of Generative Lives," *Journal of Personality and Social Psychology,* 1997, *72,* 678–694.

108 The marital bond and children: F. Furstenberg, Jr., and C. Nord, "Parenting Apart: Patterns of Childrearing After Marital Disruption," *Journal of Marriage and the Family,* 1987, *47,* 893–904; E. Hetherington, M. Stanley-Hagan, and E.

Anderson, "Marital Transitions: A Child's Perspective," *American Psychologist*, 1989, *44*, 303–312; B. Whitehead, *The Divorce Culture* (New York: Knopf, 1997).

108 *"he can provide.":* E. Hetherington, M. Bridges, and G. Insabella, "What Matters? What Does Not? Five Perspectives on the Association Between Marital Transitions and Children's Adjustment," *American Psychologist*, 1998, *53*, 167–184. The quotation appears on p. 179.

109 *"came second.":* J. Snarey, *How Fathers Care for the Next Generation* (Cambridge: Harvard University Press, 1993), p. 337. In addition to its own data, Snarey's book contains an excellent literature review on marital intimacy and parenting.

109 Exceptions and resilience among children of divorce: Hetherington et al., "Marital Transitions"; Hetherington et al., "What Matters? What Does Not?"

110 Sexual reproduction and higher forms of life: Gutin, "Why Bother?"

110 H. Gardner, *Creating Minds* (New York: Basic, 1993). While Gardner's research was not done under the rubric of "generativity," the term is clearly applicable, for the creators he studied left their influence on an entire century.

111 *"of other men.":* Einstein is quoted in Gardner, *Creating Minds*, p. 131. Quotations I make from Freud, Picasso, and Graham in the pages that follow—and from those involved in their lives—are taken from Gardner's book.

111 *"of Picasso's works.":* Gardner, *Creating Minds*, pp. 182–183.

111 The scholar who views Picasso as a "tragedy addict" is Mary Gedo. See Gardner, *Creating Minds*, p. 180.

112 *"Dr. Faust and Mephistopheles.":* Gardner, *Creating Minds*, p. 386.

113 *"and unquestioned emotional support.":* Gardner, *Creating Minds*, p. 68.

115 *"experiments with composition.":* Gardner, *Creating Minds*, p. 164.

115 *"in joint inspiration.":* Erikson, *Identity: Youth and Crisis*, p. 135.

115 *"someone else's hand.":* Gardner, *Creating Minds*, p. 185.

116 *"as its embodiment.":* Gardner, *Creating Minds*, pp. 272–273.

117 *"accessible to an audience.":* Gardner, *Creating Minds*, p. 279.

118 *"and you are surrounded.":* J. Miles, *God: A Biography* (New York: Knopf, 1995), p. 409.

118 On Leeuwenhoek: A. Schierbeek, *Measuring the Invisible World* (London: Abelard-Schuman, 1959), pp. 87–88.

119 Memory for one's contribution to a group product: A. Greenwald, "The Totalitarian Ego," *American Psychologist*, 1980, *35*, 603–618.

119 Erik Erikson's view of his own originality: P. Roazen, *Erik H. Erikson* (New York: Free Press, 1976); D. McAdams, "Three Voices of Erik Erikson," *Contemporary Psychology*, 1997, *42*, 575–578. Erikson, a disciple of Freud, wrote volumes on identity; Freud, the master, mentioned it only once in his own voluminous writings. Yet Erikson continually cited Freud's single use of the concept—a case, says Roazen, "of a disciple trying to foist off an original idea onto the founder of psychoanalysis."

120 *"to care more than this.":* J. Kotre, *Outliving the Self* (Baltimore: Johns Hopkins University Press, 1984; New York: Norton, 1996), p. 111. "Jo Biondi" is a pseudonym.

120 *"and about loneliness.":* Kotre, *Outliving the Self*, p. 108.

120 D. Bakan, *The Duality of Human Existence* (Chicago: Rand McNally, 1966). The brief quotations describing agency and communion are from pp. 14–15.

121 Agency, communion, and generativity: D. McAdams, B. Hoffman, E. Mansfield, and R. Day, "Themes of Agency and Communion in Significant Autobiographical Scenes," *Journal of Personality*, 1996, 64, 339–377. The research reported in this article was conducted on adults of all ages; the results held for both sexes.

121 E. Mansfield and D. McAdams, "Generativity and Themes of Agency and Communion in Adult Autobiography," *Personality and Social Psychology Bulletin*, 1996, 22, 721–731.

122 The sum of power and intimacy motivation relates to generativity: D. McAdams, K. Ruetzel, and J. Foley, "Complexity and Generativity at Mid-Life: Relations Among Social Motives, Ego Development, and Adults' Plans for the Future," *Journal of Personality and Social Psychology*, 1986, 50, 800–807.

122 Longitudinal study of women who combine agency and communion: B. Peterson and A. Stewart, "Antecedents and Contexts of Generativity Motivation at Midlife," *Psychology and Aging*, 1996, 11, 21–33.

122 While the God of Genesis is an agentic creator, He is not completely so, for He gives human beings the freedom to choose. But even this freedom has agentic strings attached, for God makes it clear that if humans make the wrong choices, He will punish them.

122 God's first reference to Himself as a father: II Samuel 7:14.

122 *"does not know what love is."*: Miles, *God*, p. 238. In his book, Miles construes God as a literary character whose personality unfolds in the pages of the Tanakh (the Hebrew Bible).

122 *"the soul's omniscient companion."*: Miles, *God*, p. 236.

123 *"You, O Lord, know it well."*: Psalms 139:1–4.

123 Agency and communion in men and women: D. Gutmann, *Reclaimed Powers* (New York: Basic, 1987).

123 *"that is what he told me."*: D. Levinson, *The Seasons of a Man's Life* (New York: Knopf, 1978), pp. 307–308.

123 *"was very important to me."*: J. Kotre and G. Zajic, "The Life Course of Work," *Seasons of Life Audiotapes*, Program 22 (Ann Arbor and Washington, DC: The University of Michigan and the Corporation for Public Broadcasting, 1990).

124 *"that I have mattered."*: Kotre, *Outliving the Self*, pp. 110–111.

124 I have condensed and adapted the story of "The Golden Tree" from H. Schwartz, *Elijah's Violin and Other Jewish Fairy Tales* (New York: Harper & Row, 1983). Another condensation appears in Allan Chinen's *Once Upon a Midlife* (New York: G. P. Putnam's Sons, 1992).

127 Allan Chinen's interpretation of "The Golden Tree" can be found in his book *Once Upon a Midlife*.

Chapter Seven. Selecting and Letting Go

Page

130 The Biblical account of the flood can be found in Genesis 6–9.

130 The *Qur'an*'s account of Noah's son: Surah XI, v. 42–43.

131   The Biblical account of Abraham and Isaac: Genesis 12–22.

131   The *Qur'an*'s detail about Abraham's son can found in Surah XXXVII, v. 102ff.

131   The number of eggs present in a woman's ovaries: J. Hargrove and E. Eisenberg, "Menopause," *Office Gynecology*, 1995, *79*, 1337–1356. The two million eggs present at birth were twelve million just three months earlier, at six months' gestational age.

131   The number of sperm: J. Hyde, *Understanding Human Sexuality*, 2nd ed. (New York: McGraw-Hill, 1982).

132   Twins conceived and born: L. Wright, "Double Mystery," *The New Yorker*, August 7, 1995, pp. 45–62.

133   *"He was perfectly normal."*: J. Kotre and S. Millett, "And Then We Knew," *Seasons of Life Audiotapes*, Program 3 (Ann Arbor, Michigan, and Washington, DC: The University of Michigan and the Corporation for Public Broadcasting).

133   *"she told me all that story"* and *"That's all written in her life."*: J. Kotre, *Outliving the Self* (Baltimore: Johns Hopkins University Press, 1984; New York: Norton, 1996), pp. 206 and 218.

134   *"was going for the orphans"* and *"of the whole thing."*: A. Colby and W. Damon, *Some Do Care* (New York: Free Press, 1992), pp. 44 and 126–127.

135   *"the rest of the year."*: This father-coach is quoted in J. Snarey and P. Clark, "A Generative Drama: Scenes From a Father-Son Relationship," in D. McAdams and E. de St. Aubin (eds.), *Generativity and Adult Development* (Washington, DC: American Psychological Association, 1998), p. 53.

135   *"water through my fingers."*: Kotre, *Outliving the Self*, p. 110.

136   *" 'I'm very angry at you.' "*: Kotre, *Outliving the Self*, p. 76.

137   *"a whole generation of performers."*: S. Lee, "Generativity and the Life Course of Martha Graham," in McAdams and de St. Aubin, *Generativity and Adult Development*, p. 444. Late in her career, Graham was persuaded that her dances should outlive her ability to perform them, and she consented to filming. By that time, however, much of her early work had been lost.

137   *"admit your mortality."*: H. Gardner, *Creating Minds* (New York: Basic, 1993), p. 304.

137   *"and deeply rewarding experience."*: Lee, "Generativity and the Life Course of Martha Graham," p. 441.

137   *"to go out and be free."*: Kotre, *Outliving the Self*, pp. 106 and 108.

Chapter Eight. Responding to Outcome

Page

144   *"to pay for medicine."*: O. Lewis, *The Children of Sanchez* (New York: Random House, 1961), pp. 481 and 485–486.

144   *"I've ruined everybody's life."*: J. Kotre, *Outliving the Self* (Baltimore: Johns Hopkins University Press, 1984; New York: Norton, 1996), p. 81.

144   *"do himself some injury."*: W. Heisenberg, *Physics and Beyond*, translated by A. Pomerans (New York: Harper & Row, 1971), p. 193.

145   *"but that is all.":* Heisenberg, *Physics and Beyond,* p. 195.

145   *"history had never seen.":* Erikson's treatment of Luther can be found in *Young Man Luther* (New York: Norton, 1958). The words of Luther are drawn from this book. Erikson's words are from pp. 234 and 242.

145   *"I think they are.":* J. Kotre and E. Hall, *Seasons of Life* (Boston: Little, Brown, 1990; Ann Arbor: University of Michigan Press, 1997), p. 278.

146   *"to go to dream.":* Kotre and Hall, *Seasons of Life,* p. 16. Some of this man's words appear in J. Kotre, "Late Adulthood," *Seasons of Life Television Series,* Program 5 (Ann Arbor: The University of Michigan; Pittsburgh, PA: WQED; and Washington, DC: The Corporation for Public Broadcasting; 1990).

146   Shelley's "Ozymandias," A. Witherspoon (ed.), *The College Survey of English Literature* (New York: Harcourt Brace, 1942), p. 834.

147   B. Schwartz, "The Reconstruction of Abraham Lincoln," in D. Middleton and D. Edwards, *Collective Remembering* (London: Sage, 1990).

149   The story of Kujum-Chantu is from C. Long, *Alpha: The Myths of Creation* (New York: Braziller, 1963), p. 35. Long's source was V. Elwin, *Myths of the North East Frontier of India* (Calcutta: Sree Saraswaty, 1958), p. 8.

149   *"that leads to life.":* Matthew 7:14.

149   *"the full grain in the ear.":* Mark 4:28.

150   The parable of the sower: Matthew 13:4–9; Mark 4:3–9; Luke 8:5–8. For a lengthier discussion of this parable, see J. Kotre, "Sowing the Seed: A Christian Archetype of Fruitfulness," *Spirituality Today,* 1980, *32,* 129–137. For more on outcome, see J. Kotre, "Generative Outcome," *Journal of Aging Studies,* 1995, *9,* 33–41.

150   The parable of the weeds and the wheat appears in Matthew 13:24–30. In some translations, the weeds appear as "tares" or "darnel."

151   *"I've got to impact.":* Kotre, *Outliving the Self,* p. 54.

151   *"in parents' own lives.":* C. Ryff, Y. Lee, M. Essex, and P. Schmutte, "My Children and Me: Midlife Evaluations of Grown Children and Self," *Psychology and Aging,* 1994, *9,* 195–205.

151   *"Better never to have started.":* A. Greeley, "More Useful Life" (Universal Press Syndicate, 1979). The book referred to is J. Kotre, *The Best of Times, the Worst of Times* (Chicago: Nelson-Hall, 1978).

151   Research on highly esteemed creators: D. Simonton, *Scientific Genius* (New York: Cambridge University Press, 1989) and *Psychology, Science, and History* (New Haven: Yale University Press, 1990).

152   *"that others fulfilled for me.":* Kotre and Hall, *Seasons of Life,* p. 298.

153   The *Bhagavad Gita* on nonattachment is cited in E. Erikson, *Gandhi's Truth* (New York: Norton, 1969), p. 252.

153   *"and without modesty.":* C. Lewis, *The Great Divorce* (New York: Macmillan, 1946), p. 80.

153   *"the energy of the center.":* J. Campbell, *The Power of Myth* (New York: Doubleday, 1988), p. 218.

154   *"Effort is"* and *"in my time.":* L. Daloz, C. Keen, J. Keen, and S. Parks, *Common Fire* (Boston: Beacon, 1996), pp. 200 and 203.

154 The Buddhist advice was conveyed in M. Csikszentmihalyi, "Finding Flow," *Psychology Today*, July/August 1997, p. 71. In several books Csikszentmihalyi has described a state of "flow" that is like what Joseph Campbell calls the "energy of the center" (*Flow* [New York: Harper and Row, 1990]; *Creativity* [New York: HarperCollins, 1996]; and *Finding Flow* [New York: Basic, 1997]). Flow is an experience of activity that is so spontaneous and absorbing that nothing else seems to matter. "The roof could fall in and, if it missed you, you would be unaware of it," said a chess player (*Flow*, p. 54). A rock climber: "All I can remember is the last thirty seconds, and all I can think ahead is the next five minutes" (*Flow*, p. 58). Flow is so pleasurable that it is sought, not for what it produces, but as an end in itself.

Flow is not generativity, however, though it can easily lead to it. For one thing, generativity can entail years of sheer tedium in which nothing at all "flows" but from which much results. Just ask Florence Nightingale.

Chapter Nine. *Never Too Soon, Never Too Late*

Page

158 Generativity in young adults: The most comprehensive review of research on this subject can be found in A. Stewart and E. Vandewater, "The Course of Generativity," in D. McAdams and E. de St. Aubin (eds.), *Generativity and Adult Development* (Washington, DC: American Psychological Association, 1998). Stewart and Vandewater's chapter presents data on generative desire in two longitudinal samples of college women.

159 *"I just wasn't ready for this.":* D. Levinson, *The Seasons of a Woman's Life* (New York: Knopf, 1996), p. 107. A companion volume to *The Seasons of a Man's Life* (New York: Knopf, 1978), this book is a rich description of women's experience in their 20s, 30s, and early 40s.

159 *"the birth of our child.":* J. Kotre and E. Hall, *Seasons of Life* (Boston: Little, Brown, 1990; Ann Arbor: University of Michigan Press, 1997).

160 *"connected with that.":* B. Cohler, A. Hostetler, and A. Boxer, "Generativity, Social Context, and Lived Experience: Narratives of Gay Men in Middle Adulthood," in McAdams and de St. Aubin, *Generativity and Adult Development*, p. 284.

160 Schedules of creative output: D. Simonton, "Age and Outstanding Achievement: What Do We Know After a Century of Research?" *Psychological Bulletin*, 1988, *104*, 251–267.

160 *"you've blown it.":* Levinson, *The Seasons of a Man's Life*, p. 271.

161 *"how lonely this land could feel.":* D. Cole, *After Great Pain* (New York: Summit, 1992), pp. 148–149.

161 Generativity chill and its effects: J. Snarey, *How Fathers Care for the Next Generation* (Cambridge: Harvard University Press, 1993), pp. 23–24. Also: J. Snarey, L. Son, V. Kuehne, S. Hauser, and G. Vaillant, "The Role of Parenting in Men's Psychosocial Development: A Longitudinal Study of Early Adulthood Infertility and Midlife Generativity," *Developmental Psychology*, 1987, *23*, 593–603.

161 *"all those years."*: Cole, *After Great Pain*, pp. 183 and 208.

162 Baby faces and adult care: K. Lorenz, "Part and Parcel in Animal and Human Societies: A Methodological Discussion," in R. Martin (ed. and trans.), *Studies in Animal and Human Behavior*, vol. 2 (Cambridge: Harvard University Press, 1971), pp. 115–195. Also: B. Bogin, "Evolutionary Hypotheses for Human Childhood," *Yearbook of Physical Anthropology*, 1997, *40*, 63–89.

162 The effects of having children on broad generative concern: D. McAdams, and E. de St. Aubin, "A Theory of Generativity and Its Assessment Through Self-Report, Behavioral Acts, and Narrative Themes in Autobiography," *Journal of Personality and Social Psychology*, 1992, *62*, 1003–1015. The test used was the Loyola Generativity Scale.

162 *"a moral metaphor and model for good citizenry."*: Snarey, *How Fathers Care for the Next Generation*, p. 24.

162 From "proximal" to "distal" roles: S. MacDermid, C. Franz, and L. De Reus, "Generativity: At the Crossroads of Social Roles and Personality," in McAdams and de St. Aubin, *Generativity and Adult Development*.

163 Women in their 60s giving birth: F. D'Emilio, "Autumn's Child," *Ann Arbor News*, July 23, 1997, p. C1. In *New Passages* (New York: Random House, 1995), Gail Sheehy mentions the case of the Italian woman, Rosanna Della Corte, in an eye-opening description of the lengths to which some women go to live out the "fantasy of fertility forever."

163 Sterilization in the United States: W. Mosher, "Contraceptive Practice in the United States, 1982–1988," *Family Planning Perspectives*, 1990, *22*, 198–205; J. Forrest and R. Fordyce, "Women's Contraceptive Attitudes and Use in 1992," *Family Planning Perspectives*, 1993, *25*, 175–179.

163 *"an octopus, overextended."*: D. Levinson, *The Seasons of a Woman's Life*, pp. 174–175.

163 *"a lot of deferred stuff."*: Cohler, Hostetler, and Boxer, "Generativity, Social Context, and Lived Experience," p. 285.

164 *"take care of themselves."*: Kotre and Hall, *Seasons of Life*, p. 293.

164 *"want to step out of it?"*: J. Kotre, *Outliving the Self* (Baltimore: Johns Hopkins University Press, 1984; New York: Norton, 1996), p. 81.

165 *"and not messing up."*: Kotre, *Outliving the Self*, p. 88.

165 *"If only he could see them now!"*: Kotre, *Outliving the Self*, p. 81.

165 *"all these things with our daughter"* and *"all summer long."*: J. Kotre and S. Millett, "Three Grandparents," *Seasons of Life Audiotapes*, Program 25 (Ann Arbor, Michigan, and Washington, DC: The University of Michigan and the Corporation for Public Broadcasting, 1990).

166 *"who cared about people."*: J. Kotre, "Middle Adulthood, " *Seasons of Life Television Series*, Program 4 "Middle Adulthood" (Ann Arbor: The University of Michigan; Pittsburgh, PA: WQED; and Washington, DC: The Corporation for Public Broadcasting; 1990).

166 Levels of generativity in middle age: C. Ryff, and S. Heincke, "Subjective Organization of Personality in Adulthood and Aging," *Journal of Personality and Social Psychology*, 1983, *44*, 807–816. See also D. McAdams, E. de St. Aubin,

and R. Logan, "Generativity Among Young, Midlife, and Older Adults," *Psychology and Aging,* 1993, *2,* 221–230.

For empirical work exploring the relationship in middle age between generative desire and actual generative realization, see B. Peterson, "Case Studies of Midlife Generativity: Analyzing Motivation and Realization," in McAdams and de St. Aubin, *Generativity and Adult Development.* For a summary of research on the timing of generativity across the life span, see Stewart and Vandewater, "The Course of Generativity."

167 Vera Brittain's diaries: B. Peterson and A. Stewart, "Using Personal and Fictional Documents to Assess Psychosocial Development: A Case Study of Vera Brittain's Generativity," *Psychology and Aging,* 1990, *5,* 400–411. Brittain's novels showed the same pattern as her diaries, though not as dramatically.

167 *"it makes me feel good.":* Sheehy, *New Passages,* p. 79.

167 *"than my successes"* and *"as we are collected together.":* Kotre and Hall, *Seasons of Life,* pp. 315–317.

168 A review of research on the fear of death can be found in R. Kalish, "The Social Context of Death and Dying," in R. Binstock and E. Shanas (eds.), *Handbook of Aging and the Social Sciences,* 2nd ed. (New York: Van Nostrand Reinhold, 1985).

168 The "midlife crisis" among artists: E. Jaques, "Death and the Mid-Life Crisis," *International Journal of Psychoanalysis,* 1965, *46,* 502–514. In large-scale studies since Jaques's time, there has been little evidence for a *universal* midlife crisis.

169 *"I am the bottom line.":* The farmer's story, though not this quotation, can be found in Kotre and Hall, *Seasons of Life.*

169 The story of the conjure woman: W. Hooks, *Freedom's Fruit* (New York: Knopf, 1996).

172 *"will leave this gift with me.":* J. Kotre, *White Gloves* (New York: Free Press, 1995; New York: Norton, 1996), p. 232.

173 *"and restore lost balance.":* A. Assmann, "Wholesome Knowledge: Concepts of Wisdom in a Historical and Cross-Cultural Perspective," in D. Featherman (ed.), *Life-Span Development and Behavior,* vol. 12 (Hillsdale, NJ: Erlbaum, 1994), p. 194.

173 *"not projects.":* A. Chinen, *In the Ever After* (Wilmette, IL: Chiron, 1989), p. 36.

173 Wisdom is not restricted to late adulthood: P. Baltes and U. Staudinger, "The Search for a Psychology of Wisdom," *Current Directions in Psychological Science,* 1993, *2,* 75–80.

174 Aging in developing countries: C. Holden, "New Populations of Old Add to Poor Nations' Burdens," *Science,* July 5, 1996, *273,* 46–48.

175 The eleven-to-one ratio in U.S. federal spending: P. Peterson, "Will America Grow Up Before It Grows Old?" *The Atlantic Monthly,* May 1996, *277,* 55–86.

175 Data on older populations and decreasing per-pupil spending: J. Tilove, "Gray vs. Brown?" *Ann Arbor News,* November 30, 1997, pp. A3ff. (syndicated by the Newhouse News Service). Tilove cites the work of MIT economist James Poterba. I might add that not only will the United States be "browning" in the

years ahead, with more and more of the youngest generation being people of color, it will also be "feminizing," with more and more of the oldest generation being women.

175 Data on age and poverty: C. Taeuber, "Women in Our Aging Society: Golden Years or Increased Dependency?" *USA Today Magazine,* September 1993.

175 Social Security data: Peterson, "Will America Grow Up Before It Grows Old?" If you take what the average one-earner couple paid into Social Security, Peterson says, add what their employers did, and add interest, that couple still comes out $123,000 ahead.

175 *"card wool.":* M. Csikszentmihalyi, *Flow* (New York: Harper & Row, 1990), p. 146.

176 *"wishing for more leisure.":* Csikszentmihalyi, *Flow,* p. 158.

176 *"satisfying work as well?"* Peterson, "Will America Grow Up Before It Grows Old?" p. 73.

176 *"but independent.":* Kotre and Hall, *Seasons of Life,* p. 326.

176 Reversal of early-retirement trend: M. Benson, "Fewer Opt for Early Retirement," *Ann Arbor News,* July 25, 1997, pp. A1ff. (syndicated by the Newhouse News Service).

177 Erikson on grand-generativity: E. Erikson, J. Erikson, and H. Kivnick, *Vital Involvement in Old Age* (New York: Norton, 1986), pp. 74–75.

178 Luke Skywalker, Princess Leia, Ben Kenobi, and Yoda, of course, are all characters from the *Star Wars* trilogy.

178 *"personal satisfaction, you know?":* Kotre and Hall, *Seasons of Life,* p. 346.

178 *"the most brilliant paper ever written.":* Kotre and Hall, *Seasons of Life,* p. 360.

178 Generativity's decline in late adulthood: McAdams, de St. Aubin, and Logan, "Generativity Among Young, Midlife, and Older Adults." The older adults in this study were between 67 and 72 years of age. The decline reported was in generative concern and in the number of generative acts.

178 *"biting strategically.":* This and other study quotes are from L. Daloz, C. Keen, J. Keen, and S. Parks, *Common Fire* (Boston: Beacon, 1996), p. 204.

178 D. Simonton, "The Swan-Song Phenomenon: Last-Work Effects for 172 Classical Composers," *Psychology and Aging,* 1989, 4, 42–47.
Distilling the essence of one's work, and of oneself, is of course another form of selecting. In this connection, professional readers might wish to consult P. Baltes, and M. Baltes, "Psychological Perspectives on Successful Aging: The Model of Selective Optimization with Compensation," in P. Baltes and M. Baltes, *Successful Aging* (New York: Cambridge University Press, 1990). Also: L. Carstensen, "Evidence for a Life-Span Theory of Socioemotional Selectivity," *Current Directions in Psychological Science,* 1995, 4, 151–156.

179 *"with your fellow humans.":* "Holding On: The Last Words of Henry Roth," *Forward,* October 20, 1995, pp. 1 and 9.

179 Morrie Schwartz: M. Albom, *Tuesdays with Morrie* (New York: Doubleday, 1997).

179 *"overwhelming differences in output.":* J. Gleick, *Chaos* (New York: Penguin, 1987), p. 8.

180   *"the way I used to."*: Chinen, *In the Ever After,* p. 81.

180   Medicare spending: J. Califano, "Physician-Assisted Living," *America,* November 14, 1998, pp. 10–12.

180   The survey data on living wills was reported in Peterson, "Will American Grow Up Before It Grows Old?"

180   *"not to fear death."*: E. Erikson, *Childhood and Society* (New York: Norton, 1963), p. 269.

180   A condensation of "The Shining Fish" can be found in Chinen, *In the Ever After.*

182   The longitudinal study of working-class boys: G. Vaillant and E. Milofsky, "Natural History of Male Psychological Health: IX. Empirical Evidence for Erikson's Model of the Life Cycle," *American Journal of Psychiatry, 137,* 1348–1359.

183   In *Altering Fate: Why the Past Does Not Predict the Future* (New York: Guilford, 1997), developmental psychiatrist Michael Lewis presents a thorough case regarding the failure of longitudinal research to predict much in the way of life outcomes.

183   *"as teleology."*: E. Erikson, *Gandhi's Truth* (New York: Norton, 1970), p. 98.

Chapter Ten. The Corruption of Generativity

Page

185   *"We surrounded him with our reverence."*: S. Naipaul, *Journey to Nowhere* (New York: Simon & Schuster, 1980), p. 301. In addition to sources listed in these notes, I would recommend for an understanding of Jim Jones's life the account of Lawrence Wright in "Orphans of Jonestown," *The New Yorker,* November 22, 1993, pp. 66–89. Wright's article is built around conversations with three of Jones's surviving sons.

185   *"What a legacy!"*: T. Reiterman, *Raven* (New York: Dutton, 1982), p. 599. Tim Reiterman is a journalist who was attached to the party that was ambushed by Jones's security guards just as the mass suicide was beginning. Five were killed in the attack. Reiterman was one of those injured.

185   Jones's tape recording was made in Guyana in September of 1977. A partial transcript, published in the *Guyana Chronicle* on December 6, 1978, is cited in both Naipaul, *Journey to Nowhere,* and Reiterman, *Raven.*

186   *"as white trash."*: Naipaul, *Journey,* p. 236.

187   *"I'm standing there. Alone."*: Reiterman, *Raven,* pp. 16–17.

189   *"the world contains."*: Timothy Stoen's paternity document is cited in Reiterman, *Raven,* p. 131.

190   *"have given you all these things."*: Jones's sermon, preserved on videotape, is cited in Reiterman, *Raven,* p. 149.

191   *"I truly am happy!"*: Naipaul, *Journey,* pp. 72–81.

191   *"and not letting us suffer."*: This letter appears in a set of photographs adjacent to p. 451 in Reiterman, *Raven.*

192   *"demonstrably psychotic."*: A. Storr, *Feet of Clay* (New York: Free Press, 1996), p. 4.

193 D. Bakan, *The Duality of Human Existence* (Chicago: Rand McNally, 1966). Bakan's treatment of Satan often draws upon that of personality psychologist Henry Murray: H. Murray, "The Personality and Career of Satan," *Journal of Social Issues,* 1962, *18,* 36–54.

194 *"somebody else from Jonestown."*: Odell Rhodes, quoted in E. Feinsod, *Awake in a Nightmare* (New York: Norton, 1981) p. 209.

195 On the distinction between agentic and communal knowledge, see Bakan, *The Duality of Human Existence,* p. 61.

196 *"constitute the greatest threat."*: Storr, *Feet of Clay,* p. 3.

196 *"is not shooting immoderately."*: E. Klee, W. Dressen, and V. Riess (eds.), *"The Good Old Days"* (New York: Free Press, 1991), pp. 158 and 167.

196 *"that we could designate."*: R. Rhodes, *Dark Sun* (New York: Simon & Schuster, 1995), pp. 528–529.

196 *"the tendency toward infanticide arises."*: Bakan, *The Duality of Human Existence,* p. 68.

197 *"we all eat."*: B. Gill, *Many Masks* (New York: Ballantine, 1987), p. 170.

198 *"or watched stunned."*: Klee, Dressen, and Riess, *"The Good Old Days,"* p. xxi.

198 *"to an ideology that supports it."*: E. Staub, *The Roots of Evil* (Cambridge: Cambridge University Press, 1989), pp. 17–18.

199 *"Caring was infectious."*: P. Hallie, *Lest Innocent Blood Be Shed* (New York: Harper & Row, 1979), p. 114.

Chapter Eleven. Of Skin and Spirit

Page

201 The "noosphere": I drew this term from the writings of the Jesuit paleontologist Pierre Teilhard de Chardin. See *The Phenomenon of Man* (New York: Harper & Row, 1959). I later learned that it had been coined by the French philosopher Edouard Le Roy and also adopted by the Russian scientist Vladimir Vernadsky. See the latter's article, "The Biosphere and the Noosphere," *American Scientist,* 1945, *33,* 1–12. See also L. Margulis and D. Sagan, *What Is Life?* (New York: Simon & Schuster, 1995).

203 The "sounds of apprenticeship": J. Burke and R. Ornstein, *The Axemaker's Gift* (New York: G. P. Putnam's Sons, 1995), p. 21.

204 *"jewelry and oil lamps."*: Burke and Ornstein, *The Axemaker's Gift,* p. 46.

207 *"paleontology of consciousness."*: J. Jaynes, *The Origin of Consciousness in the Breakdown of the Bicameral Mind* (New York: Houghton Mifflin, 1976), p. 216.

207 "vision," "faith," and "desire": S. Lee, "Generativity and the Life Course of Martha Graham," in D. McAdams and E. de St. Aubin (eds.), *Generativity and Adult Development* (Washington, DC: American Psychological Association, 1998), p. 443.

208 On Plato, see the *Symposium* and J. Wakefield, "Immortality and the Externalization of the Self: Plato's Unrecognized Theory of Generativity," in McAdams and de St. Aubin, *Generativity and Adult Development.*

209 Macaques and langurs: S. Hrdy, "Nepotist and altruist: The behavior of old

females among macaques and langur monkeys," in P. Amoss and S. Harrell (eds.), *Other Ways of Growing Old* (Stanford: Stanford University Press, 1981).

210 For more on infertility in the human life cycle, see B. Bogin and H. Smith, "Evolution of the Human Life Cycle," *American Journal of Human Biology*, 1996, *8*, 703–716.

210 Generativity as an ethical orientation: E. Erikson, *Life History and the Historical Moment* (New York: Norton, 1975), p. 207; D. Browning, *Generative Man* (New York: Westminster, 1973); J. Kotre, "Generative Humanity," *America*, December 20, 1975, pp. 434–437.

210 *"but ethically binding."*: J. Snarey, *How Fathers Care for the Next Generation* (Cambridge: Harvard University Press, 1993), p. 27.

210 One recent and comprehensive study on the relationship of generativity to psychological well-being: C. Keyes and C. Ryff, "Generativity in Adult Lives: Social Structural Contours and Quality of Life Consequences," in McAdams and de St. Aubin, *Generativity and Adult Development*.

211 *"self-sacrifice or suffering."*: D. Dollahite, B. Slife, and A. Hawkins, "Family Generativity and Generative Counseling: Helping Families Keep Faith with the Next Generation," in McAdams and de St. Aubin, *Generativity and Adult Development*, p. 474. Dollahite and Hawkins have produced an award-winning web site entitled *Fatherwork* (http://fatherwork.byu.edu). It is worth checking out.

Chapter Twelve. The Gift

Page

212 "The Gift" is a condensation and adaptation of "Story of Wali Dad the Simple-Hearted," in A. Lang (ed.), *The Brown Fairy Book* (London: Longmans, Green, 1904). It was called to my attention by Allan Chinen in *In the Ever After* (Wilmette, IL: Chiron, 1989). Chinen called his version "The Simple Grasscutter."

214 *"shelter in its branches."*: Gospel of Matthew 13:31–32.

215 *"that are necessary."*: The quotations in this paragraph are from J. Kotre and E. Hall, *Seasons of Life* (Boston: Little, Brown, 1990; Ann Arbor: University of Michigan Press, 1997), pp. 348 and 383.

219 *"of the community."*: E. Erikson, *Childhood and Society* (New York: Norton, 1963), p. 267.

Index

Index

Printed in the United States
By Bookmasters